Marx and Russia

THE BLOOMSBURY HISTORY OF MODERN RUSSIA SERIES

Series Editors:

Jonathan Smele (Queen Mary, University of London, UK) and
Michael Melancon (Auburn University, USA)

This ambitious and unique series offers readers the latest views on aspects of the modern history of what has been and remains one of the most powerful and important countries in the world. In a series of books aimed at students, leading academics and experts from across the world portray, in a thematic manner, a broad variety of aspects of the Russian experience, over extended periods of time, from the reign of Peter the Great in the early eighteenth century to the Putin era at the beginning of the twenty-first.

Published:

Crime and Punishment in Russia: A Comparative History from Peter the Great to Vladimir Putin, Jonathan Daly

Peasants in Russia from Serfdom to Stalin: Accommodation, Survival, Resistance, Boris B. Gorshkov

Forthcoming:

Dissidents, Émigrés and Revolutionaries in Russia: Anti-State Activism in International Perspective, 1848–2015, Charlotte Alston

The History of the Russian Worker: Life and Change from Peter the Great to Vladimir Putin, Alice Pate

Law and the Russian State: Russia's Legal Evolution from Peter the Great to Vladimir Putin, William Pomeranz

A Modern History of Russian Childhood: From Imperialism to the End of the Soviet Era, Elizabeth White

Marx and Russia

The fate of a doctrine

James D. White

BLOOMSBURY ACADEMIC
LONDON • NEW YORK • OXFORD • NEW DELHI • SYDNEY

BLOOMSBURY ACADEMIC
Bloomsbury Publishing Plc
50 Bedford Square, London, WC1B 3DP, UK
1385 Broadway, New York, NY 10018, USA

BLOOMSBURY, BLOOMSBURY ACADEMIC and the Diana logo are trademarks of
Bloomsbury Publishing Plc

First published in Great Britain 2019
Reprinted 2019

Cover image: Karl Marx, 1933 by Gustav Klutsis (1895–1938). (© Heritage Image
Partnership Ltd / Alamy Stock Photo)

A catalogue record for this book is available from the British Library.

A catalog record for this book is available from the Library of Congress.

ISBN: HB: 978-1-4742-2407-9
PB: 978-1-4742-2406-2
ePDF: 978-1-4742-2408-6
eBook: 978-1-4742-2409-3

Series: The Bloomsbury History of Modern Russia Series

Typeset by Newgen KnowledgeWorks Pvt. Ltd., Chennai, India
Printed and bound in Great Britain

To find out more about our authors and books visit www.bloomsbury.com
and sign up for our newsletters.

CONTENTS

PREFACE

The present work is the history of Marxist ideas in Russia. It was in Russia that Marxism had its greatest impact and produced some of the most well-known Marxist theoreticians: men like Plekhanov, Lenin, Bukharin and Trotsky. Tracing the development of Marxist ideas in Russia is one aspect of the subject of this book. The other is investigating Marx's own involvement with Russia, his intensive study of its economy and society in the last decade of his life. What motivated him to do this provides a unique insight into the nature and dynamics of his project. This work is therefore about a reciprocal relationship: Russians' interest in Marx and Marx's interest in Russia.

Marx and Russia is a study in Russian intellectual history, in the history of ideas. However, since ideas do not exist in a vacuum, it is necessary to supply the political and economic background in which they originated and developed. For example, to understand the attraction that Russia of the 1870s had for Marx, one has to know the provisions of the 1861 peasant reform and how they were implemented. Similarly, the way in which the Bolsheviks came to power in 1917 explains a great deal about theoretical developments in the 1920s. Inter-party rivalries also had their part to play in determining how conceptions were crafted to serve particular political ends.

Existing works which treat the subject of Marxist ideas in Russia and the Soviet Union, such as Leszek Kolakowski's *Main Currents of Marxism* (Kolakowski 1992) and Gustav Wetter's *Dialectical Materialism* (Wetter 1964), concentrate on Marxist philosophical ideas. However, in tracing the history of Marxist ideas in Russia, one discovers that these involve a broad range of subject areas. Sometimes the issues at stake are philosophical, sometimes economic, sometimes political, sometimes historiographical and so on. I have accordingly interpreted the term 'Marxist ideas' broadly to include ideas and theories that in some way take their inspiration from Marx.

Another major difference between Kolakowski's book and the present study is that, whereas Kolakowski treats the various thinkers in isolation from one another, I present the development of Marxist ideas in Russia as a continuous narrative. This narrative approach has the advantage that it brings out the continuities between one thinker and another, and reveals the ways in which Marx's doctrines were interpreted in response to particular situations. Moreover, what may be important for a thinker viewed individually can be of lesser importance when that thinker is taken as a link in a historical narrative, and vice versa.

A feature of the narrative approach is that it brings into prominence key thinkers who have fallen into obscurity, or whose names have been deliberately omitted from the historical record. The present work reconstructs the parts played by Nikolai Sieber, Maxim Kovalevsky and Alexander Bogdanov in the development of Marxist ideas in Russia. Sieber was the first person to introduce Marx's ideas to the Russian reading public, and was the only commentator on Marx's economics whom Marx himself endorsed. Kovalevsky was a collaborator of Marx's, whose sociological writings Marx valued highly and Rosa Luxemburg incorporated into her seminal study *The Accumulation of Capital*. Bogdanov was the most original thinker of the Russian revolutionary era. His influence extended from 1897, when he published his textbook on Marxist political economy, to the industrialization debates of the 1920s. Rudolf Hilferding was influential in the history of Marxism in Russia, but his name was subsequently consigned to oblivion. His book *Das Finanzkapital* provides the key to the economic policies Lenin advocated in 1917.

Chronologically, I begin *Marx and Russia* at the start of the 1870s, when Marx began an intensive study of Russia's economy and society, and take it up to 1938 when Stalin published his *History of the Communist Party of the Soviet Union (Bolsheviks). A Short Course*. I have chosen Stalin's *Short Course* as a terminal point for two reasons. The first is that this book represents a culmination of what has gone before. It brings to a logical conclusion the party control on historical writing that had been instituted almost as soon as the Bolsheviks came to power. The book decided the outcome of a debate on Russian imperialism that had waged since 1925. But, most importantly, it incorporated and perpetuated the ideological mythology that had been generated by Plekhanov and Lenin, and now formed the Leninist ideology of the Stalin regime. The second reason is that the *Short Course* marks a major landmark in the history of Marxist thought in Russia. It presented Marxist thought and its history in Russia in the way Stalin wanted it to be perceived by the population of the Soviet Union. In this form it was an instrument of Stalin's despotic rule, and had very little in it that remained of the conceptions that had inspired Marx's work.

In the main, the sources I have used are primary ones, the actual texts written by the thinkers discussed in the languages of the original. Where possible, I have cited English versions of the works used, so that the original texts can be consulted more easily. Often, however, I have altered the wording in order to standardize how various terms are translated and/or to bring the translation closer to the original.

I have not followed the convention of translating '*narodnichestvo*' as 'populism' for reasons that emerge from the chapter on Plekhanov, and because the English word has connotations that are at variance with the

Russian original. I have been sparing in my use of the terms 'Marxism' and 'Marxist', as their current usage is imprecise, and where I do use them it is in the sense of 'Marx's ideas' or 'pertaining to Marx's thinking'; I do not attach any further qualification to the term whatsoever.

For his encouragement to take up the present project my thanks are due to Jonathan Smele. It would have been impossible to undertake it without the resources on Russian and Soviet studies in Glasgow University Library. Thanks must go to the subject librarian Kay Munro for her help in accessing materials, and to the staff of the Library's Special Collections Department for making the unique holdings of the Trotsky Collection available to me. A debt of gratitude is due to John Lowrie, Ian Thatcher, Nijole White and Paul Zarembka, who have given me valuable assistance and support in my work on this book.

1

Marx and Russia

Marx's 'Critique of Political Economy'

The history of Marxism in Russia begins with Marx himself. At the start of the 1870s Marx began an intensive study of Russia, its economy and its society, which led him to modify his conceptions in the light of what he found. Simultaneously, to understand the economic processes taking place in their country following the liberation of the serfs in 1861, the Russians began to take an interest in Marx and his economic doctrines. It is this mutual relationship that provides an insight both into Marx's thought in the last years of his life and the direction taken by the development of Marxism in Russia.

What led Marx to embark upon his study of Russia? This has to do with the way he intended to follow up the publication of the first volume of *Das Kapital* in 1867. Marx intended that there would be three volumes of *Das Kapital*, which would form part of a more extensive work called 'The Critique of Political Economy'. In volume one, Marx described the production process of capital, how commodities came into being and were exchanged. The third volume, which already existed in draft, dealt with the various ways in which income was derived from capital, such as profit, rent and the like. Marx had left the writing of the second volume to the last in order to ensure that it would fit seamlessly between the first and the third volumes, so that all three would form a continuous sequence. This second volume would deal with how capital circulated and reproduced itself.

One can see from Marx's outlines and drafts how important the subject of circulation was for the argument that *Das Kapital* would make. For in its circulations, capital does two important things. One is that it expands ever outwards, bringing more and more areas under its sway. The other action of capital as it circulates is what Marx called 'subsumption', that is, making the spheres in which it functions more and more capitalist, so that eventually everything becomes a capitalist commodity. The end result would be to make capitalism the 'universal' system so that it would extend throughout the world and replace all previous forms of economic organization.

There was also a philosophical dimension to this scheme of things, which is why *Das Kapital* is such an intricate work. Marx structured his exposition of the capitalist system on analogy with the layout of Hegel's *Science of Logic*. There Hegel sets out to show that the Absolute Idea, the knowledge, say, that an inventor would have of his machine, is not obtained by communing directly with nature, as Schelling's prevailing philosophical school at the time maintained, but by conscious reasoning using concepts. He made his case in a way calculated to convince his contemporaries, though modern readers of his work might not appreciate Hegel's mode of argument. At the centre of Hegel's *Logic* is the Concept (*Begriff*), the entity so despised by Hegel's contemporaries as a symbol of plodding mediocrity, and this is what moves from the most rudimentary awareness to absolute knowledge. The route the Concept takes is one linking together in a continuous progression all the philosophical conceptions or 'categories' of Hegel's day, such as the syllogism, quantity, quality, measure and so on. Hegel's Concept moves in a peculiar way: it passes through the phases of Universality (the phase of abstraction), Particularity (the phase of concreteness) and Individuality (the phase of concrete Universality). Hegel calls the cyclical movement of the Concept through its three phases 'dialectics' or 'logic'.

Marx's 'Critique of Political Economy' was to be structured in like manner, though in this case, the linked categories would not be philosophical but economic. The progression would be from the most rudimentary category of capitalism, the commodity, to its most complex, the world market. He would show that 'the tendency to create the world market is directly given in the Concept of capital itself' (Marx 1973: 408). Marx's drafts show that he grouped the phenomena of capitalism under the headings of Universality, Particularity and Individuality. This is how he designated the phases undergone by a commodity in its circulation, so that the cycle of Money-Commodity-Money (M-C-M) was designated as Universality, Particularity and Individuality (U-P-I) (Marx 1970: 94). The three volumes of *Das Kapital* were also designated in this way, so that in Marx's system, as in Hegel's, each part of the system was identical to the system as a whole.

But why should the capitalist economy emulate Hegel's *Logic*? What does Marx mean by this? He thinks that Hegel's system of philosophy is valid up to a point, but it is based entirely on abstractions. The system that Hegel sees in philosophy is in reality the system of the capitalist economy, but Hegel views it in a distorted or 'reflected' way, because his standpoint is that of the individual in bourgeois society. But if one adopts the viewpoint of the collectivity of mankind one can appreciate the illusions which the individualism of capitalist society creates for what they are (Marx 1976: 102). If it had been completed, Marx's 'Critique of Political Economy' would have made all of its arguments explicit.

Although he knew exactly what he had to say in volume two and although he already had sketched this out in preliminary drafts, Marx was never able to finish the crucial second volume of *Das Kapital*. And consequently he was unable to complete his intended 'Critique of Political Economy'. What went so badly wrong?

The snag that Marx encountered came just at the time that he was working on the final draft of the first volume of *Das Kapital*. When he looked for evidence that the circulation and expanded reproduction of capital absorbed earlier types of social and economic formations, it was not to be found. On the contrary, there were numerous examples of traditional rural communities surviving in a capitalist environment and, ironically enough, one of them was near his native town of Trier in Germany. In March 1868 in a letter to Engels Marx cursed himself for the 'judicial blindness' that prevented him from seeing what was obvious; he had been too carried away by the structure of his system to notice the actual situation on the ground. But if Marx had got his economics wrong, its Hegelian structure was no longer appropriate. This is implied in the letter to Engels where Marx makes a reference to the terms Universal and Particular:

> But what would Hegel say if in the next world he was to learn that the Universal [*Allgemeine*] in Old German and Old Norse means nothing but the common land, and the Particular [*Sundre, Besondere*] nothing but the separate property divided off from the common land? So the logical categories are coming damn well out of 'our intercourse' after all. (Marx and Engels 1987a: 558)

From 1868 onwards these and other Hegelian terms, which previously had pervaded Marx's writings, cease to appear.

The above passage is significant not simply as the one in which Marx abandoned the Hegelian underpinnings of *Das Kapital* but also for its insight into what Marx meant by 'materialism'. This is contained in the observation that: 'the logical categories are coming ... out of "our intercourse"', which is a reference to Ludwig Feuerbach's argument that logical abstractions have no independent existence, that they are products of the relationship between people in society. In this case Marx implies that the terms Universal and Particular can be resolved into the practices of everyday life.

Compared with the drafts which preceded it, volume one of *Das Kapital* shows that Marx had already gone some way to removing mentions of the action of capital to 'subsume' earlier forms of economic organization. 'Chapter 6' in which 'subsumption' was mentioned at some length was discarded. Instead of proceeding with volume two, in 1872 Marx published a second edition of volume one, this time removing much – but not all – of the philosophical vocabulary. In the French translation published between 1872 and 1875 he not only removed all of the Hegelian terminology but also rewrote substantial parts of it, inserting passages to make it clear that capital did not inevitably carry all before it, or that economic development was necessarily unidirectional. Marx illustrated the possibility of reverse development with the example of Northern Italy at the end of the fifteenth century, where emancipated peasants streamed into the towns, but because there was insufficient industry to absorb them, they returned to the countryside where they made a livelihood from small-scale cultivation (Marx 1872: 315).

To indicate that any remaining Hegelian terminology in the second German edition of *Das Kapital* did not advance the argument but was only a mode of expression, Marx declared in the Postscript that in contrast to the dismissive attitude to Hegel in contemporary intellectual circles, he had 'openly avowed myself a pupil of the great thinker, and even, here and there in the chapter on the theory of value, coquetted with the mode of expression peculiar to him' (Marx 1976: 102–3). The declaration did not appear in the French edition of *Das Kapital*, since there it no longer applied.

To be sure, Marx had done much more than 'coquetted' with Hegel's form of expression, and Hegel's influence had gone well beyond the first chapter of *Das Kapital*. These comments, therefore, were not a statement of what Marx's debt to Hegel had been in the past, but about how Marx wanted that debt to be understood in the future, that is, not as an essential part of his system, but as a form of expression.

During the 1870s Marx returned repeatedly to his manuscript of volume two, showing that he had not entirely lost hope of completing it. It was in connection with his studies of the circulation of capital and what its effects were on traditional agrarian communities that Marx took up the study of Russia. For Marx's purpose there could not be a better subject for study than Russia. The country was undergoing one of the most profound and far-reaching changes in its history. Russia's defeat in the Crimean War had emphasized that to compete militarily with the Western powers it would have to modernize its flagging economy and its social institutions. The reform on which all others depended was to bring an end to serfdom. Nothing could be done to reform the army, the educational system or the judiciary as long as twenty-two million of Russia's population remained outside the control of the state, as the private property of the landowners. The liberation of the serfs in 1861 was the first of a series of reforms in which Russia's armed forces, its legal and educational system were brought more into line with corresponding institutions in Western Europe. The liberation of the serfs was a first tentative step towards moving the Russian economy in the direction of a Western market economy.

The abolition of serfdom

By the mid-nineteenth century the Russian government could draw upon considerable experience of liberating serfs in the Empire. Between 1817 and

1819 the serfs had been liberated in the Baltic provinces of Estland, Livland and Kurland. This had not been an act of magnanimity by the German landowners, but a means of avoiding improved conditions of renting land to the peasants that Alexander I would have imposed. In the eyes of the Baltic aristocracy the tsar's regulations would have infringed on their right of ownership to the land. The liberation of the serfs was a means to protect this ownership, and consequently the serfs were liberated without land. Having no other means to support themselves, the peasants were forced to work for their former employers, often on worse terms than before. Their desperation erupted in uprisings in the 1850s. When the landowners of the neighbouring Lithuanian province of Kovno petitioned the government to liberate their serfs without land, Alexander II made it plain that the liberation that he contemplated would be one that would provide allotments of land to the freed peasants.

As in the Baltic provinces, most landowners of the Russian interior, especially those of the fertile southern 'black soil' region, were determined to cling on to their absolute ownership of the land, and this principle was embodied in the corresponding legislation of 1861. They were compensated for the land ceded to their peasants by an advance from the government which would be repaid over time by the peasants. The abolition of serfdom, moreover, would not be implemented immediately, but phased in over a period of nine years, during which the peasants would be 'temporarily obligated' and still perform their accustomed services to the landowner, whether it be labour service (*barshchina*) or payments in money or of kind (*obrok*). Often the allotments the peasants received under the 1861 legislation were smaller than those that they had formerly rented from the landowner, since the latter was permitted to 'cut off' portions of peasant land in order that his estate would be at least one third of its former size. Although the reform of 1961 gave Russian peasants their personal freedom, the conditions, restrictions and payments with which this was hedged caused widespread discontent, many believing that this was not their real liberation; that the genuine one was still to come.

What the Russian government wanted to avoid at all costs was the formation of a proletariat, a class of rootless workers who would roam the country creating disturbances that would threaten the existing social order. They had seen the destructive power of the proletariats in the rebellions that had engulfed the countries of Western Europe in 1848, and the Russian authorities were determined to do everything they could to avoid it. Liberating the peasants with land was one method the Russian government used to maintain social stability. Another measure of this kind was the maintenance of the peasant commune. The land was given, not to individual peasants, or even to peasant families, but to the commune.

Haxthausen

In the period prior to the liberation of the serfs the peasant commune had been the subject of lively public discussion. This had been initiated by the book about Russia written by the German scholar August von Haxthausen. Haxthausen was an adherent of the Romantic Movement in Germany. He deplored the drab uniformity of the society that the French revolution had left in its wake, and looked to Medieval times for the social ideal. Like his friends, the Brothers Grimm, Haxthausen collected folk stories and folk songs, considering that the peasants were the bearers of national culture rather than the educated metropolitan elite. His first publication was a study of village life in two north German provinces, for which he was awarded the title of Privy Councillor by the Prussian king and was also commissioned to make a similar study of the provinces of the Prussian monarchy. It was while working on this study that Haxthausen received the invitation from tsar Nicholas I to travel round Russia and write an account of the country and its people (Haxthausen 1972: 17–21).

The book that Haxthausen produced at the end of his travels in Russia has much in common with his studies of the north German and Prussian provinces. Haxthausen paid special attention to the Russian peasant commune because he was familiar with a similar institution in Germany. He recognized that the peasant communes were autonomous and self-governing, and that their practice of redistributing the land at their disposal prevented the emergence of inequalities among the families that composed them. As in his studies on German village communities, Haxthausen stressed the role of the Russian peasant commune in maintaining social stability and shielding Russia from the corrosive influence of the socialist doctrines that so afflicted Western Europe. He was able to declare that Russia was immune from this kind of socialist agitation because 'the utopia of the European revolutionaries is already there, fully embodied in the life of the people' (Haxthausen 1972: 10). Haxthausen's book, which met with the approval of the Russian authorities, was an influence on the liberation legislation in 1861.

Among the Russian intelligentsia the peasant commune acquired an ideological significance. It was placed within the framework of current German philosophy, every development of which, as Haxthausen observed, was followed with keen interest in Russia. To the current called the 'Slavophiles', some of whose members Haxthausen met in Moscow (Haxthausen 1972: 226), the commune imbued Russia with a spirit of fellowship and cooperation which was entirely lacking in the individualistic and egotistical societies of Western Europe.

During the 1840s the Russian liberal Alexander Herzen, in company with the camp of the 'Westerners', placed too great a value on individualism to agree with the Slavophiles on the superiority of Russia in this respect over the West. Once in exile in Paris, and disillusioned by the failure of the 1848 revolution, however, Herzen's ideas began to change in a direction more akin to the Slavophile way of thinking. He now regarded Western Europe in the same light as the Slavophiles – as the world of the past, now suffering decay and decrepitude. Russia, on the other hand, he thought of as the embodiment of youth and vigour. Whereas European society was enervated by petty-bourgeois individualism, Russian society, based on the peasant commune, was integrated and whole, so that communism was the natural condition of the Russian people. It was with Russia, Herzen considered, that the future lay.

Herzen expressed these ideas in a series of articles in French between 1849 and 1850. In the article 'The Russian People and Socialism' he drew the contrast between Russia and Europe in a particularly evocative way. He posed the question:

> Will old Europe have the strength to infuse new blood into its veins and fling itself headlong into the boundless future, to which it is being precipitously borne by an irresistible force over the ruins of its ancestral home, the fragments of past civilisations, and the trampled treasures of modern culture? ... In the midst of this chaos ... of a world falling into dust at the foot of the cradle of the future, men's eyes involuntarily turn to the East. (Herzen 1956: 472–3)

By the 'East' Herzen of course meant Russia, and he went on to elaborate on the social solidarity of the Russian peasant commune which, he observed, it had required the Prussian scholar Haxthausen to bring to public attention (Herzen 1956: 498).

Marx was dismissive of Herzen's conception of 'Russian socialism' for a number of reasons. One was the antipathy of the Young Hegelians to the Romantic school to which Haxthausen belonged, an antipathy that Marx shared. Marx believed that Haxthausen had been duped by the Russian authorities. In a letter to Engels written in October 1858, Marx observed that when a revolutionary movement began to develop in Russia 'we shall have proof of the full extent to which the worthy Privy Councillor Haxthausen has allowed himself to be hoodwinked by the "authorities" and by the peasants those authorities have trained'(Marx and Engels 1983: 346). Moreover, Marx had a personal antipathy towards Herzen, and even more so towards Herzen's friend and associate, the anarchist Mikhail Bakunin. And of course the idea of a special kind of Russian socialism was in conflict with Marx's conception of socialism as being universal, on a world scale.

In his book *A Contribution to the Critique of Political Economy* published in 1859, Marx observed, clearly with Herzen in mind, that:

> It is an absurdly biased view that is gaining ground at the present time, according to which the form of communal property which has its origins in

nature is a specifically Slavonic, or even exclusively Russian, phenomenon. It is an early form which can be found among the Romans, Teutons and Celts, and of which a whole collection of diverse patterns ... is still in existence in India. (Marx 1970: 33)

A much more vehement rebuttal of Herzen's conception of 'Russian socialism' appears in the Postscript to the first volume of *Das Kapital* published in 1867. This was:

If on the continent of Europe the influence of capitalist production continues to develop as it has done up till now, enervating the human race by overwork, the division of labour, subordination to machines, the maiming of women and children, making life wretched, etc., hand in hand with competition in the size of national armies, national debts, taxes, sophisticated warfare etc., then the rejuvenation of Europe by the knout and the obligatory infusion of Kalmyk blood so earnestly prophesied by the half-Russian and full Muscovite Herzen may become inevitable. (This belletrist, incidentally, has noted that he made his discoveries on 'Russian' communism, not in Russia, but in the work of the Prussian Privy Councillor Haxthausen). (Marx 1867: 763)

This passage was written at a time when Marx was confident that the scheme of capitalist development that he had envisioned in his drafts could be supported by evidence. His realization by the following year that traditional agrarian society would not yield so easily to the inroads of capitalism caused Marx to revise his attitude to Herzen's conceptions, if not to Herzen himself. Accordingly, the caustic remarks about Herzen's 'Russian socialism' were removed from the 1872 edition as well as all subsequent editions of *Das Kapital*.

The debate on the peasant commune

The 1861 reform did much to stimulate debate on the origins and nature of the Russian peasant commune. The Russian historian V. A. Aleksandrov has pointed out that whereas before 1850 only four works had been published in Russia on the peasant commune, between 1856 and 1860 the number soared to 99, and by 1880 it had reached 546 (Aleksandrov 1976: 3).

It was the liberal thinker B. N. Chicherin who initiated much of the discussion surrounding the peasant commune in the second half of the 1850s. In 1856 he published an article entitled 'A Survey of the History of the Development of the Agrarian Commune in Russia' in the journal of the Westerners *Russkii Vestnik* (Russian Herald) which challenged the interpretation put on the peasant commune by Haxthausen, the Slavophiles and Herzen, who had all assumed that the commune in Russia was the survival of an ancient social order.

Chicherin's article undermined this assumption completely. For from archival documents he had discovered that in medieval Russia peasants had owned land, sold it, bequeathed it to heirs and donated it to monasteries, all as individual private property. This led him to conclude that a process of evolution had taken place by which an original patriarchal or clan commune had developed into the modern type with common ownership of land and periodic redivision.

From the fifteenth century onwards concepts of the State began to develop in Russia, and these new principles occasioned changes in the commune. It was transformed from a possessionary institution into an estate (*soslovie*) and a State one, owing obligations not only to the landowner but also to the government. Between the fifteenth and the seventeenth centuries changes were effected which facilitated the fulfilment of these obligations. One such change was the attachment of the peasants to the land to meet the objections raised by communes that many of their members had departed, increasing the tax burden on those who remained.

The culmination of this process was Peter the Great's poll tax which was introduced in 1722. It was this tax which, in Chicherin's view, shaped the modern peasant commune and gave it its characteristic features. Since the tax fell upon individuals, it followed that each one should receive a certain portion of land to enable him to raise enough money to pay it. And since the tax burden was the same for everyone, it was reasonable that the portion of land received ought also to be equal. As, moreover, any increase in the population was liable to create inequalities, repartitions were required to restore parity to the land holdings.

In the same year as his article appeared Chicherin also published his findings in book form under the title, *Regional Institutions in Russia in the XVII Century*. I. D. Beliaev replied to Chicherin in the Slavophile journal *Russkaia Beseda* (Russian conversation). In Beliaev's opinion the commune had not been created by the government, but had arisen out of the way of life of the Russian people; the government had only made use of 'what already existed in the manners and customs of the people'. Like Chicherin, Beliaev too published his views in book form; his *Peasants in Russia* appeared in 1860 (White 1996: 217–20).

If there was controversy about the origins of the peasant commune, there was a great deal more unanimity about its future. By the time the debate on the commune was conducted it was generally accepted that the institution was not peculiarly Russian and that it had once existed in the countries of Western Europe. It survived in Russia only through that country's social and economic backwardness. The implication was that if Russia were to follow the economic development of the West then the commune must inevitably disappear. The peasant reform of 1861 was widely held by Slavophiles and Westerners alike to be a significant step in this direction.

The only prominent writer in Russia at that time to advance the view that the peasant commune was not destined to disintegrate was N. G. Chernyshevsky. A follower of Feuerbach and deeply influenced by German philosophy, Chernyshevsky discussed the future of the peasant commune in an article entitled 'Critique of Philosophical Prejudices against Communal Ownership', published in 1858. In it he challenged the widely held assumption that communal landownership must inevitably give way in the course of historical development to private property in land.

According to Chernyshevsky, the conclusion drawn by orthodox economists was that since communal ownership was a primitive form of agrarian relations, and private property a more advanced form, there was every reason to prefer private to common property. This was a logical position, and one which implied that trying to preserve the peasant commune would be to fly in the face of progress and the natural course of historical development.

The argument deployed by Chernyshevsky in defence of the commune was that historical development was not as simple as the orthodox economists believed. The newest German philosophy, that of Schelling and Hegel, had discovered that in all spheres of existence the universal pattern of development was a return to the point of departure. Chernyshevsky stated:

> We are not followers of Hegel, and even less of Schelling. But we recognise that both of these systems have given great service to the science of discovering universal patterns of development. The basic result of these discoveries is expressed in the following axiom: 'In respect of form, the higher stage of development is similar to the initial one, that which was its point of departure'. (Chernyshevsky 1950: 362)

This is the essence of Schelling's system; it was made more precise and detailed by Hegel.

Having established the general principle, Chernyshevsky could now argue that private property was not the highest, but only an intermediate stage in the development of property relations. The highest form of landownership would be the negation of private property, the return to the communal type. There was every reason to retain the peasant commune, therefore, rather than to welcome its disintegration, because it could bring about the direct transition to the highest form of property ownership. As a socialist, Chernyshevsky saw in the commune a means of attaining socialism without having to pass through a capitalist stage. This objective conditioned his approach to economic questions in general.

In the sphere of economic theory Chernyshevsky's major work was his translation of and commentary on John Stuart Mill's *Principles of Political Economy*. This was originally published in the journal *Sovremennik* (Contemporary) in 1860, but appeared in 1869 and 1870 as volumes III and IV of the edition of Chernyshevsky's writings published in Geneva. The work consisted of two parts: (1) a translation of the first Book of Mill's treatise with 'additions and notes' by Chernyshevsky, and (2) 'Studies in Political Economy (according to Mill)', which was a brief exposition of the second, third, fourth and fifth Books of Mill's work with commentaries by Chernyshevsky.

According to Chernyshevsky, the purpose of this voluminous work was to provide the younger generation with a reliable source from which to learn about Adam Smith's system. He regarded Mill as the most brilliant representative of the Smithian school and someone from whom much could be learnt. But, at the same time, Chernyshevsky could not accept the individualist assumptions on which classical political economy was based, so much so that he found it necessary not only to expound Mill's ideas, but also to take issue with some of the most fundamental of them.

Chernyshevsky was thus able to use Mill's principles in two ways. He was able to take up and reinforce Mill's criticisms of the capitalist system and use them as a platform for his own socialist ideas. On the other hand, Mill's clear and comprehensive exposition of classical political economy could be used by Chernyshevsky as a starting point for demonstrating the system's inherent irrationality and inhumanity.

Chernyshevsky repeatedly stressed the difference in approach to economics between Mill and himself. This was that, whereas Mill adopted the viewpoint of economic individualism, Chernyshevsky espoused the point of view of society or humanity. In Chernyshevsky's opinion: 'Science regards all subjects from the point of view of humanity or society, and when it speaks of benefit it must of course have in mind the benefit of society, if no explicit reservation is made limiting the sense of the word'(Chernyshevsky 1949: 155). As a social science, Chernyshevsky believed, political economy could do no other than take society as its subject.

It was to the benefit of society in Russia, Chernyshevsky believed, to avoid the proletarianization of the peasantry. For this reason, he advocated that they be adequately provided with land, and that the commune should be preserved. He referred in his commentary on Mill's *Principles* to articles he had published earlier, written in defence of communal ownership. He thought it fortunate that the institution had survived in Russia and that it would continue to survive if one did not 'contrary to any need and common-sense, attempt to destroy it'. The commune, he considered, should be preserved and improved to remove its disadvantages (Chernyshevsky 1949: 403).

In articles written before 1861, Chernyshevsky argued in favour of a low rate of redemption payment for peasant allotments, and even for a redemption that would be paid by all groups in society, since all would benefit from a liberated peasantry. He was therefore bitterly disappointed by the actual terms of the 1861 statutes. In 1862, he wrote an open letter to Alexander II entitled 'Letters without an Address' criticizing the 1861 reform. This was only published in 1874, eight years after Chernyshevsky had been exiled to Siberia, convicted on dubious evidence of subversive activities (Koniushaia 1948: 3–17).

Marx first came to know of Chernyshevsky in 1867 through A. A. Serno-Solovevich, an associate of Chernyshevsky's living in exile in Geneva. It was initially in order to read Chernyshevsky's economic works that Marx began to teach himself Russian at the beginning of 1870. By January of the following year he could read in it fairly fluently.

Marx's annotations on the essay 'Critique of Philosophical Prejudices against Communal Ownership' register his agreement with Chernyshevsky. All the stages in Chernyshevsky's argument were underlined, as was the 'axiom' on which the argument was based, that is, 'In respect of form, the higher stage of development is similar to the initial one, that which was its point of departure'. This was underlined by Marx on the two instances it occurred in the text. He also noted with approval Chernyshevsky's qualification: 'of course, while the two forms are similar, the content at the end is immeasurably richer and higher than at the beginning' (Nikolaevsky 1929: 391).

Marx read Chernyshevsky's commentary on Mill's *Principles of Political Economy* with equal care, and here too Chernyshevsky's ideas paralleled Marx's own. The commentary on Mill was a critique of classical political economy from the point of view of 'society' or 'humanity', and 'society', moreover, was conceived in the concrete form of the peasant commune, a position Marx had recently adopted.

It is significant that in such an extensive work Marx's annotations show relatively few points of disagreement with Chernyshevsky. Most of these, moreover, were on points of factual detail, as when, for example, Chernyshevsky stated that Mill had been the first British economist to concern himself with the question of small peasant proprietorship. Here Marx noted: 'It's a mistake'. Marx also queried Chernyshevsky's judgement that Mill's sketch of economic history had been written in a masterly fashion (Chernyshevsky 1937: XX).

Marx made his high regard for Chernyshevsky known in the Postscript to the second edition of *Das Kapital*, where he remarked:

The Continental revolution of 1848 also had its reaction in England. Men who still claimed some scientific standing and aspired to be something more than mere sophists and sycophants of the ruling classes tried to harmonise the political economy of capital with the claims, no longer to be ignored, of the proletariat. Hence the insipid syncretism, of which John Stuart Mill is the best representative. It is a declaration of bankruptcy by 'bourgeois' economics, which has already been illuminated in a masterly fashion by the great Russian scholar and critic N. Chernyshevsky, in his *Outlines of Political Economy according to Mill*. (Marx 1976: 97–8)

The Russian translation of *Das Kapital*

Marx intended to make Chernyshevsky's work better known in the West. In his letters to Nikolai Danielson, his contact in Russia, Marx informed him that, in addition to using Chernyshevsky's economic works in the second volume of *Das Kapital*, he wanted to write something on Chernyshevsky's life and personality; he therefore asked Danielson to provide the requisite information. This was done, but the projected biography of Chernyshevsky never materialized.

The desire of the radical Russian intelligentsia to discover what the capitalist system had in store for the country inspired the appearance of Chernyshevsky's commentary on Mill. It also stimulated the interest in Marx's *Das Kapital* in the same circles. It was natural, therefore, that Marx's first contacts in Russia should be with the group of Chernyshevsky's young followers in St Petersburg, consisting of N. F. Danielson, G. A. Lopatin, N. N. Liubavin and M. F. Negreskul. All but Liubavin were employed at the Society for Mutual Credit, where Danielson was to remain for the rest of his working life (Grin 1985: 12). It was a post which allowed Danielson to gain access to all kinds of materials relating to the economic situation in Russia, and this was to prove extremely useful to Marx.

Danielson first made contact with Marx in September 1868. In the 'Introduction' to a collection of letters Marx had written to him, and which was published in 1908, Danielson explained how this correspondence had come about. He recalled that when he first read Marx's *Das Kapital* in 1867, he was so impressed that he began at once to make arrangements to have it translated into Russian. He succeeded in finding a publisher; this was N. P. Poliakov, a man with radical sympathies who specialized in publishing works from Western Europe. All that remained was to find a translator. Danielson's first letter to Marx in September 1868 informed him of these arrangements (Marx and Engels 1908: 1).

Finding a suitable translator proved to be no easy matter. Negreskul and Liubavin first approached Mikhail Bakunin, and although the latter undertook the translation and accepted payment in advance, his work was found to be inadequate and was produced only as a result of constant exhortation and after great delays. Bakunin found the work tedious, and to free him from his obligation, his associate Sergei Nechaev sent a letter to Liubavin stating that if he did not leave Bakunin in peace there would be unpleasant consequences. Since Nechaev had been involved in the murder of a fellow revolutionary in Russia, Liubavin had every reason to take the threat seriously (Carr 1933: 299). In the spring of 1870 Lopatin went to Geneva and on Poliakov's behalf released Bakunin from his undertaking and recovered the money the publisher had advanced. He also made known Nechaev's criminal activities in Russia.

After spending two weeks in Geneva, Lopatin went to Paris where he received a letter of introduction to Marx from his son-in-law Paul Lafargue. He then crossed to England and found lodgings in Brighton, from where he visited Marx in London on 2 July 1870. Three days later Marx communicated to Engels his impressions of the young Russian:

> He is still very young, was 2 years in prison, then 8 months in a fortress in the Caucasus, from where he escaped. He is the son of an impoverished nobleman, and supported himself at St Petersburg University by giving lessons. Now he lives very miserably doing translations for Russia ... . (Marx and Engels 1988: 530)

With Marx's help, Lopatin made a thorough study of *Das Kapital*. He became familiar not only with the first volume but also with the overall structure of the work as a whole and what the remaining volumes would contain. He impressed Marx by his understanding of how the argument and the arrangement of the material would proceed. According to P. L. Lavrov:

> There were few people of whom Karl Marx spoke to me with such warmth as of Herman Lopatin. There was, in his words, hardly anyone who understood so well what he was doing and what he intended to accomplish in the forthcoming volumes of his work as Lopatin did. And in this respect the distinguished teacher of socialism was very demanding of the people he befriended. (Antonov 1962: 37)

The fact that Lopatin and, through Lopatin, Danielson understood what was to be contained in the subsequent volumes of Marx's work was very important. It meant that Danielson in St Petersburg knew exactly what kind of materials Marx required and was able to supply them as they became available.

It was while studying *Das Kapital* in this first-hand way that Lopatin embarked on its translation into Russian. He did this in a most thorough and systematic manner, taking great care to devise suitable equivalents for the terminology Marx had used, and checking quotations from the *Blue Books* with the original text in the British Museum. Altogether Lopatin translated about a third of the volume, comprising the chapters 'The Transformation of Money into Capital', 'The Production of Absolute Surplus Value' and part of 'The Production of Relative Surplus Value'.

Significantly, Lopatin began his translation from the second chapter. By the summer of 1870 Marx had decided to rewrite the first chapter, dispensing with its Hegelian terminology, and he expected to have it ready by the time the translation was finished. This turned out not to be the case, and the Russian translation came out with the same first chapter as the original German edition.

Lopatin ended his translation work abruptly in November 1870. Marx's admiration for Chernyshevsky had convinced Lopatin of the need to 'give back to the world the great publicist and citizen'. Consequently he decided to try to rescue Chernyshevsky from Siberia. But before setting out for Siberia he left his translation with Danielson, explaining Marx's intention to rework the first chapter for the Russian version. As it happened, Lopatin's rescue attempt failed and he himself was arrested and imprisoned at Tobolsk. He was able to escape and make his way abroad only in 1873 (Marx and Engels 1908: 1–3).

The translation of *Das Kapital* fell to Danielson, who reached the end of the volume in October 1871. As Marx was preoccupied with the affairs of the International, he was unable to provide a rewritten first chapter. In November, Marx wrote to Danielson not to wait but to translate the first chapter as it stood. Since this chapter and the appendix 'The Value Form' which accompanied it were especially intricate, Danielson handed them over for translation to Liubavin (Grin 1985: 74). The completed Russian version was finally published in March 1872. Marx, who by that time could read Russian fluently, was delighted with the translation and found the work of the three translators to be 'masterly' (Marx and Engels 1989b: 386).

Marx's studies of Russia

Just how extensive Marx's study of Russia was can be judged from the catalogue of Russian-language material in his possession that he compiled in 1881. This was headed 'Russisches in my bookstall' and contained 115 titles comprising 150 separate volumes. When Danielson invited Marx to write on the subject of Russian agrarian relations in 1877, he could do so in the confidence that the latter was as familiar with all the available sources on the subject as any scholar in Russia (Rudiak 1979: 17–22).

The Russian works that Marx read covered three main areas of investigation: (1) the history of the Russian peasant commune; (2) the peasant reform of 1861; and (3) Russian economic development from 1861 to the present time. One may consider Marx's study of Russia under these three heads.

(1) Relatively few of the Russian works that Marx read were on the history of the peasant commune. Those that were on that subject centred around the debate between Chicherin and Beliaev. In March 1873 Marx requested Danielson to send him details of the debate, indicating that his sympathies were not with Chicherin:

You would much oblige me in giving me some information on the views of Chicherin, relating to the historical development of communal property in Russia; and on his polemics on that subject with Beliaev ... all historical analogy speaks against Chicherin. How should it come to happen that in Russia the same institution had been simply introduced as a fiscal measure, as a concomitant incident of serfdom, while everywhere else it was of spontaneous growth and marked a necessary phase of development of free peoples? (Marx and Engels 1989b: 487)

Danielson not only sent Marx the relevant works by Chicherin, Beliaev and other authors but also accompanied them by a lengthy disquisition of his own, complete with bibliography, on how the controversy had developed (Marx and Engels 1967: 288–308).

Marx left no annotations in Chicherin's book, but in Beliaev's he made several notes. These show that he was interested to see on what grounds Beliaev based his argument that communal landownership had existed prior to serfdom. Marx in general found Beliaev's case unconvincing. His impression of Beliaev's book was the same as that of Chicherin's: it was unable to support its arguments with documentary evidence (Nikolaevskii 1929: 403).

(2) Marx devoted a considerable amount of attention to examining how the 1861 legislation had been framed and what its provisions were. He was deeply influenced in this respect by Chernyshevsky's 'Letters without an Address' and it was this essay which provided the framework for his own interpretation of the reform. His first attempt at writing on the subject, a draft entitled 'On the Emancipation of the Russian Serfs', was a summary of Chernyshevsky's Letters. His more detailed manuscript entitled 'Notes on the 1861 Reform and Russia's Post-Reform Development', written probably in 1880–81, drew upon a wider range of sources, but retained the same structure and interpretation as Chernyshevsky's work.

Marx's sources for the 1861 reform were extremely good. His notes show that he had used Haxthausen's book, *The Agrarian Constitution of Russia* (Haxthausen 1866) and A. I. Skrebitsky's four-volume collection of documents on the reform, *Peasant Affairs in the Reign of Alexander II* (Skrebitskii 1862). These two works were connected with one another, and shared a common first-hand source of information. Haxthausen had always been an enthusiastic supporter of peasant liberation in Russia, and he had made his views known to Alexander II when the latter had visited Berlin in 1857. Due to his keen interest in Russian affairs, Haxthausen was kept informed of how the reform was progressing. The Chairman of the Editorial Commission Ya. I. Rostovtsev sent him copies of all the relevant documents and the proceedings of the Commission. These were the materials on which Haxthausen's book, *The Agrarian Constitution of Russia*, was based.

As Haxthausen required his materials translated into German, he enlisted the help of the Russian ophthalmic surgeon Alexander Skrebitsky, who was in Berlin on business in 1860. Skrebitsky not only helped Haxthausen with the research for his book but also edited and published the collection of documents that Rostovtsev had made available. Haxthausen's book and Skrebitsky's collection were among Marx's main materials in compiling the manuscript, 'Notes on the 1861 Reform and Russia's Post-Reform Development' (Haxthausen 1866: 6).

It was from the reports of the Commission's proceedings in Skrebitsky's collection that Marx found proof that the reform of 1861 was deliberately designed to impose financial burdens on the peasantry in order to make them dependent on the landowners, so that the latter would continue to have plentiful and cheap labour at their disposal. This aspect of the proposed legislation was thrown into relief when two members of the Commission objected to the inconsistency of making the peasants' freedom dependent on their purchase of land. Marx found their intervention to be highly significant as it was symptomatic of the spirit in which the legislation was framed.

It is interesting to note that when the Russian Marxist historians N. A. Rozhkov and M. N. Pokrovsky wrote about the 1861 liberation in the early twentieth century they assumed that the 'Marxist' approach to the subject would be to trace the measure to its economic roots, to show that it was driven by the economic interests of the landowners (Tsagolov 1956: 63). As Marx's notes published in the 1940s show, this was not at all the approach that he himself took to the question.

(3) By far the most extensive and most detailed of Marx's studies of Russia were on the period after 1861 and concerned the consequences of the reform for Russia's economic development. They concerned in particular the implications of the reform for the circulation and accumulation of capital, and the ways in which peasants were transformed into proletarians.

A work which had an important bearing on these questions was the one which Marx first read in Russian. This was N. Flerovsky's *The Condition of the Working Class in Russia* (Flerovskii 1869), a book published in St Petersburg by Poliakov and sent to Marx by Danielson in October 1869. Flerovsky was the pseudonym of V. V. Bervi, the son of a professor of physiology at Kazan University. Bervi studied law there, and through his father's connections became a high-ranking civil servant in St Petersburg. But his opposition to arbitrary acts of repression by the government led to his arrest in 1862. Bervi spent many years in internal exile, but he used his experiences to gather material for his book on the life and economic situation of the common people in the various parts of Russia.

Despite its title, Flerovsky's book concerned mostly the Russian peasants. It was these peasants that he referred to as workers. Like Marx, he reserved the term 'proletarians' for those who had been uprooted from the land and relied exclusively on wages for a livelihood. Bervi was interested, moreover, in how workers became proletarians, a feature of his work that Marx found especially valuable. But besides this, Flerovsky's book provided Marx with a wealth of information about the life and culture of the population of the Russian Empire, both Russians and the minority nationalities. As he remarked to Engels: 'this is the most important book which has appeared since your *Condition of the Working Class*. The family life of the Russian peasants – the awful beating to death of wives, the vodka and the concubines is well described' (Marx and Engels 1967: 25). This kind of description, in Marx's opinion, made a refreshing change from Herzen's presentation of Russia as some kind of 'communistic Eldorado'.

Marx's daughter, Jenny, in a letter to Kugelmann on 30 October 1869 indicated the use to which Flerovsky's book was to be put: 'The book has come at an opportune time. Moor [i.e. Marx J. W.] intends to publish the facts contained in it in his second volume'(Rudiak 1979: 29). As Marx had not read the book at that time, not knowing sufficient Russian, its relevance for the second volume must have been communicated to him by Danielson and Lopatin.

The most important statistical source Marx used was the collection *Reports of the Fiscal Commission*. This Commission had been established by the Ministry of Finance shortly before the 1861 reform to look into the way taxes and levies were collected. It continued in existence until the early 1880s and in that time issued something in the region of 70 volumes of its findings. In 1875 Danielson loaned ten of these volumes to Marx, who made extensive notes from them before sending them back to St Petersburg. These volumes provided valuable first-hand information on the current economic processes in Russia.

Danielson used the materials he sent to Marx for his own studies of the Russian economy, and the resulting article entitled 'A Sketch of Our Post-Reform Social Economy' was published in the journal *Slovo* (Word) for October 1880 (Danielson 1880). A copy was sent to Marx. The article is of considerable interest because in it Danielson, in advance of Marx, attempted to set out a scheme of how the circulation of capital applied to Russia's economic development since 1861.

In Danielson's view, there were two kinds of economic principle in operation in Russia. One was the collective principle that had been sanctioned in the 1861 legislation; the other was the individualist capitalist principle that the same legislation had simultaneously fostered. A number of factors, he considered, combined to effect the circulation of capital in Russia. These included the operation of State policy, the construction of railways, the increase in the grain trade and the vast expansion of credit. Danielson's article explained how these factors were interconnected. He began by pointing out that in order to stimulate railway construction the government subsidized private railway companies. In examining the income of the railway companies, Danielson found an apparent paradox in that although their indebtedness to the state was considerable and increasing steadily, the profits of the railway companies were enormous. The paradox was to be explained by the fact that whereas the income from the profitable companies was retained by the private companies, the losses of the remainder were borne by the exchequer (Danielson 1880: 85).

How, Danielson inquired, could such great losses to the state be recovered? The answer was in the enormous expansion in trade which had taken place over the last decade or so, especially the trade in grain. In the period in question the export of grain had increased rapidly, and grain was the chief item of freight carried by the railways. Danielson went on to argue that not only the railways but also the banks and the credit institutions lived off peasant agriculture. And, of course, it was from taxing the peasants that much of the government's income was derived. In Danielson's view, both railways and the provision of credit were the means by which the circulation of commodities took place. In the West, their appearance had given a stimulus to commodity production, to the development of science and the increased productivity of labour. In Russia the circulation of commodities had had none of these effects. For, according to Danielson, 'to maintain our economic independence we have deployed our energies not on the development of capitalist production itself, but on its result, on banks and railways' (Danielson 1880: 103).

The full significance of Danielson's article emerges when it is read in conjunction with Marx's manuscript entitled 'Notes on the 1861 Reform and Russia's Post-Reform Development'. It uses Danielson's figures and follows the structure of his article, arranging the material in practically the same order as the original. The account of the circulation of capital in Marx's manuscript represented a significant departure from the way he had approached the question previously. For here the circulation was not simply that of one capital among many but of the whole national economy. By taking the nation as his unit, Marx seemed to indicate that the circuit of capital by which the peasantry was increasingly expropriated and which expanded the capitalist class was one which was completed only on a national scale, and which involved the agency of the government. In other words, capital did not circulate in Russia locally, and one need not look in the peasant communities themselves for the force which created proletarians on the one hand and capitalists on the other. This position was of course consistent with Marx's failure to discover any instance of original accumulation that did not involve state intervention (Koniushaia 1952: 22–8).

An important work which Marx read and took notes from was V. P. Vorontsov's *The Fate of Capitalism in Russia* published in 1882 (Koniushaia 1985: 156, 177, 180, 215, 234, 240–4). The author acknowledged his debt to Danielson's 1880 article 'A Sketch of Our Post-Reform Social Economy', and in the course of his work examined the implication of the Russian state's involvement in the circulation process of capital. Vorontsov noted that large-scale industry existed largely through the support of the government; it was supported by tariffs, subsidies and state orders. The advantage it thus obtained enabled it to undercut and ruin the small-scale domestic industries.

The resources to subsidize the large-scale industry, moreover, were wrung from the peasantry by the tax system, which forced them to sell their agricultural produce at disadvantageous prices. The peasant commune no longer afforded its members protection as it became largely a mechanism for enforcing the system of mutual responsibility. As a result, peasants were leaving it in increasing numbers (Karataev 1958: 475–81).

The poverty of the population, Vorontsov argued, provided large-scale industry with a very limited market for the sale of its products, thus ensuring that it would continue to be an artificial growth requiring state support. On the other hand, foreign markets were closed to the products of Russian industry because the low productivity of labour in Russia made it impossible for them to compete with goods produced abroad. Internally, moreover, the productivity of Russian industry was high enough for it to employ only a small proportion of the peasants it had uprooted from the countryside.

Vorontsov thought, therefore, that in Russia capitalism did not have the conditions requisite for its natural development and so had to be propagated artificially by the government. He believed that these attempts were doing positive harm; by destroying the existing economic organization, peasants were being subjected to untold hardship and misery. He therefore thought that the policy should be reversed (Karataev 1958: 472).

In noting the problem that Russia did not employ the peasants it had uprooted, Vorontsov had discovered a piece of evidence which confirmed that Marx's early conception of the circulation of capital was untenable. For not only was it possible for capital to circulate without dispossessing the peasants but it was also possible for them to be expropriated without their being transformed into industrial proletarians. There was, as a result, no inevitability about the ambit of capitalism being constantly extended. It followed that even the model of circulation which Danielson (and Marx) had drawn up, involving the Russian state, would not guarantee the expanded reproduction of capital.

Despite several attempts in the 1870s to complete the volume of *Das Kapital* concerned with the circulation of capital, the work remained in the form of unfinished drafts and rough notes that after Marx's death it fell to Engels to make something of them. It was not only this particular volume that remained incomplete: so too did the projected general work, 'The Critique of Political Economy'. That meant that the objective of showing the logical progression from the commodity to the world market was unachieved. And although Marx did leave in draft a critique of classical political economy from Adam Smith, he did not, as Hegelian methodology implied, return to his point of departure, the philosophical presuppositions of his system, and examine the phenomenon of 'reflection' by which the categories of political economy appeared as categories of philosophy in human consciousness.

Marx's system as he left it had sufficient depth of analysis to attract dedicated followers, but because it was unfinished, it left the way open for an infinity of interpretations. The removal of the philosophical underpinnings from *Das Kapital* encouraged attempts to make good the philosophical dimension which it apparently lacked. The associated removal of references to capital's expanded reproduction raised the question of whether capitalism was destined to take root in Russia. *Das Kapital* and the problems it raised provided the dynamic that prompted the development of Marxist ideas, and accounts for many aspects of the history of Marxism in Russia.

2

Marx's Russian 'Scientific Friends'

Nikolai Sieber

The Russian reading public did not have to wait for the appearance of the translation of *Das Kapital* into Russian. As early as 1871, a young economist at Kiev University, Nikolai Sieber, published a dissertation which gave an exposition of Marx's economic doctrines. Sieber (Ziber) is an unjustly overlooked figure in the history of Marxism in Russia. He was born in 1844 in the Crimea. His father was a Swiss who had settled in Russia, his mother being a Ukrainian of French descent. Although Sieber was brought up in Russia and thought of himself as Russian, he remained a Swiss subject throughout his life. He was educated at the *gimnaziia* in Simferopol and entered the law faculty of Kiev University in 1863. He was fortunate to have as his teacher N. C. Bunge, who later became the Minister of Finance under Alexander III. Bunge was an adherent of the Smith and Ricardo school, but was also very receptive to the latest developments in economic thinking. Sieber graduated from Kiev University in 1866, and, encouraged by Bunge, decided to embark on an academic career, and to specialize in the study of political economy (Kleinbort 1923: 11–12). For his master's dissertation, Sieber set out to show how Marx's ideas were an elaboration on the ideas of the classical economists. The dissertation, entitled, *David Ricardo's Theory of Value and Capital in Connection with the Latest Contributions and Interpretations* was presented in 1871 and published in Kiev in the same year (Ziber 1871).

As the title of Sieber's dissertation implies, its main focus was on the theory of value which Sieber considered to be the fundamental concept in political economy and the one which gave coherence to all the rest. Although ostensibly the dominant figure in Sieber's dissertation was Ricardo, it was really Ricardo and his predecessors seen through the prism of Marx's *Das Kapital*. In Sieber's view – as in Marx's – Adam Smith and his school had been misled into believing that value was an intrinsic quality of commodities rather than the product of social relations. Sieber also, in company with Marx, reproached the classical economists with having based their conceptions on the economic activities of individuals rather than of societies, and therefore having missed the social significance of the value phenomenon. In Sieber's view, however, Ricardo was of all the representatives of the classical school the best exponent of the theory of value because he was aware that labour was the element that imparted value to commodities.

If one compares Sieber's chapter on Marx's theory of value with the first German edition of *Das Kapital* one can see how Sieber arrived at his exposition. He had taken Marx's appendix entitled 'The Value Form' and merged it with material taken from the first chapter of the book to present a continuous argument. The other change Sieber made compared to Marx's original text was more significant: he had eliminated the philosophical dimension systematically and completely. There was no trace in Sieber's commentary of any of the Hegelian vocabulary that had been so characteristic of the first edition of *Das Kapital*'s first chapter. In his dissertation Sieber refers briefly to what he had done, explaining that he had felt that Marx's form of expression had got in the way of his otherwise valuable contribution to economic thought.

> The peculiar language and the quite laconic manner of expression does little to facilitate the comprehension of his ideas, and in some cases has led to the accusation that he employs a metaphysical approach to the investigation of value. With the exception of a few places in the chapter where perhaps some statements are indeed made which do not really correspond to the truth, the accusation seems to me unjust. As far as the theory itself is concerned, Marx's method is the deductive method of the whole English school, and both its faults and its merits are those shared by the best of the theoretical economists. (Ziber 1871: 169–70)

In response to Marx's request, Danielson sent him Sieber's book in December 1872. Marx was deeply impressed by it and it is significant that the only marginal note which he made was a criticism of a highly specialized order.

The second edition of *Das Kapital* must have been the source of enormous gratification to Sieber because it vindicated his own presentation of Marx's work in his dissertation. For one thing, for the sake of increased clarity, Marx had eliminated the appendix 'The Value Form' and incorporated its material into the body of the first section, just as Sieber had done. Besides this, Marx had gone a long way towards eliminating the philosophical dimension from his work, so that in the second edition only vestiges of this remained. In this too Sieber had anticipated what Marx had done. What for Sieber must have been most encouraging of all was the mention made of his dissertation in the Postscript. There Marx observed:

> As early as 1871, N. Sieber (Ziber) Professor of political economy at the university of Kiev in his work *David Ricardo's Theory of Value and Capital* referred to my theory of value, money and capital as in its fundamentals a necessary sequel to the teaching of Smith and Ricardo. What surprises a Western European on reading this excellent work is the consistent comprehension it shows of the purely theoretical standpoint. (Marx 1976: 99)

No doubt encouraged by Marx's favourable response to his work and by the changes Marx had made to the second edition of *Das Kapital*, in 1874 Sieber embarked upon a series of articles in the journals *Znanie* (Knowledge) and *Slovo* (Word) designed to make Marx's ideas understandable to the Russian reading public. The first article in this series entitled 'Marx's Economic Theory' went over some of the same ground that had been covered in Sieber's dissertation, namely the theory of value. In it Sieber explained that he had not encountered many people who were able to comprehend Marx's ideas, and that the main obstacle to their doing so was Marx's abstruse mode of expression. According to Sieber:

> Some – and these constitute the majority – are barred on the way to an elucidation of the essence of the matter by Marx's doctrine of the forms of value; others, by the difficult, and, if the truth be told, somewhat scholastic language in which a considerable part of the book is written; and others again are put off by the unaccustomed complexity of the subject and the ponderous argumentation encased in the impenetrable armour of Hegelian contradictions. (Sieber 2011: 155–6)

In Sieber's view, the presence of the 'Hegelian contradictions' had been entirely detrimental to a comprehension of Marx's work because few readers had managed 'to distinguish in it what is significant from what is of small importance, who have noticed what constituted the core elements or the framework of the whole theoretical edifice from the detail which only serves to decorate it' (Sieber 2011: 155). Sieber obviously believed that many of Marx's readers had been misled into thinking that the Hegelian terminology was a structural element rather than a decorative detail.

While in agreement with the substance of what Marx said, Sieber was critical of the approach Marx had taken. He thought it regrettable that Marx had begun his study of capital with the examination of the most complex forms of human economy, with capitalist production, rather than with the simpler forms of economic organization. Nor did he see why Marx should commence with an abstract analysis of value and utility rather than with the real relations which underlay these abstractions. In Sieber's view, a historical approach to the study of capital would have been possible and desirable (Sieber 2011: 164).

In noting the absence of a historical dimension in Marx's approach to capital in a revised version of his dissertation published in1885, Sieber observed:

> One can only regret that the author of *Das Kapital* ... should have limited himself to studying the forms of labour combination and the movement of these forms within capitalist society alone. That is why we do not find in his work an account of the social cooperation at previous stages of economic development. Even the feudal handicraft order, which gave rise to capitalist manufacture, is passed over in silence. And yet it is precisely the knowledge of this order which is of enormous importance in giving the necessary understanding of the capitalist modes of the succeeding period. It is to be hoped that someone else will undertake the beneficent work of filling where necessary this and other gaps left by Marx in the great series of changing forms of social cooperation. (Ziber 1959a: 388)

Sieber even suggested the kind of sources that could be used for the purpose. 'What a mass of material', he remarked, 'having a bearing ... on the relations of production of hunting, fishing and nomadic peoples, lies buried in countless travellers' tales' (Ziber 1959a: 405). This was the kind of material that Sieber himself was to employ in articles on village communities throughout the world, and in his major work on pre-capitalist forms of social cooperation, *Studies in the History of Primitive Economic Culture*, published in 1883 (Ziber 1959b).

Through his Russian contacts, Marx had received a copy of Sieber's article 'Marx's Economic Theory' by February–March 1875 (Rudiak 1979: 73). Marx read the article with some care, and fortunately the notes he made on it have been preserved. Considering the somewhat critical nature of Sieber's article, these notes are perhaps more remarkable for what they do not say than what they do. Marx does not defend his use of 'Hegelian contradictions', dispute the place Sieber allots to him in the history of economic thought or try to justify beginning his work with abstractions. He finds no fault with the way Sieber has expounded his theory of value. Marx only finds fault with Sieber for his response to an esoteric point that a German critic had raised (Marx 1927: 61).

It was in 1879 that Marx gave Sieber perhaps his most substantial endorsement. In commenting on the textbook on economics by Alfred Wagner, Marx noted:

> Mr Wagner could have discovered, both from *Das Kapital* and from Sieber's work (if he knew Russian) the difference between me and

Ricardo, who in fact concerned himself with labour only as a measure of value-magnitude and on that account found no connection between his theory of value and the essence of money. (Marx and Engels 1989a: 534)

As Lavrov had observed, Marx was not one to be liberal in his praise, especially where the interpretation of his ideas was concerned. Sieber has the distinction of being the only commentator on Marx's work that Marx approved of.

Sieber defends Marx

Sieber was to act not just as the popularizer of Marx's works in Russia but also as their champion. He took up his pen to counter the attacks on *Das Kapital* by two critics who approached Marx's book from the point of view of classical liberal economics, Yu. G. Zhukovsky and Chicherin. In 1877 Zhukovsky, a follower of Ricardo, published a lengthy review of Marx's *Das Kapital* in the journal *Vestnik Evropy* (European Herald). Zhukovsky raised several objections to Marx's work. As far as methodology was concerned, he had the impression that Marx was still very much influenced by Hegel, so that his approach was formalistic, paying insufficient attention to the actual content of economic affairs. Nor could Zhukovsky believe Marx's contention that only human labour created surplus value. He was of the opinion that anything which bore fruit, be it a tree, livestock or the earth, all were capable of providing exchange value. Zhukovsky thought too that Marx's account of the origins of capitalism, the expropriation of the peasants and the formation of a proletariat, had a fortuitous quality about it; Marx had traced the beginnings of capitalism in Europe to the liberation of the peasantry without land, but this clearly implied that in other places, if the peasants were not so liberated, then capitalism would not develop (Zhukovsky 1877: 67–72).

Sieber's reply appeared in the journal *Otechestvennye zapiski* (Notes of the Fatherland) in November 1877. In regard to Zhukovsky's objections to Marx's philosophical approach, Sieber conceded that Marx would have done no harm by 'reducing somewhat the dialectical side of his exposition' (Ziber 1959a: 562). But, on the other hand, he pointed out that, in the case of value, the metaphysical approach was necessary because in capitalist society perceptions of value were metaphysical. Marx's treatment of the subject duly reflected this fact. Sieber then explained how exchange value represented the essential unity of humanity through the prism of the division of labour and the fragmentation of society (Ziber 1959a: 564). In response to Zhukovsky's idea that exchange value was created not only by human labour but also by Nature, Sieber emphasized that it was human labour which constituted the sole source of exchange value, something, he added, that Zhukovsky, as an authority on David Ricardo, ought to know full well.

Sieber was eager to defend Marx against Zhukovsky's charge that he had presented the origins of capitalism as a fortuitous event rather than as a Natural process and quoted from the Russian translation of *Das Kapital* one of the few passages in which Marx suggested that the development of capitalism was a universal and necessary phenomenon:

> The small (medieval) means of production presupposes the fragmentation of the land and the means of production. It excludes both the concentration of the latter and the cooperation of labour in the given process of production, the social control and the regulation of the forces of Nature – in a word, it excludes the development of social productive forces. It is compatible only with narrow, primitive conditions of production and society. At a certain stage of development it itself provides the material means within the society, passions and forces which feel themselves fettered by that society. It has to be destroyed and it is destroyed. Its destruction, the transformation of the individualised and scattered means of production into socially-concentrated ones, i.e. the transformation of the petty property of the many into the vast property of the few ... forms the original history of capital. (Ziber 1959a: 583–4)

In Sieber's view this passage demonstrated three things: (1) that Marx did not consider capitalist development to be in any way accidental or fortuitous, but represented 'the necessary consequence of the development of social cooperation'; (2) that in Marx's opinion, despite the rift it created in society, capitalist production constituted 'not a reactionary, but a progressive social phenomenon'; (3) that Marx obviously considered that the expropriation of the small landowners and the socialization of the workers to be one and the same phenomenon (Ziber 1959a: 583–4).

It is indicative of how well Sieber understood Marx's ideas, that he could reconstruct accurately what Marx's original intention had been, despite the fact that explicit indications of it had been almost completely removed from the published work. Sieber had correctly taken capitalism to be a universal relation of production, and that its development implied the destruction of all earlier social and economic forms. As, moreover, it led to the socialization of the workers and the creation of a socialist society, the development of capitalism should be seen as a progressive phenomenon. As Marx had observed, Sieber's understanding of theory was impressive. But the problem was that by the time Sieber wrote, some fundamental aspects of the theory he was defending had been abandoned by its author.

In the following year, Chicherin published an article attacking Marx's *Das Kapital* in the journal *Sbornik gosudarstvennykh znanii* (Compendium of Statecraft) (Chicherin 1998). The article was couched in much the same terms as Zhukovsky's had been, and when he replied to Chicherin in *Slovo* in February 1879, Sieber could note that both critics shared some key misapprehensions. In a passage which brought out the metaphysical character of exchange value, he observed:

> But to people it appears as though things exchange themselves one for another, that things themselves have exchange value etc. and that the labour embodied in the thing given is reflected in the thing received. Here lies the whole groundlessness of the refutations of Mr Chicherin, and before him of Mr Zhukovsky, that neither the one nor the other could understand, or wanted to understand, as he should the circumstance that Marx presents to the reader the whole doctrine of value and its forms not on his own behalf, but as the peculiar way people at a given stage of social development necessarily understand their mutual relations, based on the social division of labour. In fact, every exchange value, every reflection or expression of it etc. represents nothing but a myth, while what exists is only socially-divided labour, which by force of the unity of human nature, seeks for itself unification and finds it in the strange and monstrous form of commodities and money. (Ziber 1900a: 697)

Marx followed Sieber's literary output closely, and Danielson sent him the journals in which Sieber's articles appeared, including Sieber's polemics with Zhukovsky and Chicherin. Marx had certainly read Sieber's article against Zhukovsky, and possibly that against Chicherin.

Sieber was not the only defender of Marx's *Das Kapital* against Zhukovsky. The journalist N. K. Mikhailovsky, who had written a favourable review of the Russian translation of the work in 1872 (Karataev 1958: 160–8), also wrote an article in reply to Zhukovsky's criticisms. It appeared in *Otechestvennye zapiski* under the title of 'Karl Marx before the Tribunal of Mr. Zhukovsky'. Danielson sent this article to Marx along with Sieber's reply to Zhukovsky and one of a similar nature written in reply to criticism of *Das Kapital* by Chicherin. On 15 November 1878, Marx wrote to Danielson:

> Of the polemics of Chicherin and other people against me, I have seen nothing, save what you sent me in 1877 (one article of Sieber, and the other, I think of Mikhailovsky, both in the 'Fatherlandish Annals', in reply to that queer would be Encyclopedist Mr. Zhukovsky). Prof. Kovalevsky, who is here, told me that there had been rather lively polemics on the 'Capital'. (Marx and Engels 1991: 343)

M. M. Kovalevsky, another of Marx's Russian acquaintances, had obviously exaggerated the scale of the polemic and the number of participants, for the articles Marx enumerated constituted its entirety. The contribution by Mikhailovsky, however, gave the interchange especial significance because it highlighted the question of the universality of capitalism raised by Zhukovsky and prompted Marx to formulate where he now stood on the issue.

In his article, Mikhailovsky paid a great deal of attention to the connection between the growth of capitalism and the expropriation of the peasantry. Like Sieber, Mikhailovsky understood Marx to mean that he conceived the development of capitalism, not as a fortuitous occurrence, but as a universal process. But it was on this very point that he took issue with Marx; Mikhailovsky's position was that if the peasants were not expropriated – as in Russia they were not – then capitalism need not develop. He was unable to reconcile himself, therefore, with Marx's 'historico-philosophical theory' which decreed that all countries must undergo a capitalist phase, and that this phase would be 'progressive'.

Citing the passages in the chapter on 'Primitive Accumulation' in which Marx spoke of the expropriation of the peasants, the establishment of capitalist private property and its subsequent abolition by the 'negation of the negation', Mikhailovsky held this to be 'Marx's historico-philosophical view'. He then considered it from the point of view of a Russian who accepted the validity of this theory. Such a person, Mikhailovsky thought, would have an ambivalent attitude towards the development of capitalism in his country. For whereas, on the one hand, it would bring the benefit of the socialization of labour and the eventual 'possession in common of the land and the means of production produced by labour itself', on the other, the cost of this benefit in terms of human suffering would be enormous (Mikhailovskii 1897: 169–70).

To illustrate the fact that the horrors of capitalism were recognized by Marx himself, Mikhailovsky, somewhat mischievously, cited not any of the cases documented in the body of Das Kapital but what he described as the 'irritable outburst' of the author in the first edition of the work denouncing Herzen and his conception of Russian socialism (Mikhailovskii 1897: 171).

Mikhailovsky interpreted Marx's attitude to Herzen as demonstrating that the author of Das Kapital refused to allow the possibility that any country might escape the terrible fate of capitalist development – which indeed had been the case when Marx first encountered Herzen's conception of socialism based on the peasant commune. But if, in Mikhailovsky's view, all countries were fated to undergo capitalist development to achieve the socialization of labour, there would be a strange paradox in the case of Russia because what capitalism was supposed to achieve was already an established fact there. It meant that in Russia the producer would be separated from the means of production in order that he should be later reunited with them – and all at the tremendous human cost, all the 'maimings of women and children', that Marx had described so graphically (Mikhailovskii 1897: 172).

On reading Mikhailovsky's article Marx wrote a reply in the form of a letter to the editorial board of Otechestvennye zapiski. He began by saying that if Mikhailovsky, a clever man, had been able to find a single passage on the treatment of 'primitive accumulation' that supported his contentions, he would have quoted it; failing this, he had seized upon something more insubstantial: the remarks on Herzen in the appendix of the first German edition of *Das Kapital*. Marx denied that these remarks could serve as evidence of his own estimation of the efforts of Russians to find a different path of development for their country from that followed by Western Europe. As proof of this Marx referred Mikhailovsky to the Afterword to the second edition of *Das Kapital* where Chernyshevsky, who, like Herzen, held that a non-capitalist path of development was possible for Russia, was spoken of with approval. Thus, Marx claimed, Mikhailovsky might just as well conclude that the author of *Das Kapital* shared the views of Chernyshevsky as that he rejected those of Herzen (Marx and Engels 1989a: 199).

This was less an argument than a debating point. While formally correct, it took no account of the evolution in views Marx had undergone between the time he formed his opinion of Herzen and when he formed his impression of Chernyshevsky.

Marx then alluded to his studies of Russia and stated his conclusion that the development of capitalism in Russia was not inevitable:

> In order that I might be able to judge the matter of Russia's modern economic development in an informed way, I learnt Russian and then for long years studied official publications and other Russian materials relating to this subject. I came to the following conclusion: if Russia continues to follow the path she has followed since 1861, she will lose the finest chance ever offered by history to any people and undergo all the fatal vicissitudes of the capitalist regime. (Marx and Engels 1989a: 199)

He then turned his attention to the question of the chapter on original capitalist accumulation extensively discussed by Mikhailovsky. He emphasized that this did not 'claim to do more than trace the path by which in Western Europe the capitalist economic order emerged from the feudal economic order'. Here Marx quoted the passage from the French edition of *Das Kapital* to the effect that: 'It has as yet been accomplished in a radical fashion only in England ... But all the other countries of Western Europe are going through the same movement'. The passage had appeared only in the French translation of *Das Kapital* published two years earlier.

On the implications of his study of capitalism in Western Europe for Russia, Marx said the following:

> If Russia is tending to become a capitalist nation after the example of the Western-European countries – and during the last few years she has taken a lot of trouble in that direction – she will not succeed without first having transformed a good part of her peasants into proletarians; and after that, once taken into the bosom of the capitalist regime, she will experience its pitiless laws like other profane peoples. That is all. (Marx and Engels 1989a: 200)

In this connection Marx complained that Mikhailovsky had distorted his meaning:

> But that is too little for my critic. He feels he absolutely must metamorphose my historical sketch of the genesis of capitalism in Western Europe into a historico-philosophical theory of the universal path (*marche générale*) every people is fated to tread ... But I beg his pardon. He is simultaneously honouring and shaming me too much. (Marx and Engels 1989a: 200)

The contention that Mikhailovsky had misrepresented the argument of *Das Kapital* was an astonishing accusation. It imposed retrospectively on *Das Kapital* an interpretation completely at variance with the spirit in which it was conceived. Marx had never regarded the development of capitalism as merely historical, merely empirical. He had conceived of capitalism as a universal system, the outward manifestation of man's inner species being. *Das Kapital* had limited itself to the development of capitalism on the historical plane only because Marx had been unable to discover the more essential and logical steps in the process.

Marx ended his letter by giving an example to illustrate the proposition that history offered a great variety of possibilities, making it impossible to employ *a priori* historical schemes:

> In different places in 'Capital' I allude to the fate which overtook the plebeians of ancient Rome. They were originally free peasants, each cultivating his own piece of land on his own account. In the course of Roman history they were expropriated ... What happened? The Roman proletarians became not wage-labourers, but a mob of do-nothings ... and alongside them there developed a mode of production which was not capitalist but based on slavery. (Marx and Engels 1989a: 200)

Danielson, who translated Marx's letter from the original French into Russian for publication, succeeded in tracking down the places of *Das Kapital* in which the Roman proletarians were allegedly alluded to. These amounted to the single footnote Marx had inserted in the French translation. Like the passage limiting the application of the treatment of the development of capitalism to Western Europe, it had appeared there for the first time (Marx and Engels 1908: 113).

Marx did not actually send the letter to *Otechestvennye zapiski*. It was discovered after Marx's death by Engels, who gave a copy to Lopatin in 1883 to be passed on to Danielson for publication. According to Danielson, Engels had told Lopatin that Marx had wanted to send the letter, but 'had been persuaded not to'. Danielson later gave the same information in rather more detail, when he stated that Marx had written the letter for publication in *Otechestvennye zapiski*, 'But – due to the assurances of one of his Russian 'scientific friends' that it could not appear in a Russian journal – the letter was not sent ... ' The expression 'scientific friends' referred to Kovalevsky, and was contained in the letter from Marx to Danielson of 19 September 1879.

Engels explained elsewhere that Marx was afraid that his name alone would threaten the existence of the journal in which his reply appeared (Grin 1985: 132). Danielson's emphasis, in both cases, on the advice Marx received rather than any objective problems of publication could indicate some scepticism on his part about potential danger to the journal. In fact he had written to Marx on 19 March 1877, specifically suggesting that the latter should write an article on the peasant commune for *Otechestvennye zapiski* (Marx and Engels 1967: 339).

There was a difficulty that could not have escaped the notice of Marx or Kovalevsky. It was that the next issue of *Otechestvennye zapiski*, directly following the one in which Mikhailovsky's article appeared, contained the one written by Sieber against Zhukovsky. This maintained that Marx believed the development of capitalism to be a universal phenomenon, and had supported this with a quotation from *Das Kapital*, that Marx had denied to Mikhailovsky existed. Publication of the letter would have created a ridiculous and lamentable situation in which Marx appeared to support Zhukovsky's interpretation of *Das Kapital* and disown that of his 'supporter' Sieber. As Mikhailovsky later observed:

Karl Marx's letter appeared only in 1888 and I do not know how Sieber, by then deceased, would have reacted to the arguments in it. But at that time, in 1878, he was firmly of the opinion that the process formulated by Marx was universally obligatory. (Mikhailovskii 1909: 327)

One may depend upon it that the irony would not have been lost on Mikhailovsky – or the Russian reading public in general – if the letter had been published a decade earlier.

Marx's remaining silent, however, had important consequences for perceptions of his doctrines in Russia. Marx had done nothing to contradict the interpretation of his ideas that Sieber had put forward in his reply to Zhukovsky. As far as the Russian public were concerned, therefore, Marx had propounded a universally obligatory scheme of economic development. This perception was reinforced by the fact that Mikhailovsky had criticized Marx for proposing a 'historico-philosophical theory' which was obligatory for all countries. The implication could only be that this was indeed the character of Marx's economic theory. Once established, the perception acquired considerable momentum and resilience, so that even when Marx's letter was eventually published it proved difficult to shake.

Maxim Kovalevsky

Despite Kovalevsky's eminence as a pioneer of sociology and his importance in the development of Marxist thought, he remains a relatively unknown figure. This is partly because he lived a substantial part of his life outside Russia, and so tends to fall beyond the purview of historians of Russian social thought. Moreover, although Russian social and political developments were always at the centre of Kovalevsky's attention, he approached them in a comparative perspective, and seldom published works specifically about Russia. In this way, his relevance to Russian studies is not always appreciated.

Maksim Maksimovich Kovalevsky was born on 27 August 1851 in Kharkov, the son of a wealthy landowner. His early education was at home with French and German governesses and tutors from whom he acquired the facility with languages that he would later employ in his scholarly research. Kovalevsky studied law at Kharkov University where his main teacher was D. I. Kachenovsky, an admirer of the British form of government. Since he could not openly campaign for parliamentary government in Russia, Kachenovsky did this indirectly by publishing studies in the constitutional history of Britain and other European countries. This would be a method that Kovalevsky himself would later adopt.

It was Kachenovsky who introduced Kovalevsky to the positivist philosophy of Auguste Comte. Comte's works were banned in Russia, but expositions of them by his English followers John Stuart Mill and George Lewes were available even in Russian translation. It is easy to see what the attraction of positivism would be for people like Kachenovsky, who looked forward to a time when Russia would have a constitutional government. According to Comte, humanity passed through three stages of intellectual development, the Religious, the Metaphysical and the Positive. This was a progression from the times when people's views were determined by superstition and fetishism to modern times when the outlook of humanity was derived from scientific methods of empirical observation and experiment. Corresponding to the intellectual stages was progress in society from the feudal or militaristic society to industrial society whose institutions were based on order and progress. Comte, therefore, assured Kachenovsky and his pupil that the laws of history which had been derived from objective empirical observation would eventually lead to the establishment in Russia of the kind of regime that they so desired.

Kachenovsky's death in 1872 deprived Kovalevsky of his preferred supervisor for his master's dissertation. Accordingly, he left Kharkov to continue his postgraduate studies at Moscow University. In order to collect material for his research, Kovalevsky went on an extended trip to Western Europe. Having spent the winter semester of 1872 in Berlin, Kovalevsky went on to Paris, where he began research for a dissertation on the history of French administrative law (White 2016: 94–6).

While In Paris Kovalevsky made contact with the émigré Russians living there, including the writer Ivan Turgenev and his fellow-Positivist Grigorii Vyrubov. Vyrubov, who had trained as a chemist, had lived in Paris since 1864, where he had befriended Emile Littré, one of the most eminent of Comte's followers. In 1867 Vyrubov together with Littré had founded the journal *La philosophie positiviste* to promote positivist teachings. Vyrubov's journal had been one of the few to review *Das Kapital* on its appearance. The review, by E. V. De Roberty, had been largely unfavourable, finding in Marx's work too much of dialectics and too little of the inductive method. Danielson wrote to Vyrubov in protest, pointing out the original contribution to economic science that Marx had made (Volodin and Itenberg 1983: 86–7). Marx himself referred to De Roberty's review in the Afterword to the second edition of *Das Kapital*, justifying his method by quoting approvingly what Sieber had said in this regard in his dissertation. This was that: 'As far as the theory itself is concerned, Marx's method is the deductive method of the whole English school, and both its faults and its merits are those shared by the best of the theoretical economists' (Marx 1976: 99–100).

In 1875 Kovalevsky contributed a review of Sir Henry Sumner Maine's book *Lectures on the Early History of Institutions* to Vyrubov's journal. He was much impressed by the book and recommended it to the journal's readership because its treatment of the origins of private property, classes and kingship could not but be of interest to Positivists. As Kovalevsky went on to indicate, Maine had already written two books, *Ancient Law* and *Village Communities in the East and West*. There, drawing together existing accounts of rural communities in the Classical world, Germany, Russia, India and Anglo-Saxon England, Maine had shown that all of them had remarkably similar modes of social organization. Inspired by Maine's comparative method, and seeing the scholarly value of placing the Russian peasant commune in the context of world social evolution, in 1876 Kovalevsky published a small monograph on the dissolution of communal landownership in the Swiss Canton of Vaud. In the preface he made it clear that his main concern was to examine the implications of the dissolution of communal landownership for the future of Russian society (Kovalevskii 1876).

From Vyrubov Kovalevsky received letters of introduction to representatives of Positivism in England. In London Kovalevsky's first contact was George Lewes, the author of the book on Comte's philosophy with which Kovalevsky was already familiar. Lewes had a wide circle of friends, and that being so Kovalevsky could not have had a better guide to the intellectual elite of London of the day. This was particularly the case since Lewes's partner was the famous novelist George Eliot, whose works Kovalevsky had read in Russian translation.

Around Lewes and Eliot there revolved the wider circle of English Positivists. Among these, Frederic Harrison was of especial interest to Kovalevsky because he had been a pupil of Maine, and indeed had encouraged his former tutor to publish his lectures as *Ancient Law*. Harrison saw in the legal categories Maine employed a parallel with the Comtean stages of the religious, the metaphysical and the scientific. Along with his friends Edward Beesly and John Bridges, Harrison had been introduced to Comte's ideas by Richard Congreve, their tutor at Wadham College, Oxford. The four men formed the nucleus of the orthodox wing of the Comtists in England (White 2016: 97).

It was through Harrison that Kovalevsky was able to meet Maine, and through Maine's influence Kovalevsky was able to gain access to the archive and library of the India Office where he found rich and little-used material on the Indian agrarian commune and the part played by the policy of the British colonists on its fate. Kovalevsky would use this material in the production of a comparative study of the destruction of the agrarian commune by the British in India, the Spanish in South America and the French in Algeria. The result was the book *Communal Landownership* which was published in 1879.

Communal Landownership is in its way a continuation of Kovalevsky's earlier book on Canton Vaud, since the main theme is the dissolution of communal landownership. But the later work has the additional feature of dealing with territories under foreign occupation. This is a feature that is to be explained by the intellectual environment in which the book was written, by the influence of the English Positivists. In the *Course de politique positive*, which had been translated by Richard Congreve and his friends, Comte had insisted that politics should be subordinated to morals. This applied not only to domestic politics but to international relations as well. Comte condemned the colonial conquests of his own country and expressed the hope that the Arabs should expel the French from Algeria. On Comte's suggestion, Congreve launched a campaign for the return of Gibraltar to Spain, and subsequently published a pamphlet demanding the withdrawal of the British from India. He regarded the British occupation of India as immoral and compared it to the cruelty and avarice of the Spanish conquerors of Mexico and Peru in the sixteenth century. Congreve repeated this comparison in his essay in *International Policy*, a symposium in which he and his Positivist friends condemned British colonialism. In his chapter 'England at Sea' Beesly too argued that justice required that the British should recognize their duty to withdraw from India and shape their policy towards that end. He indicated that this course of action was in accordance with what Comte would have wished, since Comte had urged that France abandon not just Algeria but Corsica as well (White 2016: 100–1).

As Kovalevsky's reminiscences imply, there was no hermetic separation between the English Positivists and Marx's circle of followers. There was not only contact but also a fair amount of cooperation between the groups. In the 1860s Harrison and Beesly gave support to the workers during the 1859–60 builders' strike in London. Beesly chaired the meeting in September

1864 at which the International Working Men's Association (the First International) was formed (Ryazanov 1924: 111–12). The anti-colonialist motif formed the substance of Beesly's speech at the inaugural meeting of the International. There he condemned the colonial policy of the British in Gibraltar, Ireland, China, Japan and New Zealand. He compared the actions of the British in these territories to those of the Russians in Poland. This anti-colonialist aspect of Positivist doctrine is a prominent characteristic of Kovalevsky's book *Communal Landownership*.

It is worth noting that Marx was present on the platform at the formation of the International, and later performed the important function of drawing up the rules of the new organization. The preamble to these rules began with the proposition that 'The emancipation of the working classes shall be conquered by the working classes themselves.' This fundamental programmatic principle is one that had a wide resonance in the Russian revolutionary movement.

Communal landownership

It was, Kovalevsky explained, the aim of his book *Communal Landownership* to study the development of private property in countries that, until now, had not been subject to comparative-historical investigation. The project had begun three years earlier with the monograph on the dissolution of communal property in one of the cantons of French Switzerland, and, in his view, the findings of that research were valid on an international scale. It was Kovalevsky's contention that what undermined the common ownership of land was the 'conflict of interest' within the community, the conflict between the more wealthy among the agrarian population who desired the dissolution of communal property and the less wealthy who desired its retention. This was a process, Kovalevsky believed, which would take place sooner or later in all countries, and that the emergence of private property out of common ownership was a universal phenomenon.

But whereas the action of 'internal necessity' was likely to be a gradual one, in colonial countries the individualization of immobile property as well as its centralization in a few hands had been effected within some two or three decades. This was the consequence of the legislative and administrative measures of this or that foreign government which was likely to be unfamiliar with local conditions and the social structure of the native populations. Nevertheless, although the artificial and fortuitous causes brought about by colonial rule served to accelerate the dissolution of common land ownership, in the end it led to the same results as the spontaneous ones: to the rapid transformation of small property into major property and the concentration of land ownership in the hands of a small class of capitalist-usurers (Kovalevskii 1879: 20).

From Maine's work and the research of Lewis Morgan, Kovalevsky had formed a conception not only of how communal landownership came to an end but also how it had originated in the first place. The agrarian commune had arisen out of the clan commune, whose sense of kinship rested on the conception that every member of the group was descended from a common ancestor. This conception was preserved in the course of centuries and survived even after the transition of the clan commune to the village community. Kovalevsky also followed Maine in viewing the emergence of feudal relations as one of the consequences of the break-up of communal landownership. This too was a process which took place much more rapidly in colonial countries.

In surveying the phenomenon of communal landownership in those countries that had been subject to foreign domination Kovalevsky was able to show its evolution through different stages. The first chapter dealt with the most primitive types of social organization, those observed among the American Indians by Morgan and among the tribes of Mexico and Peru before the Spanish conquest. He then turned to the agrarian organization of India and the influence upon it by the rule of the Moguls and subsequently by the British. The final section was devoted to the way the French rule in Algeria had transformed traditional Islamic society by replacing the common ownership of land by individual property. Throughout the book Kovalevsky made references to the situation in his own country, where processes of a comparable kind were at work to undermine the collective ownership of land in the Russian peasant commune. The reader of Kovalevsky's work could be left in little doubt where the chief concerns of the author lay.

Collaboration with Marx

According to Kovalevsky, his first meeting with Marx, which took place in 1875, was inauspicious. Marx spent most of the time denouncing émigré Russians, Herzen and Bakunin in particular. But later in the year, when Kovalevsky and Marx met up in Karlsbad, where both had repaired for health reasons, a lasting friendship was established on the basis of common scholarly interests. Kovalevsky, however, had doubts about the validity of Marx's methodology, as he mentioned in a letter to the economist I. I. Yanzhul, dated 15 October 1875:

> In Karlsbad I spent many happy hours in Marx's company. He is a most noble and a most gifted person. It is a great pity that he was and remains a Hegelian, and that therefore his scientific constructions are built on sand. While in Karlsbad I read well over half of his book which he presented me with, and I found in it fresh proof that any departure from the Positive method and, most of all the application of the maxim: '*les*

grandes idées viennent du coeur,' inevitably lead to frequent unconscious misconceptions. (Kazakov 1969: 100)

In London Kovalevsky visited Marx practically every week, and these visits ended only in 1876 when Kovalevsky obtained a professorship at Moscow University and returned to Russia. A correspondence then began between the two men. Unfortunately none of Marx's letters to Kovalevsky have survived since they were burnt by Kovalevsky's associate I. I. Ivaniukov when he feared a raid by the tsarist police on his home (*Maksim Kovalevsky 1851–1916*. Sbornik statei, 1918: 17).

Marx received a copy of Kovalevsky's *Communal Landownership* from the author in 1879, and Marx's detailed notes from it are of considerable interest because they show how he viewed the evolution of social and economic systems in the last years of his life. For the most part the notes follow Kovalevsky's text rather closely, often translating into German long passages from Kovalevsky's book.

One may conveniently divide Marx's commentary on Kovalevsky's book into two categories: there were the aspects that Marx agreed with, and those to which he took exception. To the first category belong those sections of the book where Kovalevsky showed how the agrarian policies of the colonial powers had served to undermine communal landownership. Thus, in the case of the British in India, paraphrasing Kovalevsky, Marx observed:

British officials in India, as well as the publicists like Sir Henry Maine, who rely on them, describe the dissolution of communal ownership of land in the Punjab as if it took place as the inevitable consequence of economic progress, despite the affectionate attitude of the British towards this archaic form. The truth is rather that the British themselves are the chief (active) culprits responsible for this dissolution – to their own danger. (Harstick 1977: 88)

An aspect of Kovalevsky's work with which Marx disagreed was a fundamental one: it was Kovalevsky's cherished conception that sooner or later communal landownership would be replaced by private property, through 'conflicts of interest' that were generated within the community. It was the conception that led Kovalevsky to argue that the legislation of the occupying powers only accelerated a process that would be accomplished in any case. But why should conflicts of interest inevitably arise everywhere? This was something Kovalevsky did not explain, and the omission was noticed by Marx (Harstick 1977: 269).

With regard to the conceptions Kovalevsky had expounded in *Communal Landownership* Marx's position was as follows: he agreed completely with Kovalevsky that the action of government policy was capable of undermining communal landownership. But he did not agree that communal landownership would have been destroyed in any case by more long-term natural causes. He believed that without governmental interference communal forms of ownership were resilient enough to survive.

Marx's letter to Vera Zasulich

One use that Marx put Kovalevsky's researches to was in replying to a query he received from Vera Zasulich, a young Russian socialist, in February 1881. Zasulich wrote to Marx from her exile in Geneva to inquire if it were true, as his disciples in Russia asserted, that the agrarian commune was an archaic form bound to disappear in the course of history; or was it possible that it could serve as a basis for a socialist society. The answer to this question, Zasulich assured Marx, was crucial for Russian socialists. For if the peasant commune could serve as a basis for socialism, then all their efforts would be bent towards its preservation; if not, then all that remained would be to conduct propaganda among the urban workers and wait for capitalism in Russia to develop to a point that would make a socialist revolution possible.

On 8 March Marx sent in reply a short letter similar to the one he had drafted in response to Mikhailovsky's article in *Otechestvennye zapiski* four years earlier. It contained the same quotations from the French version of *Das Kapital* and concluded by stating that:

> The analysis in *Capital* therefore provides no reason either for or against the vitality of the rural commune. But the special study I have made of it, and for which I consulted original sources for materials, has convinced me that this commune is the fulcrum of social regeneration in Russia, but in order that it might function as such, the harmful influences assailing it on all sides must first be eliminated and then assure it of the normal conditions for spontaneous development. (Marx and Engels 1989a: 370–1)

The preparatory drafts which Marx made for the letter attempted to give a much fuller account of how the Russian commune might develop in the light of its past history and the economic situation in which it now found itself.

In arguing for the survival of the peasant commune Marx emphasized that its demise was not decreed by historical inevitability. He pointed out that in the French edition of *Das Kapital* where the expropriation of the peasants was discussed, he had 'expressly limited the "historical inevitability" of this process to the countries of Western Europe' (Marx and Engels 1989a: 346).

In the first draft of the letter, Marx quoted the passage from the chapter on 'Primitive Accumulation' that described 'the transformation of the petty property of the many into the vast property of the few', that Sieber had interpreted as showing the universalist character of capitalist development. Marx had to assume that Zasulich had read Sieber's article, and so had to address himself to Sieber's argument. In response to this Marx points out that the passage quoted could not possibly apply to Russia, because the peasants had never owned their land as private property (Marx and Engels 1989a: 346). While it was natural that Marx would want to contest the argument Sieber had presented in the article against Zhukovsky, he would realize that he could not do so without seeming to enter into a polemic with Sieber, his most valued supporter and commentator. The second draft makes the point about peasant property without reproducing the quotation, but without the quotation it is not clear to what end the point is made. In the third draft, the point about peasant ownership of land has been rewritten in such a way as to make it less like a dispute on the passage Sieber quoted (Marx and Engels 1989a: 365). But, however framed, Marx's reply to Zasulich could still be construed as a polemic against Sieber. Taking this circumstance into account, one can understand why Marx did not send Zasulich a reply that contained the material in the drafts, but confined himself to a short letter summarizing his conclusions, cautioning that they were not suitable for publication.

Marx pointed out to Zasulich that although it might be said that institutions analogous to the peasant commune had disappeared in other European countries this did not mean that the same had to take place in Russia. Even when the disappearance of village communities was attributed to spontaneous forces, in reality the cause had been deliberate policy. The example Marx gave was one he had found in Kovalevsky's book:

When reading the histories of primitive communities written by bourgeois writers it is necessary to be on one's guard. They do not even shrink from falsehoods. Sir Henry Maine, for example, who was a keen collaborator of the British Government in carrying out the violent destruction of the Indian communes, hypocritically assures us that all the government's noble efforts to support the communes were thwarted by the spontaneous forces of economic laws! (Marx and Engels 1989a: 359)

In this connection Marx contended that the one considerable advantage that Russia had was that, unlike India, it was not subject to colonial rule.

According to Marx, what was threatening the life of the Russian commune was the same thing which had undermined the commune in India: it was neither historical inevitability nor a theory; it was oppression by the State and exploitation by capitalist intruders, who had been made powerful at the expense of the peasants by the self same state. In what might have been a veiled reference to Kovalevsky, Marx intimated that the Russian liberals were rather keen on establishing capitalism in Russia by abolishing communal property and expropriating the peasantry, but he did not think that their wish would necessarily become reality. Therefore, Marx reasoned, what was needed to protect the peasant commune was a revolution in Russia (Marx and Engels 1989a: 359–60).

Marx believed that if such a revolution took place, Russia would be well placed to construct a socialist system on the basis of the commune because it existed contemporaneously with Western capitalism. Had this not been so, and Russia had been isolated from the rest of the world, then the communes would have had to perish to give way to the capitalist system, so that its high level of economic development could be reached. But as this was not the case, Russia could reap the fruits with which capitalist society had enriched humanity without passing through the capitalist regime (Marx and Engels 1989a: 532–3).

One must note here that although Marx spoke of Western capitalism's domination of the world market, he did not suggest at any point that the commerce with Western capitalism might lead to the dissolution of the agrarian commune rather than its enrichment. Indeed, he could hardly have done so since he had discovered that primitive communes could thrive in a capitalist environment. This was true both at a local level and on an international scale.

One prominent feature of the drafts of Marx's letter to Vera Zasulich was the attention it gave to the dynamics of the peasant commune, to its evolution from more primitive types of social organization. This was an element that Marx had adopted from Kovalevsky's book, and Kovalevsky, in his turn, had taken from the researches of Henry Sumner Maine and Lewis Morgan. Marx pointed out that the Russian peasant commune was a relatively modern example of the type, and that, whereas earlier communities had been based on blood ties between their members, the Russian peasant commune was the first social grouping that was independent of natural kinship (Marx and Engels 1989a: 351). This made it better equipped to survive in the modern world. On the whole, the drafts of the letter to Vera Zasulich are more optimistic about the future perspectives of the Russian peasant commune than the letter itself.

Kovalevsky and Sieber

Not only Kovalevsky but Sieber too published a study of the evolution of peasant communities in connection with the emergence of capitalism. This was *Studies in the History of Primitive Economic Culture* which appeared in 1883 (Ziber 1959b). In it Sieber had made use of a large number of accounts by European travellers of primitive peoples in various parts of the world. He also drew upon most of the scholarly works on the subject then available: studies by Maine, Bachofen, Morgan, Levaleyé, McLennan and Kovalevsky.

A great part of Sieber's work was devoted to nomadic hunting and fishing peoples, examining how these and other activities were carried on collectively wherever they had been recorded. He also showed that among these peoples private property was unknown; this had developed gradually and at higher cultural levels, first in relation to movable, and subsequently to immovable property. Sieber emphasized, however, that even the most primitive peoples were well aware of property and considered themselves to own collectively the territory over which they hunted.

Sieber believed that the principles of collectivism were carried over from the nomadic to the settled condition, and viewed the practice of equalization of allotments and the redivision of the land in this light. Unlike Kovalevsky, he did not regard these phenomena as the product of later evolution and the weakening of the consanguine principle.

Marx would have discussed Sieber's researches with him because Sieber and the economist N. A. Kablukov visited Marx and Engels in January 1881. Kablukov recalls:

In the second half of 1880 I lived in London, studying every day in the library of the British Museum and spending some time in the company of N. I. Sieber, who was then working on his book *Studies in the History of Primitive Economic Culture*, on which we talked a great deal. I went with him several times to visit K. Marx and F. Engels, who made us very welcome and introduced us to their families. (*Russkie sovremenniki o K. Markse i F. Engel'se*, 1969: 78)

In a letter dated 19 February 1881 Marx informed Danielson:

Last month we had several Russian visitors including Professor Sieber (he has now gone to Zurich) and Mr. Kablukov (from Moscow). They worked for whole days at a time in the British Museum. (Marx and Engels 1992: 64)

It was immediately after this visit that Marx embarked on an intensive reading of Morgan, Maine and Lubbock, that is, the writers that featured prominently in Sieber's work. Marx made very extensive notes on them, especially on Morgan's *Ancient Society*, which he had received from Kovalevsky. But at the time of his death in 1883 he had not utilized them even in a draft work. It is not absolutely certain how Marx intended to use them, but the context suggests it would have been to account for the emergence of capitalism, in particular, the circulation of capital, from earlier collectivist society.

It was also just after he was visited by Sieber and Kablukov that Marx received Vera Zasulich's letter. When he sent his reply, Marx probably sent a copy to Sieber, which would explain the references to the 'conversation with Sieber' and the 'letter to Sieber' referred to in the exchange of views between Polish socialists in Swiss exile in 1883–84.

Thus, in response to the contention of Adam Zakrzewski that in a letter to 'friends in the East' Marx had stated most categorically that 'certain economic formations, obligatory in one place, can be with advantage omitted in another', Adam Sasiedzki argued:

> As for the mention of the letter written to friends in the East, the author probably has in mind the letter written to Vera Zasulich and the conversation of the author of *Das Kapital* with Sieber. Well, in neither the one nor the other is a categorical, let alone a 'most categorical', statement made in any way whatever. On the contrary, from the letter, although it is couched in a very conditional form, one can only draw the following conclusion: Russia has no special path. I have read the letter. What it says is more or less this: if the Russian peasant commune has enough strength in the struggle against capitalist individualism, Russia can (but can and not will be able!) achieve with the help of the peasant commune the realization of the rights of labour, which the West will achieve with the help of capitalist development. The other results of studies of the Great Russian peasant commune are the following: the peasant commune has been considerably undermined by the increasing unprecedented development of capitalism in Russia. In a few years or a few decades the peasant commune will be a thing of the past. (Falkowski and Kowalik 1957: 150)

According to Stanislaw Krusinski:

> In this respect, reference to Marx's letter written to Sieber is unfounded from two points of view. First, Marx in his letter recognises only very conditionally the possibility of retaining the Russian peasant commune, and second, although he himself believed in that possibility, he could not, despite his enormous fund of knowledge, know the peasant commune better than those who had studied it intensively on the spot over many years. (Falkowski and Kowalik 1957: 221)

It was after his meeting with Marx and after the possible receipt of a copy of the letter to Vera Zasulich that Sieber published his review of V. P. Vorontsov's book *The Fate of Capitalism in Russia* in *Vol'noe slovo* (Free Word) in 1883. The question arises: What does the review reveal about Sieber's views following his conversations with Marx?

In Sieber's opinion, Vorontsov's antipathy to capitalism had led him to attribute to the Russian autocracy a beneficence and permanence which it did not possess. Like Marx at this time, Sieber was convinced that tsarism was about to be overthrown. What had brought Russia to this state of affairs was the growing complexity of its social organization, the division of the country into town and village, the division of the people into different classes and the influence of Western Europe. In this situation it was necessary that the old communal order of agriculture, in which each community lived an independent and isolated existence, allowing the domination over it of the tyranny of the tsar and his officials, should give way to a more advanced form of organization.

Capitalism, Sieber conceded, had its faults; it divided people into classes, it enriched some and impoverished others; it engendered extreme egotism in society and undermined the health of the workers. But at the same time capitalism immeasurably weakened political power, brought together the working classes of all peoples and socialized production and consumption. For Sieber, capitalism was a universal phenomenon, encountered in every society at a certain stage of its development, if certain conditions for its development were present. In Russia, admittedly, capitalism had not developed fully, not through any inherent flaw in its nature, but because it had come on the scene later than in other countries. It would be possible to ameliorate the adverse consequences of capitalism, but to try to eliminate it completely, before it had eliminated itself, would be a futile undertaking (Ziber 1959b: 672–3).

The review of Vorontsov's book was to be one of Sieber's last publications. He fell ill with a degenerative disease in 1884 and died in Yalta four years later at the age of only forty-four. Sieber's early death was a factor in determining the direction taken by Marxism in Russia. Without Sieber's authority as the commentator on Marx's work whom Marx himself endorsed, the way was cleared for the emergence of G. V. Plekhanov, 'the father of Russian Marxism', who was much influenced by Engels's interpretation of Marx's intellectual legacy. The lasting value of Sieber's works is that they show us Marx's ideas as they were in Marx's lifetime, in a state still unaffected by gloss that Engels later put upon them.

3

Engels

Engels as editor

The evidence relating to the last decade of Marx's life suggests that the trajectory of his thinking was away from the Hegelian philosophical constructs that had characterized the preliminary drafts of *Das Kapital* and its first published edition, towards more empirical studies of economics and society. On this basis, it would be reasonable to suppose that those who followed Marx would take up where he had left off and, by using the extensive Russian material that Marx had collected, apply themselves to examining how the circulation and expanded reproduction of capital impacted on a traditional pre-capitalist society. Could one, for example, do as Sieber had suggested, and recast the content of *Das Kapital* in concrete historical rather than in abstract terms? That Marxist thought in Russia did not develop in this way is due, in the first instance, to the activities of Friedrich Engels.

From the correspondence between the two men it is clear that Engels did not keep abreast of the direction of Marx's thought and, in particular, did not appreciate the importance of Russian sources for the study of capitalist development. On the contrary, he considered Marx's preoccupation with Russia to be an unnecessary diversion which only served to postpone the completion of the remaining volumes of *Das Kapital*. According to Paul Lafargue, he had once remarked that he would gladly take all the materials Marx had accumulated on Russian agriculture and throw them on the fire (Lafargue 1905: 560).

After Marx's death Engels was horrified to discover that so much work remained to be done on volumes two and three of *Das Kapital* and he made it manifest to Danielson that he held him responsible for the lack of progress (Marx and Engels 1908: v). When Engels himself prepared volumes two and three for publication he made no attempt to incorporate

into them any of the Russian material on which Marx had spent so much
time. Engels explained to Lavrov that, in view of his advanced age and the
pressure of work, it would be impossible for him to begin from scratch
the kind of Russian studies that Marx had pursued (Marx and Engels
1995: 87). Accordingly, in 1884, he made Lavrov a gift of Marx's extensive
Russian library. Engels was of necessity committed to the assumption that
Marx's Russian studies were marginal to his overall project, and that the
remaining volumes of *Das Kapital* could be published without the inclusion
of the Russian material. This departure was much deplored by those who
recognized the significance of Marx's Russian studies, and had contributed
towards them.

In July 1884 Kovalevsky wrote in a letter to Lavrov:

> You know of course that Marx's notes on Russia, made in the past few
> years, are not to go into Volume II. What if one were to insist that they
> be printed, at least in extract, in your journal? His notes on the Reports
> of the Fiscal Commission are in all probability extremely interesting.
> (*Russkie sovremenniki o K. Markse i F. Engel'se*, 1969: 206)

As might be expected, Danielson was very disappointed by Engels's decision
(Marx and Engels 1908: v). So too was Kovalevsky's friend, the economist
A. I. Chuprov, who knew the extent and importance of Marx's Russian
studies. In a letter to Danielson of 11 January 1886 he remarked that:

> It would be a very great pity indeed if Marx's enormous preparatory
> work were to disappear without trace. Couldn't one ask the Editor to
> publish these works, if even in the form of fragmentary notes, if not all,
> then at least those containing the imprint of their author's thoughts and
> personality. (*Ocherki po istorii 'Kapitala' K. Marksa*, 1983: 363)

Engels, however, did not take this course, and volumes two and three of
Das Kapital appeared much as they had first been drafted in the 1860s. The
only mention Engels made of Marx's Russian studies was a short paragraph
in the preface to volume three, where he stated that Marx intended these
to be used in a new version of the section on ground rent. In Marx's
presentation, ground rent was one of the various forms of surplus value. To
class his studies of Russia under this head was to reduce their significance
immeasurably. It made their omission from *Das Kapital* seem no doubt
regrettable, but a relatively minor matter, certainly not one which would
affect the overall argument of the work.

The exclusion of Marx's Russian material not only kept from the public
domain a great part of his activity but also glossed over the problem which
had originally led Marx to undertake the study of Russian conditions.
Engels's decision to omit the Russian material, therefore, suggests that he
did not fully understand the kind of difficulties Marx had encountered

when writing *Das Kapital*, and therefore the kind of structure the work was intended to have. Engels apparently had little patience with theoretical niceties. In a letter to August Bebel in August 1883, he said that Marx had kept quiet about his lack of progress with *Das Kapital* because he knew that otherwise he, Engels, 'would give him no peace, day or night, until the book was finished and in print' (Marx and Engels 1995: 53). Clearly Engels attached more importance to publication than finding answers to difficult economic problems.

A product of Engels's lack of understanding of the direction of Marx's research was the book *The Origin of the Family, Private Property and the State* (1884), whose main source was Lewis Morgan's *Ancient Society*. Morgan's book had been given to Marx by Kovalevsky, who had first become acquainted with Morgan's work from Maine, who had used *Systems of Consanguinity and Marriage* extensively in his *History of Institutions*. It was natural that Kovalevsky should send Marx the later work, which he obtained in America. Its significance was that it showed an earlier stage in the evolution of the village community, and Marx used it in this way when writing the drafts of the letter to Vera Zasulich. This was also the context in which Sieber referred to it in his book on primitive economic culture. A book which was based on Morgan's study and in keeping with Marx's line of thought would have been about the evolution of the village community and its relationship to emergent capitalism, using the rich material on this subject afforded by the Russian sources. Engels's book, however, concentrates on the evolution of the family, which is a topic far removed from that of the circulation and reproduction of capital. It is symptomatic that when referring to Morgan's *Ancient Society* in a letter to Lavrov in February 1884 Engels remarked: 'Marx mentioned it, but my head was full of other things at the time and he never referred to it again' (Marx and Engels 1995: 103).

The Origin of the Family appeared the year after Marx's death, and to produce it so quickly had meant consulting rather few sources. In June 1891, after preparing the fourth edition of the work, Engels admitted in a letter to Laura Lafargue: 'I had to read the whole literature on the subject (which, *entre nous*, I had not done when I wrote the book – with a cheek worthy of my younger days) and to my great astonishment I find that I had guessed the contents of all those unread books pretty correctly – a good deal better luck than I had deserved' (Marx and Engels 2001: 202). According to Hans-Peter Harstick, who examined Engels's preparatory materials for *The Origin of the Family*, the notes Engels made for the first edition of the book comprised only 26 pages, with extracts from MacLennan, Lubbock, Giraud-Teulon, Bancroft, Agassiz and Bachofen (Harstick 1977: xlviii). Though he utilized later works of Kovalevsky on the evolution of the family for the fourth edition, Engels never made use of his *Communal Landownership* or Sieber's *Studies in the History of Primitive Economic Culture*.

Modernizing dialectics

A work that fundamentally severed the links with the philosophical current that had formed the theoretical framework of *Das Kapital* was Engels's book *Anti-Dühring* (see Marx and Engels 1987b). As Engels explained in the preface to this work, he was taking advantage of the polemic with the German academic Eugen Dühring to provide an exposition of 'the dialectical method and of the communist world outlook' that he and Marx had adopted. However, this exposition did not attempt to recreate the intellectual context which had given rise to Marx's conception of the 'Critique of Political Economy'. On the contrary, what Engels set out to do was to expound the dialectical method as it would be formulated at the present time, updating this method in the light of recent developments in the natural sciences.

Prior to the publication of *Anti-Dühring* in 1877 Engels had been working for two years on a manuscript which he called the 'Dialectics of Nature', which remained unpublished until 1924. In it he brought his knowledge of the natural sciences to bear on Hegelian philosophy to establish how much of it remained valid when put to the test of the latest scientific discoveries.

Since Marx and Engels had commenced their literary activities in the 1840s there had been a number of fundamental scientific developments. The three most important of these mentioned by Engels were: the discovery of the living cell; the discovery of the conservation of energy; and, above all, Darwin's theory of evolution. This, in combination with advances in the science of geology, showed that the Earth and life upon it were in continuous change. These developments had rendered the philosophies of Nature propounded by such writers as Schelling and Hegel obsolete. As Engels observed in 1858, if Hegel were to write the *Philosophy of Nature* in the present day, he would have to contend with a mass of new information (Marx and Engels 1983: 326).

In particular, new discoveries had made untenable the doctrine, subscribed to by generations of philosophers, that Nature was constant and unchanging over time. As Engels observed, 'natural philosophy, particularly in the Hegelian form, was lacking in that it did not recognise any development of Nature in time, any "succession," but only "juxtaposition"'. This was, he said, due to two factors: one was the requirements of the Hegelian system itself, which attributed historical evolution only to 'Spirit', but not to Nature. The other factor was the widespread assumption that Nature was something constant and unchanging. After Darwin, this assumption was untenable (Marx and Engels 1987b: 12).

In his system Hegel makes use of the fact that in his day 'Nature' implied constancy and permanence, since he is able to use the term in some contexts as a synonym for 'Essence'. Marx, in his writings up to and including the first edition of *Das Kapital*, had adopted this Hegelian usage of the term

'Nature'. Here he had followed thinkers from Fichte to Hegel, who had posited a progression in human history from 'Nature' to 'Society.' Marx associates Nature with Particularity and Society with Universality. Thus, for example, with Marx use value is Natural and Particular; exchange value is Social and Universal (White 1996: 163–4).

In 'Dialectics of Nature' and *Anti-Dühring* Engels was concerned to show that the Hegelian philosophy, from which he and Marx had drawn their inspiration, could be reformulated to conform with developments in modern science. He had identified three aspects of Hegelian dialectics which had modern-scientific equivalents. These were: the unity of opposites, the negation of negation and the transformation of quantity into quality. All three could be readily observed, Engels maintained, in the phenomena of everyday life. In fact, according to Engels, 'Dialectics is nothing more than the science of the general laws of motion and development of Nature, human society and thought' (Marx and Engels 1987b: 166).

To illustrate the ubiquity of the laws of dialectics as he interpreted them, Engels gave as an example the life cycle of a grain of barley. The grain was negated by its germination and the mature barley plant which took its place. After it is fertilized and produces more grains of barley, the stalk dies, and is in turn negated. As a result of this negation of the negation we have once again the original grain of barley, but not as a single unit, but ten, twenty or thirtyfold (Marx and Engels 1987b: 126).

Engels states in the preface of the second (1885) edition of *Anti-Dühring* that he had read the whole manuscript to Marx before it was printed (Marx and Engels 1987b: 9), in this way implying that Marx had approved of the contents of the work. The same implication is carried in Engels's assertion that 'the dialectical method and the communist world outlook' expounded in *Anti-Dühring* was shared by Marx and himself. But, as Terrell Carver points out, this claim was only made after Marx's death, and there is nothing in the Marx–Engels correspondence, in their works, or anywhere else to support it. In fact, during his lifetime Marx had never given any indication that he subscribed to Engels's conception of dialectics (Carver 1980: 357). In fact, the comparison between how Marx actually used Hegelian philosophy and Engels's conception of dialectics shows that there is very little in common between these two things.

In 1878 Marx presented a copy of *Anti-Dühring* to Kovalevsky, who, in turn, passed it on to Sieber. In the following year Sieber published extracts from it in the journal *Slovo* under the heading 'The Application of Dialectics to Science'. Sieber was not greatly impressed by Engels's book. He thought its polemical character had caused the material to be presented in an unsystematic way. He also believed that Engels had not adequately reproduced Dühring's philosophical and economic views, which merited much greater attention than had given them. Since Sieber had anticipated that the polemical part of the book was unlikely to interest the Russian reader, he kept this to a minimum in his article. Altogether, there was not much in Engels's book that he found worth translating for the Russian public. Accordingly, Sieber's article consists of two translated extracts from Engels's book, one from the section on 'Philosophy', and is on the history of philosophy; the other is from the section on 'Political Economy', which was written by Marx. The question of dialectics, which was a central element, does not figure prominently in Sieber's translation.

In the introductory part of his article Sieber distances himself from Engels's conception of dialectics, but attempts diplomatically to give some credit where it is due. In his judgement:

> Engels's book deserves particular attention both because of the consistency and aptness of the philosophical and socio-economic concepts it expounds, and because, in order to explain the practical application of the method of dialectical contradictions, it gives several new illustrations and factual examples, which in no small degree facilitate a close acquaintance with this so much praised and at the same time so little understood method of investigating the truth. It would probably be right to say that this is the first time in the lifetime of so-called dialectics that it is presented to the reader in such a real light.

But at the same time Sieber is unable to see in Engels's conception of dialectics anything beyond Darwin's theory of evolution. He continues:

> However, we for our part shall refrain from passing judgement as to the applicability of this method to the various branches of science, and also as to whether it constitutes – as far as any real meaning can be attached to it – a simple variation or even prototype of the methods of the theory of evolution or universal development. It is in this latter sense that its author regards it; or at least he strives to indicate a confirmation of it with the help of those truths achieved by the theory of evolution. And it must be admitted that in a certain respect quite a considerable resemblance is revealed. (Ziber 1900b: 718)

Sieber's judgement accorded fully with the approach that Engels had adopted to dialectics in *Anti-Dühring*. By eliminating from the concept of 'dialectics' any content that did not have an equivalent in modern natural science, Engels had purged the term of its philosophical connotations. One can discern in Sieber's remarks a hint of bewilderment. On the one hand, he himself had expounded Marx's works while divesting them of their Hegelian dimension. But for that very reason he was very familiar with the dialectical aspect of Marx's writings. And this most assuredly was not confined to the 'theory of evolution or universal development'.

The departure from the philosophical presuppositions that Marx intended to incorporate in 'The Critique of Political Economy' was taken further by Engels in his work *Ludwig Feuerbach and the Outcome of Classical German*

Philosophy, which first appeared as an extended review of C. N. Starcke's book on Feuerbach in *Die neue Zeit* (New Times) in 1886. Like *Anti-Dühring* and the pamphlet *Socialism Utopian and Scientific*, based upon it, *Ludwig Feuerbach* had an enormous influence in forming impressions of what Marx's doctrines were, both in Russia and elsewhere. It is short, accessible, written with literary flare, and authoritative, being written by a close associate of Marx. It is not, however, the reliable guide to the origin of Marx's ideas that it purports to be.

Despite the passages on the history of the Hegelian school in Germany, *Ludwig Feuerbach* is not a purely historical work. As in *Anti-Dühring*, Engels is concerned to bring the Hegelian philosophy that had informed Marx's thinking into line with modern natural science. The most important discovery of recent times was Darwin's theory of evolution, which established that the natural world is in a constant state of movement, and not permanently static, as was formerly believed. When Engels contemplated the Hegelian system in terms of what was mobile and what was static, he found that the part of Hegel's philosophy that was most in keeping with evolutionary thinking was the continuous self-movement of the Concept, which Hegel had termed 'dialectics'. Although Engels accepted the self-movement of the Concept, the dialectics, he rejected the Concept itself and all its related categories which formed the Hegelian system, such as the triad of Universality, Particularity and Individuality. These, Engels asserted, were products of Hegel's idealist viewpoint. This refined version of Hegel's dialectical method Engels held to be the revolutionary part of Hegelian philosophy, the one he and Marx had allegedly adopted. In other words, they had taken up Hegel's dialectical method, but rejected his philosophical system. In this connection Engels repeated the definition of dialectics that he had given in *Anti-Dühring*: the science of the general laws of motion, both of the external world and of human thought (Marx and Engels 1970: 361–2).

To Hegel this idea would have seemed absurd, because for him method and system were identical; indeed this was the hallmark of the Speculative school of philosophy to which he and Schelling belonged (White 1996: 76). Moreover, the contention that Marx had taken from Hegel only a dialectical method stripped of its philosophical content is manifestly untrue, as is shown by the way Marx groups his economic categories in *Das Kapital* under the headings: Universality, Particularity and Individuality. In his 'Critique of Political Economy', Marx adopted the Hegelian system as much as he adopted the dialectical method.

It is symptomatic that in *Ludwig Feuerbach* Engels neglected to mention his own part in adapting Feuerbach's ideas to economic questions in the 1844 article 'Outlines of a Critique of Political Economy', which inspired Marx's earliest conceptions of his 'Critique of Political Economy'. In his article Engels had shown that the abstract categories of political economy such as value, trade and money, could be resolved into the common transactions of everyday life. The doctrine that abstractions, such as economic categories, did not have an existence independent of the people and things from which they were derived was called 'materialism' (Marx and Engels 1975: 418–43). To mention this article would have involved Engels in expounding philosophical conceptions which, he now maintained, had been rejected.

There were consequences of unpicking the closely integrated Hegelian system that are reflected in *Ludwig Feuerbach*. The self-movement of the Concept provided Hegel with his theory of knowledge in that the movement culminated in the identity of subjectivity and objectivity. It could account for the separation of the two in common consciousness with reference to Alienation, Externalization and Reflection – all terms used by Marx in various of his writings. The concept of Reflection, in particular, was fundamental to Marx's method, because it explained how the categories of political economy could appear as abstract philosophical categories in the minds of people. But if one removed the Concept and its ramifications, then, in Engels's words, the relation of thinking to being became the 'great basic question of philosophy'. The answers which the philosophers gave to this question, Engels stated, split them into two great camps: those who asserted the primacy of Spirit to Nature comprised the camp of idealism. The others, who regarded Nature as primary, belonged to the various schools of materialism (Marx and Engels 1970: 346). This was quite a different conception of 'materialism' from the one that Marx had used and, especially in the context of the modern scientific interpretation of dialectics, raised the question of what constituted 'matter', a problem that was to plague later generations of Russian Marxists.

In his *Die neue Zeit* article Engels put forward a theory of knowledge that regarded practice as the criterion of objectivity. He argued that the best confirmation of the accuracy of our knowledge was the effectiveness of our actions. If, for example, people were able to conduct experiments that yielded predictable results, if they could reproduce artificially the processes of Nature, this would be a refutation of Kant's idea that one could not know 'things-in-themselves' (Engels 1886: 152).

In 1888, in a separate edition of *Ludwig Feuerbach*, Engels was able to adduce what he held to be documentary proof that Marx shared this 'practical' criterion of truth. This took the form of an appendix containing Marx's 'Theses on Feuerbach', published for the first time. These, Engels explained, were 'notes hurriedly scribbled down for later elaboration, absolutely not intended for publication, but invaluable as the first document in which are embodied the brilliant seeds of the new world outlook' (Engels 1888: VII).

The eleven theses on Feuerbach ended with the famous aphorism: 'Philosophers have hitherto explained the world in various ways. The point, however, is to change it'. It is remarkable that of all Marx's voluminous writings so much emphasis should have been placed on a brief note that it never occurred to the writer to publish. Yet it has been regarded as the apotheosis of Marxist thought, and has been traced back to the work of the

Polish thinker August Cieszkowski. What has been overlooked, however, is that Marx's famous aphorism is in fact a paraphrase of the statement by Arnold Ruge that: 'Our times are only understood by philosophy, and it is the task of our times to see to it that they not only understand philosophy, but are moved to action by it' (Ruge 1840: 2254). A comparison of the two formulations shows that Marx was by far the better writer, but the thought that he expresses is Ruge's. What is significant is that, in implying that Marx had a 'practical' theory of knowledge, Engels was unable to show this with reference to the considerable body of Marx's published work. His only evidence was an unpublished rough note embodying the conception of Marx's former associate.

The controversy with Tkachev

In 1874 Engels had made a brief study of Russian social and economic conditions but, unlike Marx's, his purpose had been of a political and tactical nature, and had therefore only a tenuous connection with his philosophical viewpoint. The occasion was the publication of a pamphlet by P. N. Tkachev entitled *The Aims of Revolutionary Propaganda in Russia*. Tkachev, a Russian Blanquist who had fled to Western Europe in 1873, had accepted an invitation to collaborate with Lavrov in publishing his journal *Vpered!* (Forward!). But after experiencing Lavrov's autocratic approach to editing the journal and his dubious support for revolution, Tkachev had broken with Lavrov and set out his reasons for doing so in his pamphlet.

Tkachev believed that Lavrov's emphasis on the necessity for revolutionaries to educate the masses and raise their level of consciousness distracted them from the urgent task of carrying out an immediate revolution to overthrow the existing regime. He thought that the implication of Lavrov's propagandistic methods would be to postpone revolution indefinitely, and in the meantime allow the suffering of the people to continue. Lavrov, in Tkachev's opinion, had confused peaceful progress, which embraced the majority of the population, with revolution, which involved only a minority of activists, of agitators. He was deluding himself that there could be 'bloodless revolutions of which Lassalle had dreamt, the idea on which the present Western European workers' movement was based, and on which the German programme of the International was founded'. Tkachev urged that, since the peasant commune was about to be dissolved and capitalist relations were about to develop in Russia, the revolution should not be postponed (Tkachev 2010: 406–40).

Engels, stung by Tkachev's criticisms of the International, and seeing in them similarities with Bakunin's, tried to ridicule the pamphlet and its author in a series of articles in *Volksstaat* (The People's State). Tkachev, however, replied in a reasoned and effective way in a pamphlet entitled *An Open Letter to Mr. Friedrich Engels*. This elaborated on the argument he had previously put forward and reinforced his case by pointing out ways in which Russian conditions differed from those in Western Europe and made an immediate revolution both more essential and more feasible.

These included the absence of both a proletariat and a bourgeoisie, the lack of civil rights, and the fact that the State did not represent any particular class but, as it were, 'hung in the air'. On the other hand, these same factors, Tkachev argued, made it possible for a revolution to succeed in Russia at the present time. The capitalist order had not yet become entrenched; the State's lack of class support made it vulnerable to a revolutionary takeover, and the Russian people, because of their collective institutions, were 'communists by instinct'. They were therefore nearer to socialism than the people of Western Europe. But time was of the essence; the encroachments of capitalism would eventually erode these advantages. Hence, he contended that the time was ripe for a social revolution in Russia (Tkachev 2010: 441–52).

Engels replied to Tkachev in an article in *Volksstaat* entitled 'On Social Relations in Russia'. This attempted to answer Tkachev's case in a more serious way than the previous article had done. To avoid the charge of ignorance of Russian conditions, Engels had read some books from Marx's collection of Russian materials, and no doubt discussed the matter with Marx. The result was that while the article sparkled with erudition about Russia, it showed a tension between the needs of the polemic and the results of Marx's studies.

Countering Tkachev's arguments required that Engels's article showed that Russian conditions were by no means unique, and that they were only variations on the Western European pattern. This case was in fact made, Engels indicating that the commune and the *artel'* were not peculiar to Russia but had formerly existed in all European countries. As far as Tkachev's presentation of the Russian State was concerned, Engels contended that the bourgeoisie of St Petersburg, Moscow and Odessa had developed with unprecedented rapidity during the past decade based on the construction of railways and the export of agricultural produce. Moreover, the entire large-scale industry only existed due to the protective tariffs granted by the state. Thus:

> When Mr. Tkachev assures us that the Russian State has no 'roots in the economic life of the people', that it ... 'hangs in the air', methinks it is not the Russian State that hangs in the air, but rather Mr. Tkachev. (Marx and Engels 1969b: 390)

Nor did Engels agree with Tkachev that life in communes had brought the Russian people close to socialism. The complete isolation of the individual communities one from another, he argued, was the natural basis for Oriental despotism. In this way, its specific form, tsarist despotism, instead of 'hanging in the air', was the logical outcome of Russian social conditions. It was, however, conceivable that socialism in Russia might be based on the peasant commune, so avoiding the capitalist stage. But, Engels stressed, this could only happen with the proviso that the material conditions for this were created by a successful proletarian revolution in Western Europe (Marx and Engels 1969b: 394–5).

This idea went a considerable way towards admitting Tkachev's case, that the socialist revolution in Russia could be different from that in the West if carried out with sufficient speed. The factor remaining to counter Tkachev's position was the insistence that the revolution in Russia would have to coincide with one in the West. Engels did not explain why the 'material conditions' must necessarily be provided by a socialist rather than a capitalist Europe, as Marx was later to suggest. But that this was for polemical rather than purely theoretical reasons is suggested by Engels's remark:

> It is sheer nonsense for Mr. Tkachev to say that the Russian peasants, although 'proprietors' are 'nearer to socialism' than the propertyless workers of Western Europe. It is quite the contrary. If anything can save Russian communal property … it is precisely a proletarian revolution in Western Europe. (Marx and Engels 1969b: 395)

Presumably for the same consideration, the insistence on the need for a revolution in Western Europe to save the Russian commune was maintained in the preface to G. V. Plekhanov's translation of the *Communist Manifesto* published in 1882, carrying the signatures of both Marx and Engels. Its concluding sentence read: 'If the Russian revolution becomes the signal for a proletarian revolution in the West, so that the two complement each other, the present Russian common ownership of land may serve as the starting-point for a communist development' (Marx and Engels 1969a: 100–1). This was a position more in keeping with Engels's views than with Marx's.

It is likely that Engels's input to the preface was greater than Marx's. The preface was written at a time when Marx was distraught by the death of his wife the previous month, and when his own health had seriously deteriorated. Despite travelling abroad for much of 1882 in an attempt to effect a recovery, Marx died on 7 March 1883. He left *Das Kapital*, his life's work, unfinished, having charged Engels, his literary executor, to see what could be made of his unpublished manuscripts.

The publication of Marx's letter
to *Otechestvennye Zapiski*

In September 1883 Engels handed over to Lopatin a copy of Marx's letter to *Otechestvennye zapiski* for publication in the Russian press (Grin 1985: 133). This, however, proved difficult to achieve, as journals were at that time being closed down by the authorities. In March 1884 Engels sent a second copy for publication to Vera Zasulich in Switzerland. She replied to Engels that she had translated it and that it would soon appear in print, but no publication resulted (Marx and Engels 1967: 500, 504). In 1885 Lopatin managed to have lithographed copies of the letter made by the People's Will party. They bore the explanation: 'In view of the appearance in our revolutionary literature of people "more Marxist than Marx", we print this letter as an interesting document which has not yet been made public'(Marx and Engels 1967: 765). Most of the copies, however, were seized by the police.

In 1886 Lopatin arranged to have Marx's letter published in the Geneva journal edited by Lavrov, *Vestnik Narodnoi Voli* (Bulletin of the People's Will), Lavrov stating in his introductory note that:

> We have had this letter in our possession for some time, but knowing that Friedrich Engels had given it to other people for printing in Russian, we refrained from publishing it. It has not yet appeared in the Russian émigré press. Last year it was published in Russia by our comrades, but most of the copies were seized by the police. Now we have received from our comrades a translation into Russian with the request to publish it, as they did not succeed in distributing it, and it has aroused considerable interest among the socialist youth. (Marx 1886: 214)

The translation was by Danielson, who continued to try to secure its publication in one of the journals appearing legally in Russia. With Chuprov's help he finally succeeded in having it printed in *Iuridicheskii Vestnik* (Juridical Bulletin) in August 1888.

Danielson was delighted with the letter's anti-universalist tone, and he found its appearance timely since, as he recalled, 'in the 1890s there emerged in our country a doctrine against which Marx fought in such forceful expressions, and about which I often had to write to Engels'. He added that 'some of its representatives still consider this campaign of Marx's against such a supra-historical doctrine a departure from his own theory ...' (Marx and Engels 1908: 13). It emerges from Danielson's correspondence with Engels that the latter was in great measure a subscriber to the universalist doctrine that Marx and Danielson had campaigned against.

Danielson's exchange of letters with Engels began immediately after Marx's death. It was in large measure concerned with the publication of volumes two and three of *Das Kapital*. Danielson arranged to have the proofs sent to him as they became available. He then translated them into Russian, so that the Russian versions of volumes two and three appeared in the same years as the German originals, that is, in 1885 and 1894 respectively (Marx and Engels 1908: 6).

Danielson also kept Engels informed about economic developments in Russia, reporting to him the kind of information which had interested Marx, and which he himself had used in his article published in 1880. There was a lively exchange of views in 1891 and 1892 between the two men on the subject of Russian economic development, prompted by the great famine in Russia in 1891, and Danielson's conviction that it had been brought about by the way capitalism had been fostered in the country.

Like Vorontsov, Danielson believed that Russia's late entry into the capitalist arena had created special problems. He too believed that the low productivity of labour had deprived Russia of any chance to dispose of her industrial products on the foreign market. The development of capitalism in Russia, therefore, was dependent on its internal market. By destroying the handicraft industries and forcing the population to buy articles it had formerly produced for itself, capitalism created an internal market, but at the same time, by failing to employ the peasants it had uprooted, it had deprived the market of the purchasing power necessary to buy the goods produced. The famine of 1891 had been the result; peasants had roamed throughout the country looking for work or a means of sustaining themselves. Millions had died in the attempt. According to Danielson:

> Before the present disaster we had 'liberated' 20–25% of our peasants. They wandered everywhere in search of work. You see them in Siberia, in Central Asia, in the Caucasus, in Brazil. What are they to do? Go to a factory? But we know that the number of workers employed in modern industry is constantly decreasing. (Marx and Engels 1967: 601)

Danielson recognized the problem as one of capital circulation, and found support for his ideas in the recently published volume two of *Das Kapital*, where Marx noted the contradiction in capitalism: 'the workers as buyers of commodities are important for the market. But as sellers of their own commodity – labour power – capitalist society tends to keep them down to the minimum price' (Marx 1978: 391). The person Danielson mentioned in his letters as holding the universalist, supra-historical point of view was Sieber. He told Engels:

> There are economists who consider the course of development of our economic condition very desirable and progressive, because it leads to capitalism, which is a necessary step towards universal well-being. The late N.I. Sieber, for example, was wont to say that 'the Russian peasant must be boiled in the factory cauldron' if we are to reach our economic paradise. (Marx and Engels 1967: 619)

But because, Danielson argued, only a small proportion of the peasants found employment in capitalist undertakings, what took place was not the steady formation and expansion of the capitalist system but the ruin of the country and the starvation of its population.

Engels's response to Danielson was essentially the same as Sieber's had been to Vorontsov: that the processes taking place in Russia were in no way different from those undergone in every other country where capitalism had developed, and were part of the inevitable march of capitalism. Danielson was especially incensed by Engels's remark that, 'Russia will be a very different country from what she was even on 1st January 1891. And we will have to console ourselves with the idea that all this in the end must serve the cause of human progress ...' (Marx and Engels 1967: 600).

Danielson must also have felt a certain exasperation when Engels tried to convince him that:

> They are ruined as peasants; their purchasing power is reduced to a minimum, and until they, as proletarians, have settled down into new conditions of existence, they will furnish a very poor market for the newly-arisen factories. (Marx and Engels 1967: 625)

Engels did not seem able to appreciate that Danielson's point was that in Russia most peasants had no prospect of settling down to a new existence as proletarians.

A significant kind of argument which Engels deployed against Danielson was that of authority, citing the opinion of Marx. In this case it was the foreword to the Russian edition of the Communist Manifesto – which itself had been at least partly inspired by a controversy of the same kind. 'There is no doubt', Engels wrote:

> That the commune and, to a certain degree, the *artel'*, contained in themselves the embryo which in certain circumstances could have developed and saved Russia from the necessity of undergoing the torments of the capitalist regime. I fully subscribe to our author's [i.e. Marx's J.W.] letter occasioned by Zhukovsky. But both in his opinion and in mine the first necessity for this condition was a push from outside – the change in the economic system of Western Europe, the destruction of the capitalist system in those countries where it first began. Our author in the famous foreword to the famous old Manifesto written in January 1882 to the question: could not the Russian commune serve as the point of departure for a higher social development answered thus: if the change in the economic system in Russia coincides with a change in the economic system in the West, so that the two complement each other, then modern Russian agriculture could serve as the point of departure for a new social development. (Marx and Engels 1967: 645)

The debate between Engels and Danielson was to become public when Danielson set out his views in the book *Studies in Our Post-Reform National Economy* published in 1893 and Engels responded in a Postscript to his 'On Social Relations in Russia', which appeared early the following year. The Postscript, which was approximately equal in length to the original work, attempted to dispose of any suggestion that Russian development was different in kind from that of Western Europe, and it dealt very harshly with those who had questioned the inevitability of capitalism in Russia. These, such as Herzen and Tkachev, Engels said, regarded Russians as the 'chosen people'. Chernyshevsky, according to Engels, had only placed such high hopes on the peasant commune because he had not read Marx's works, especially *Das Kapital* (Marx and Engels 1969b: 399).

For the first time Engels supplied a rationale for the insistence in the 1882 foreword to the *Communist Manifesto* on a 'push from outside' in the form of a revolution in Western Europe. The reason was that in the course of centuries the Russian peasant commune had not shown any sign of evolving into anything higher; a stimulus in this direction, therefore, must necessarily come from outside (Marx and Engels 1969b: 404).

As for Marx's letter to *Otechestvennye zapiski*, Engels contended that Marx's surmise that Russia might avoid the capitalist stage and proceed directly to socialism based on the peasant commune was enunciated at a particular juncture, when the possibilities for a revolution were especially favourable. That moment had now long passed. In the meantime capitalism in Russia had taken root and the country was destined to undergo the same economic development as had the nations of Western Europe (Marx and Engels 1969b: 407).

The tenor of Engels's Postscript was not very far removed from Marx's attitude in the 1850s to Herzen's idea of Russian socialism as expressed in his remark in the first German edition of *Das Kapital* volume one, which Engels quoted at length. When Danielson persisted in his views, Engels wrote to Plekhanov:

> As for Danielson, I fear he is a lost cause ... It is impossible to discuss anything with the generation of Russians to which he belongs, which still believes in a spontaneous communist mission, which is supposed to distinguish Russia, the real holy Russia, from other profane peoples. (Marx and Engels 1967: 722)

Engels's words came as music to the ears of Plekhanov. It was Plekhanov's contention that all those who did not accept the inevitable development of capitalism in Russia should be placed in the same category as Herzen, Tkachev and the Slavophiles, that is, the '*narodniki*'. In fact, one of Plekhanov's most lasting, if not generally recognized, contributions to the history of Russian social thought was his creation of the concept of 'narodism'.

4

Plekhanov

Nikolai Sieber was the first follower of Marx in Russia, and the commentator whom Marx most approved, but the person credited with being 'the father of Russian Marxism' was Georgii Plekhanov. Plekhanov merits the title in so far as he imposed on Marx's doctrines an interpretation that gained widespread and lasting acceptance in Russia.

Plekhanov was born in 1856 in the village of Gudalovka in the province of Tambov. He was the son of a landowner. He attended a military school and entered the Mining Institute in St Petersburg in 1874. Plekhanov, however, did not complete the course, but at the end of 1875 joined a group of revolutionaries who would form the organization Land and Liberty (*Zemlia i Volia*) in 1876.

A journal by this name began to appear in October 1878, one of whose editors was Plekhanov. The first number of *Zemlia i Volia* set out the principles on which the organization intended to operate. These were in keeping with the rules of the First International, whose preamble maintained that the emancipation of the working class must be the affair of the working class itself. These were the terms in which Plekhanov's colleague on the editorial board, S. M. Kravchinsky (Stepniak), explained how Land and Liberty saw its function, and what he thought the relationship between the revolutionaries and the masses ought to be:

Revolution is the business of the popular masses. History prepares them. Revolutionaries have no right to control anything. They can only be instruments of history, the means of expressing the people's aspirations. Their role consists only in organising the people in the name of its aspirations and demands, and to advance it in the struggle to bring them about; to facilitate and accelerate that revolutionary process, which, in accordance with the irresistible laws of history, is taking place at the present time. Outside that role they are nothing; within it they are one of the most powerful factors in history. (Bogucharskii 1970: 72)

The principle that the emancipation of the working classes was the affair of the working classes themselves, and that the role of the revolutionaries with regard to the masses was a subservient one was the original meaning of '*narodnichestvo*'. This was a principle that in the 1870s Plekhanov subscribed to.

As a follower of Bakunin, Plekhanov believed that because Russian peasants lived a communal life, they were inherently revolutionary, and that all that was required was the agitation of the revolutionaries to ignite a social revolution. In this they differed from the followers of Lavrov, who thought that the masses should be prepared by prolonged education and propaganda before a social revolution was possible. What the Bakuninists and Lavrovists were agreed upon was that political activity was futile and even harmful since it was a distraction from the social revolution. With Bakunin it was the hostility to politics which defined his anarchist ideology. For him the political sphere, that of the State, was the source of oppression and must be abolished. According to Plekhanov, Bakunin's doctrine could be summed up in the words: 'No politics! Long live the purely economic struggle!' (Plekhanov 1909: 132).

The question of the validity of political activity had been a major area of contention between Marx and Bakunin in the International. Marx advocated that the workers should take part in elections to central and local representative institutions and try to use these in the interests of the proletariat. Bakunin, on the other hand, maintained that this kind of activity represented a denial of the 'social revolution'. He could also argue in 'Marxist' terms that the state belonged to the superstructure of society, whereas the revolution must come from the social and economic base. Disagreement on this matter was one of the elements contributing to the dissolution of the International. Marx finally succeeded in having Bakunin expelled, but the latter nevertheless continued to command a great deal of sympathy and support in Russia, so that his ideas inspired the largest contingent of the young people who went 'to the people' in the mid-1870s.

The movement ended in failure. Agitation among the peasants led to no rebellion, and the peasantry in general proved to be impervious to socialist propaganda. Mass arrests of the young revolutionaries took place followed by long terms of imprisonment and banishment to Siberia. The lesson drawn by the revolutionaries was that their efforts needed better organization, and that a society should be established for the purpose. The society which came into being as a result was Land and Liberty, which maintained the apolitical stance of the Bakuninist current.

Land and Liberty distinguished itself not only from the Lavrovists but also from the followers of Tkachev. Whereas the former paid no attention to revolutionary agitation, the latter pinned their hopes for revolution on a conspiratorial seizure of power. The Tkachevists saw no need to go among the people; it was sufficient to seize State power and then use this in the interests of the common people. The Tkachevist form of revolution thereby infringed two basic principles of *narodnichestvo*: it was not the emancipation of the working classes by the working classes themselves, and it involved political action. The Tkachevists were a minority group among Russian revolutionaries, who looked upon them with suspicion (Bogucharskii 1912: 4).

Conflict within Land and Liberty arose as the question of political terror began to make inroads on the society's apolitical stance. The most celebrated instance occurred after Land and Liberty had staged a demonstration in Kazan Square in St Petersburg on 6 December 1876 and many participants had been arrested. One student, who had been taken prisoner, was flogged mercilessly for a trivial offence. As a reprisal, Vera Zasulich shot and wounded General Trepov, the Governor of St Petersburg. For this act she was put on trial but was acquitted in April 1878, to the great delight of her many sympathizers.

These developments were most unwelcome to many members of Land and Liberty who regarded assassination as a political act and, as such, contrary to the principles upheld by the organization. Terror was considered by them as an exceptional measure, one of self-defence, but not as a weapon against the State. Plekhanov was the most irreconcilable opponent of the new trend, and defended the Land and Liberty's apolitical stance.

The question of tactics was debated at Land and Liberty's congress in Voronezh in July 1879. A formal compromise was reached: it was agreed that the existing programme should be left unchanged, but that the political struggle against the government be stepped up. The settlement, however, was short-lived, and a month after the congress the organization split into two groups: the one with the more political orientation took the name People's Will (*Narodnaia Volia*), and the other representing the non-political *narodnik* orthodoxy called itself Black Repartition (*Cherny Peredel*).

The members of People's Will decided that the group that was to engage in terrorist activity would be called the 'Executive Committee', in order to imply that the members of the combat group were only the simple executors of the decisions taken by the entire 'Social-Revolutionary Party' (although no such party existed). Despite their espousal of political action in the form of acts of terrorism, the members of People's Will continued to refer to themselves as *narodniki* and to adhere to anarchist presuppositions. They rejected, for example, the struggle for political freedom on the grounds that this would only serve the interests of the bourgeoisie in enslaving the workers (Volk 1966: 69–76).

The first issue of Black Repartition's journal *Cherny Peredel* (January 1880) carried a leading article by Plekhanov explaining the reasons for political abstentionism and the need for social radicalism in terms of base and superstructure. According to Plekhanov:

> Because we regard the economic relations of society to be the base of all the rest, the root cause not only of all phenomena of political life, but also

of the mental and moral constitution of its members, radicalism must, in our view, be first and foremost economic radicalism ... an economic agrarian revolution will inevitably bring in its wake a transformation of all other social relations. (Plekhanov 1924: 114)

All other measures, Plekhanov argued, however radical they might appear, were in fact retrograde, because they not only presupposed the continued existence of the State but also action through its agency.

To avoid arrest, Plekhanov left Russia on 3 January 1880 and fled to Switzerland, settling in Geneva, where he defended the position of Black Repartition among the émigré revolutionary community. In a letter to Sorge of November 1880 Marx revealed that his sympathies lay with People's Will rather than with Plekhanov's Black Repartition. He commented:

In Russia – where *Das Kapital* is more widely read and acclaimed than anywhere else – our success is even greater. On the one hand, we have the critics (mostly young university professors, some of them personal friends of mine, some also littérateurs), on the other the terrorist Central Committee, whose recent programme ... aroused considerable ire among the anarchist Russians in Switzerland, who bring out *The Black Repartition* (to translate literally from the Russian) in Geneva. Unlike the terrorists, who risk life and limb, these men – most of whom (but not all) left Russia of their own accord – (In order to disseminate propaganda in Russia – they remove to Geneva! What a quid pro quo!). (Marx and Engels 1992: 45)

Black Repartition's apolitical stance became well-nigh impossible to justify following the assassination of Alexander II by People's Will on 1 March 1881. The fear of fresh attempts on the life of the new monarch and the fear that the assassination of the tsar nigh serve as a signal for a mass revolutionary upsurge in the country caused the Russian government to take extraordinary measures in 1881 and 1882. The flight of Alexander III from the capital to Gatchina, where he became a voluntary recluse, testifies to the panic which seized the tsar and his immediate entourage (Bogucharskii 1912: 134), a circumstance referred to by Marx and Engels in the preface to the Russian translation of the *Communist Manifesto*.

In Geneva Plekhanov read as much as he could of Marx and Engels's writings. In 1882, with the help of Vera Zasulich, he translated the *Communist Manifesto* for the Russian Social-Revolutionary Library, a series of works on socialist theory by various authors under the general editorship of Lavrov, Lev Hartmann and N. A. Morozov. At the start of 1882, on beginning his translation of the *Communist Manifesto*, Plekhanov suggested to Lavrov that Marx and Engels should be requested to supply the new Russian edition with a foreword. Lavrov duly wrote to Marx with this request, explaining that the *Manifesto* was being translated by 'a certain young man (Plekhanov), one of your most ardent followers'.

The Russian translation of the preface was published in the February 1882 issue of *Narodnaia Volia*. Its concluding paragraph containing the prognostication that 'the present Russian communal ownership of land may serve as the starting-point for a communist development' was italicized, and in the commentary which accompanied the translation Zasulich wrote:

> We have pleasure in including the 'Preface' in view of the considerable scholarly and practical interest in the questions it raises. It is especially pleasant for us to note the concluding words: we see in them confirmation of one of the basic propositions of the theory of People's Will – confirmation based on the researches of such authoritative scholars as Marx and Engels. The long-awaited continuation of Marx's celebrated work (*Das Kapital*) will of course develop with the requisite fullness, among other things, the propositions which the 'Preface' could only touch upon. (Partiia narodnoi voli 1905: 558)

The preface was Marx's first public pronouncement on the possibility of socialism in Russia being founded on the peasant commune. Zasulich, in viewing it as confirmation of the ideas of People's Will, obviously interpreted the document in the light of the letter she had received from Marx a year earlier.

Socialism and the political struggle

The revolutionaries who were behind the assassination of Alexander were hunted down relentlessly by the tsarist authorities, and by 1883 a wave of arrests had seriously weakened the People's Will organization. Lopatin, who had gone to Russia in a vain attempt to revive it, was arrested in 1884 and was sentenced to twenty years imprisonment. In Geneva members of Plekhanov's group, encouraged by Lavrov, tried to bring about a reconciliation between Black Repartition and People's Will. The journal of the new joint organization was to be *Vestnik Narodnoi Voli* (Bulletin of the People's Will), with Lavrov, Plekhanov and Lev Tikhomirov its editors. The joint organization never materialized because the terms of merger were unacceptable to Plekhanov. On 12 September 1883 he formed a new group, The Emancipation of Labour (*Osvobozhdenie Truda*).

The group's name reflected the dictum of the International Working Men's Association that 'the emancipation of the working classes must be conquered by the working classes themselves'. Accordingly, the group saw its function as preparing the ground for the emergence of a genuine workers' party by spreading socialist ideas in Russia. The group recognized the necessity for a terrorist struggle against the absolutist government, and differed from People's Will only on the question of the seizure of power by the revolutionary party and of the tasks of the immediate activity of the socialists among the working class (Plekhanov 1961: 114–15).

The Emancipation of Labour group planned to issue a series of publications under the general title of the 'Library of Contemporary Socialism'. The first item to be published was Plekhanov's pamphlet *Socialism and the Political Struggle* (Plekhanov 1961). To avoid any misunderstanding on the part of those of his readers who sympathized with the ideological current represented by the journals *Zemlia i Volia* and *Cherny Peredel*, Plekhanov reassured them that he had not diverged from the principles of *narodnichestvo*, that he still desired to work among the people, for the people, and that he still subscribed completely to the doctrine that 'the emancipation of the working classes must be conquered by the working classes themselves' (Plekhanov 1961: 57).

The main aspect of his former outlook that he wished to change was his attitude to political action. He admitted that he had been wrong on the issue of the political struggle; that political abstentionism was an entirely erroneous political tactic, which originated in Bakunin's teaching on the State. He acknowledged that in the disputes which took place in the Land and Liberty organization at the time of the split the members of People's Will were right in their stance. In the present circumstances, the campaign for political freedom was an essential one in Russia, and opened up new possibilities for effective action against the autocracy.

But while conceding that People's Will had been right on the question of political action, Plekhanov did not agree with other aspects of the group's programme. He believed that, in the light of the need for political struggle, People's Will required to reassess the theoretical bases of its programme and align these with the principles of Western Social Democracy. Plekhanov's argument was that only a revolution by the urban workers could fulfil the basic premise of *narodnichestvo*: that the emancipation of the workers should be by the workers themselves, since only the working class was capable of self-emancipation.

Having shown that one source of the error of political abstentionism was the Bakuninist doctrine of the State, Plekhanov went on to expose another misapprehension that derived from the misapplication of Marx's concept of 'base' and 'superstructure'. Political action had been excluded because, it was held, change originated in the economic base, not in the political and ideological superstructure, hence the futility of political action as a means of changing society. To this reasoning, Plekhanov, citing Engels in *Anti-Dühring*, argued that causes and effects were inter-dependent, that influences between base and superstructure went in both directions, that 'history was the greatest of dialecticians' (Plekhanov 1961: 85).

In Plekhanov's view, although People's Will understood the value of political action, their programme suggested that they would not use it to the best advantage. It spoke of the 'seizure of power by the provisional revolutionary government'. And, from the context, it was clear that what was envisaged was a government of radical intellectuals who would govern in the interests of the people. Plekhanov is decisive in rejecting any suggestion that such 'substitution' would be possible. He remarks: 'There is no more difference between heaven and earth than between the dictatorship of a class and the dictatorship of a group of radical intellectuals.' In the latter case one would have a revival in socialist dress of ancient forms of authoritarian and despotic regimes, the only difference being that national production was managed not by Peruvian 'sons of the sun' and their officials, but a socialist caste (Plekhanov 1961: 110–14). The revolution, when it came, Plekhanov pointed out, would not simply be a matter of seizing power, but of organizing all the functions of social and economic life. The kind of advanced proletariat which was capable of this task would not allow even the most sincere of its well-wishers to seize power; it would take power and carry out the socialist revolution by itself. But as Plekhanov admitted, in the Russian context, this kind of socialist revolution was not in the near future (Plekhanov 1961: 111).

Plekhanov thought that both People's Will and Black Repartition were one-sided organizations. People's Will's programme was too ambitious and took very little account of Russian reality; Black Repartition was encumbered by Bakuninist ideology. Both organizations, however, had something of value to offer the Russian revolutionary movement. According to Plekhanov:

> Our revolutionary movement, far from losing anything, will gain a great deal if the Russian *narodniki* and the Russian People's Will at last become Russian Marxists and a new, higher, standpoint reconciles all the groups existing among us, which are all right each in its own way, because despite their one-sidedness each of them expresses a definite need of Russian social life. (Plekhanov 1961: 104)

In a book published in 1912, the Russian historian Bogucharsky paraphrased Plekhanov's idea of the synthesis of the two revolutionary groups in the following way:

> The adherents of People's Will bequeathed to succeeding generations of the liberation movement in Russia the idea of the struggle for political freedom; the members of Black Repartition – the basic slogan of the whole of the previous movement: 'The emancipation of the people should be the affair of the people itself.' These two ideas were then synthesised in the Russian social-democratic movement. (Bogucharskii 1912: 373)

What Plekhanov believed to be the positive contribution of People's Will was political action; what Black Repartition contributed was the essence of *narodnichestvo*: the concept of workers' self-emancipation.

As far as the usage of the terms *narodnik* and *narodnichestvo* in *Socialism and the Political Struggle* is concerned, one notices that Plekhanov as a Marxist or a 'follower of Marx' considers himself unreservedly a '*narodnik*'.

In his discourse with the members of People's Will, moreover, Plekhanov writes not as a Marxist to non-Marxists, but as one 'follower of Marx' to other 'followers of Marx', the difference between them being on how Marx should be interpreted and how the principles of *narodnichestvo* should be upheld. There is no suggestion in *Socialism and the Political Struggle* that the adherents of People's Will belong to some non-Marxist ideological current.

Lev Tikhomirov replied to Plekhanov's pamphlet on behalf of People's Will in the second issue of *Vestnik Narodnoi Voli* in 1884 with an article entitled 'What Do We Expect from the Revolution?' The feature of Plekhanov's argument which had struck Tikhomirov most forcefully was the contention that socialism in Russia would only come after a capitalist phase. This was not a socialist programme, he thought, which took as its point of departure the country as it actually existed, but as Plekhanov thought it ought to be. Plekhanov was in the situation of having to create the class in whose name he wished to act. To do this, moreover, he had to write off the peasants, the working people who actually existed, but not being proletarians, did not qualify for Plekhanov's attention. If capitalism were really the indispensable preparation for socialism, then to be consistent Plekhanov ought to give up all thought of socialist activity and do all he could to promote capitalist development. He could, for example, help the liberals to obtain a constitution. But in that case what difference would there be between a socialist and a bourgeois? (Tikhomirov 1885: 2–3).

For Tikhomirov, the idea that it was necessary to go through the 'school of capitalism' was but one step removed from collaboration with capitalism. And until capitalism had run its course one presumably limited oneself to propaganda among the workers, still a mere 500,000 people out of a total population of 100 million – and three-quarters of these were not actually proletarians. To make matters worse, Tikhomirov pointed out, the number of workers was not increasing but remaining static. Industry was developing only with great difficulty, and with the help of the State.

In Tikhomirov's view, just because capitalism had prepared the ground for socialism in the countries of Western Europe, that did not mean that the same process would take place in Russia. It did not mean that the organization of production by competing private companies was the only or the best means of socializing the workers. In Russia the State played a bigger part in the organization of industry than private capital did. This had to do with the availability of markets. Whereas, when industry developed in the West, private companies had extensive internal and external markets with little serious competition to face, Russian industry, developing later, had little in the way of an internal market and on external markets had to face the formidable competition of European and American producers. Coming late on the scene, however, was not entirely disadvantageous to Russia. Its industry need not go through the stage of development by private enterprise; it could learn from the West's experience and proceed directly to nationalized industry (Tikhomirov 1885: 10–12).

Although, according to Tikhomirov, the Russian government had done everything in its power to foster the development of the bourgeoisie, this class remained weak both politically and economically. If the tsarist government was overthrown, it would be incapable of imposing its rule on the country. The revolution would therefore be one which would bring a popular government to power. As for the accusation that People's Will intended to seize power and rule by decree, Tikhomirov contended that Plekhanov's mode of argument was to refute things which his opponent had never said. There was no question of People's Will's imposing an authoritarian regime like the Peruvian 'sons of the sun' on the population. The government would be subject to popular control; and there would be no political compulsion since socialist measures would be introduced by economic incentives, similar to those which the tsarist government had used to foster capitalism. Socialism, Tikhomirov maintained, would be made inevitable in Russia in the near future, not through the development of capitalism and the formation of a proletariat, but by the transfer of land and State power to the peasants and working people in general (Tikhomirov 1885: 16–25).

In Tikhomirov's view the onset of the socialist revolution in Russia would be accompanied by revolutions, if not in the whole of Europe, then at least in some of its countries, possibly in Russia's nearest neighbours. This would facilitate greatly the development of Russia's national production in a socialist direction. To the possible objection that this kind of revolution had never occurred anywhere before, Tikhomirov answered that neither was there a case of a socialist order having arisen out of a capitalist order, as the historical stereotype envisaged (Tikhomirov 1885: 26–7).

Our Differences

Tikhomirov's article did not extend its scope beyond the points Plekhanov had raised in *Socialism and the Political Struggle*, and these it dealt with systematically and concisely. Plekhanov's response to 'What Do We Expect from the Revolution?', however, was the rather diffuse pamphlet *Our Differences* (1884) which set out both to counter Tikhomirov's arguments and to place them in what Plekhanov claimed to be their context in Russian intellectual history.

In *Our Differences* Plekhanov repeated the assertion, voiced in *Socialism and the Political Struggle*, that the Emancipation of Labour group was a synthesis of Black Repartition and People's Will. He professed to find the latter organization indistinguishable in its tactics from Tkachev's, and to find many similarities between Tikhomirov's 'What Do We Expect from the Revolution?' and Tkachev's 'Open Letter to Mr. Friedrich Engels'. He accused Tikhomirov of proposing to replace the initiative of a class with that of a committee, and predicted that this could only lead to the creation of a political monster similar to the ancient Chinese or Peruvian empires, to the 'revival of tsarist despotism with a communist lining'.

Plekhanov devoted a great deal of attention to discrediting the social and economic presuppositions of the People's Will programme – that in Russia the State played a much greater part in promoting economic developments than was the case in the West. He did not attempt to dispute this central proposition, but sought to undermine it by directing his arguments at related but different positions and ascribing these to his opponents in the manner Tikhomirov had indicated. Thus, the contrast between Russia and Western Europe as regards the part played by the State in the economy became in Plekhanov's presentation the doctrine of Russia's 'national uniqueness'. He then proceeded to refute this doctrine as though it was the one that Tikhomirov and People's Will actually held. He gave examples to show that in the sixteenth and seventeenth centuries the State had been interventionist in several countries in Western Europe. Consequently, it could not be said that in this respect Russia was unique. This was certainly true, but it was not relevant to the point that Tikhomirov was making.

For Tikhomirov the reason why State intervention was necessary in Russia was the difficulties facing the circulation of capital in Russia. Tikhomirov, as Plekhanov noted, had used the information in Vorontsov's book *The Fate of Capitalism in Russia* which drew attention in particular to the problem of markets. Vorontsov was the writer who took up the most extreme position on the development of Russian capitalism, but even he only argued that State intervention was necessary to overcome the obstacles to capitalism arising from its late appearance in Russia. He did not say that capitalism did not or could not exist in Russia. Plekhanov, however, argued as if the position held by his opponents was that there was no capitalist development in Russia, and that such development could not take place because of the country's 'uniqueness'. Ironically, the main work Plekhanov cited in support of his arguments was Danielson's article 'A Sketch of Our Post-Reform Economy'. Danielson, whom Plekhanov judged to have 'a more thorough knowledge of our economy ... than all the Russian revolutionaries and conservative exceptionalists put together' (Plekhanov 1961: 270), was in basic agreement with Vorontsov, but it was only when his book appeared in 1893 that Plekhanov assigned him to the category of 'exceptionalist', that is, '*narodnik*' (Plekhanov 1961: 820–6).

Although the question of the viability of the peasant commune had not been raised by Tikhomirov, and although People's Will had repeatedly mentioned how the government's economic policies were undermining the commune, Plekhanov produced facts and figures to show that the Russian agrarian commune was actually in decline. The implication was that People's Will maintained that the commune had everywhere remained immune to capitalist influence.

Plekhanov's method was effective because the false positions ascribed to his opponents taken together had a certain cogency: a belief in a special historical destiny for Russia; the impossibility of a capitalist development; and the inviolability of the peasant commune. Taken as a whole the theoretical position of People's Will seemed in this light to be a kind of neo-Slavophilism.

The great and far-reaching significance of *Our Differences*, however, was in terminology. Whereas in *Socialism and the Political Struggle* Plekhanov had referred to himself as a '*narodnik*', and had reproached People's Will for a 'complete and all-round denial of *narodism*', he now referred to the adherents of People's Will as '*narodniki*', and the neo-Slavophile doctrines they allegedly professed as '*narodism*'. The term now became detached from the principle that 'the emancipation of the working classes is the affair of the working classes themselves'. This principle, Plekhanov claimed, his own organization still upheld, but the conspiratorial People's Will denied.

The advantage of attaching the label '*narodnik*' to his adversaries, whose claim to being followers of Marx was as valid as Plekhanov's, was that they could be represented as a single current or sect within Russian socialism but not its mainstream. Plekhanov reinforced this idea by tracing the origins of '*narodism*' from Herzen and Chernyshevsky. These, he claimed, had formed the 'theoretical amalgam from which our *narodism* ... arose' (Plekhanov 1961: 187).

The point of attaching the '*narodnik*' label was to imply that there were fundamental ideological differences between People's Will and the Emancipation of Labour group, and that Plekhanov's organization represented the main current of socialism in Russia. Since Emancipation of Labour accepted terror as a legitimate means of political action, the differences between the two organizations in reality were not great. Whereas People's Will envisaged workers' participation in the socialist revolution, Emancipation of Labour insisted that the coming revolution would be a purely proletarian one and would come at the end of a capitalist stage. Plekhanov would not want to emphasize this difference, because his position on the proletarian character of the future Russian revolution was difficult to defend, as Tikhomirov had shown. Plekhanov preferred to argue about invented differences between himself and Tikhomirov rather than real ones.

The polemic with Tikhomirov ended well for Plekhanov. Tikhomirov did not reply to *Our Differences* with any detailed refutation. In 1886 he simply inserted a short paragraph in the bibliographical section of *Vestnik Narodnoi Voli* noting the publication of Plekhanov's book and explaining why he would not enter into any polemic with the author. It was impossible, he said, to do this briefly, and if one were to analyse in detail the method of argument employed 'it would be necessary to say much more about Mr. Plekhanov than about the questions he had raised'. To answer Plekhanov would require making attacks on his character, and this was something the journal had resolved not to do on its pages. In any case, Tikhomirov believed, there was no real need for him to defend himself or People's Will against Plekhanov's accusations, because their falsity would be obvious to any dispassionate reader (Tikhomirov 1886: 40).

In the short term Tikhomirov was right; *Our Differences* was not well received among Russian revolutionaries either in Russia or in emigration. But as Plekhanov's pamphlet remained unanswered, in the longer term it acquired credibility, especially after People's Will had been weakened and dispersed by mass arrests, imprisonment and internal exile. A decade after it was published a new generation of readers could take its presentation of '*narodism*' for good coin.

In retrospect, it is to be regretted that Tikhomirov did not expose the mendaciousness of Plekhanov's allegations about the supposed ideology and genealogy of '*narodism*'. For want of it many historians of the Russian revolutionary movement have been misled into thinking that the '*narodnik*' current of thought that Plekhanov described did in fact exist. The first Russian historian to be influenced by Plekhanov's conception of *narodnichestvo* was Bogucharsky, who, in his book entitled *Active narodnichestvo* published in 1912, accepted Plekhanov's contention that the *narodniki* continued the Slavophile tradition. In the West a body of literature has grown up on the subject of Russian 'populism', as '*narodnichestvo*' is conventionally translated. The most outstanding example of this is Franco Venturi's monumental *Roots of Revolution* (original Italian title *Il populismo russo*), which traces the beginnings of 'populism' from Herzen and Chernyshevsky, in the manner Plekhanov alleged. Some authors, however, have noted the amorphous nature of '*narodism*' and the difficulty of finding any documentary evidence for its existence. Albert Resis, for example, writes that: 'Russian populism ... was more a state of mind than a finished doctrine' (Resis 1970: 224).

A landmark in the historiography of 'populism' was the article '*Narodnichestvo*: A Semantic Inquiry' by Richard Pipes published in 1964 (Pipes 1964). From his reading of the literature, Pipes concluded that the term '*narodnichestvo*', used in the sense of a doctrine with Slavophile roots, propounded by Herzen and Chernyshevsky, that Russia could bypass the capitalist stage, had been coined for polemical ends by Peter Struve in his book *Critical Notes on the Economic Development of Russia*, published in 1894. Pipes was right to see the term as a polemical device rather than as an actually existing intellectual current, though he overlooked Plekhanov's role in transforming the meaning of '*narodnichestvo*'. This is surprising, considering that for application of the term Struve acknowledges his debt to Plekhanov's *Our Differences* (Struve 1893: 1).

Dialectical materialism

Plekhanov's growing interest in Marxist ideas came at a time when new works by Marx and Engels were appearing, and he was deeply influenced by these. The first such publication was an extract from Marx and Engels's book *The Holy Family* that Karl Kautsky published in the journal *Die neue Zeit* in 1885. As the book was long out of print, Kautsky wanted to give readers of the journal the opportunity to acquaint themselves with at least part of it. The extract he chose, though unrepresentative of the book as a whole, was the only one which formed an independent entity. It was entitled 'French Materialism of the Eighteenth Century' and was a short historical sketch of the various currents in French materialism, including those represented by Holbach and Helvétius (Marx 1885).

The extract made a strong impression on Plekhanov, and convinced him that eighteenth-century French materialism was a precursor of Marx's philosophy. One of Plekhanov's chief philosophical works was a book published in 1896 entitled *Essays on the History of Materialism*, and consisted of essays on Holbach, Helvétius and Marx (Plekhanov 1896). In many of Plekhanov's philosophical writings one finds references to the French materialists of the eighteenth century in connection with Marx's ideas. The full text of *The Holy Family* was published in 1902 in a collection of Marx and Engels's early works edited by Franz Mehring (Mehring 1902). The subsidiary status of the chapter on French materialism then became obvious, making it difficult for Plekhanov to maintain that this current of thought was central to the philosophy of Marxism.

The year after the appearance of the extract from *The Holy Family* Engels published his two-part article 'Ludwig Feuerbach and the Outcome of Classical German Philosophy' (Engels 1886), and in 1888 he republished it as a separate pamphlet, with the 'Theses on Feuerbach' as an appendix. Engels's *Ludwig Feuerbach* was to be an important influence on Plekhanov's conception of Marxist philosophy. In 1892 he published a Russian translation of Engels's pamphlet provided with explanatory notes. In the note which dealt with Engels's rejection of Kant's theory of knowledge, Plekhanov made a concession to Kant by saying that human sensations resembled hieroglyphics, in the sense that they did not resemble the reality that they conveyed, though they did convey faithfully the events themselves and the relations between them. This was an idea that Plekhanov was to disavow in the edition of the pamphlet published in 1905 (Plekhanov 1961: 536).

Plekhanov was also fortunate that, in the aftermath of the exchange between himself and Tikhomirov, it was not his reputation which suffered, but Tikhomirov's. By 1887 Tikhomirov had become disillusioned with revolutionary politics. He thought that People's Will had made a serious mistake by adopting the tactic of political terror, and he became convinced that, historically, more reforms to benefit the Russian people at large had come from the government rather than from any activity on the part of the revolutionaries. In the following year he withdrew publicly from the revolutionary movement, explaining his decision in a pamphlet entitled *Why I Ceased to be a Revolutionary*. He was then open to charges of treachery and perfidy, Plekhanov being prominent among his accusers. The result of Tikhomirov's change of heart was that his side of the polemic with Plekhanov was discredited, and this was the implication that Plekhanov strove to emphasize.

In 1889 Plekhanov published a pamphlet entitled *A New Champion of Autocracy* in connection with Tikhomirov's defection from the revolutionary movement. Its purpose, however, was not only to attack Tikhomirov, but to propound Plekhanov's philosophical views. He had been studying German philosophy, especially Hegel, and had intended to write a work on the subject for the 'Library of Scientific Socialism'. He had been dissuaded from doing so, however, on the grounds that literature aimed at the workers had a higher priority. The pamphlet on Tikhomirov, therefore, offered a convenient pretext for an essay on philosophy.

Plekhanov's point of departure was Tikhomirov's statement that said:

With us (and not only with us) the idea has taken root that we live in some kind of 'period of destruction', which, they believe, will end in a terrifying upheaval with rivers of blood and the blast of dynamite etc. With this – it is supposed – will begin the 'period of creativity'. This social conception, constituting something like the political reflection of Cuvier's old ideas and the school of sudden geological catastrophes, is completely mistaken. In fact, in real life, destruction and creation go hand in hand, and are even unthinkable without each other. The destruction of one phenomenon takes place precisely because within it, in its place, something else is being created, and *vice versa*, the formation of something new is nothing but the destruction of the old. (Tikhomirov 1997: 34)

This conception, Plekhanov argued, arose from the erroneous idea that Nature did not make leaps. In a reply inspired by Engels's *Anti-Dühring* Plekhanov produced some examples of what he considered to be 'leaps' in Nature: water changing into ice; the development of an insect from a chrysalis and the like, and then appealed to the authority of Hegel, citing a passage from the *Science of Logic* where the author discussed the maxim that 'Nature does not make leaps'. Plekhanov was subsequently to consider 'dialectical leaps' as an integral part of dialectics, and this idea was to pass into later conceptions of how Hegel's philosophy ought to be interpreted. It is ironical that the idea of 'leaps' should have become associated with a philosopher who did so much to stress the element of continuity in all things.

Plekhanov was to repeat his conception of dialectical 'leaps' in 1891 in his article in *Die neue Zeit*, 'On the Sixtieth Anniversary of Hegel's Death' (Plekhanov 1961). This was the work which established Plekhanov's standing in Europe as an authority on Hegel. Plekhanov went about his study of Hegel as a precursor of Marx in a quite direct way, looking in Hegel's writing for what he thought to be the embryo of Marx's ideas. His starting point was therefore not Marx's ideas, but his own understanding of what those ideas were. Not surprisingly, Plekhanov's article on Hegel was a mirror of his own philosophical conceptions.

The work Plekhanov was most concerned with in his article was Hegel's *Philosophy of History*; it was in this, he was convinced, that most of Marx's thought had originated. He professed to find in this work of Hegel's the embryo of Marx's doctrine of base and superstructure. It was Hegel's idealism, Plekhanov believed, which created the inconsistencies in his approach to history, but it was the use Hegel had made of economics that had freed him somewhat from the limitations of the idealist outlook. In this respect he had been able to point the way forward for the materialists who succeeded him. For, Plekhanov explained, post-Hegelian materialism could not simply be a return to the 'naive metaphysical materialism of the eighteenth century', which held that human judgement governed history; in the sphere of historical explanation it had to turn first and foremost to economics. To have done otherwise would not have been progress but retrogression, compared with Hegel's philosophy of history.

The latter part of this article, however, showed that although Plekhanov followed Engels's terminology, he interpreted it in the light of his own intellectual evolution. For his main concern, as in *Socialism and the Political Struggle*, was the relationship between objective factors and the possibility of human action. He was anxious to show that although historical development was determined by the economic factor, there was still room for political action. According to Plekhanov, 'dialectical materialism' (a term which neither Marx nor Engels ever used) was a doctrine which appreciated that economic necessity and freedom of action formed a synthesis, so that necessity and freedom were recognized as being interdependent. In practice this meant that once people knew the laws by which history operated they would be able to use them to transform history from an unconscious process to a conscious one (Plekhanov 1961: 477).

The famine of 1891

In 1891–92 a catastrophic famine engulfed half of European and part of Asiatic Russia. The victims were mainly peasants who died from hunger, disease and cold. It was a disaster, Plekhanov wrote, that had no parallel in modern European history; one would have to look to the barbaric despotisms of Asia to find a precedent. In his articles of the time Plekhanov described the extent of the famine and its disastrous consequences in great detail, noting the inadequate response of the authorities and the cynical ways in which the exploiting groups took advantage of the peasants' misery to advance their own interests. For Plekhanov, however, the famine was not an unmitigated disaster; he saw it as part of an objective historical process that would eventually lead to the transformation of peasants into proletarians and thus to the establishment of a socialist society in Russia. He ridiculed the apprehensions of the *narodniki* and Slavophiles on the transformation of the peasants into proletarians, because through this process the sufferings caused by the autocratic regime would be alleviated (Plekhanov 1925a: 385).

Mikhailovsky was appalled at the attitude of the Russian Marxists to the famine, which he thought unconscionable. Some, he alleged, had even gone as far as to deny aid to the famine victims on the grounds that this would 'obstruct the process of capitalist accumulation'. And what was the necessity for this accumulation of capitalism? It was nothing but the dialectical doctrine of 'economic materialism' of the negation of the negation: the peasants had to be separated from their means of production in order to be reunited with them in the socialist society. It was, in Mikhailovsky's view, the application by Russian Marxists of Hegel's abstract triad. The situation had come about that Mikhailovsky had described in his article defending *Das Kapital* from the strictures of Zhukovsky. In the face of capitalism's 'maiming of women and children' the Russian Marxists would stand by and applaud the progress that capitalism was making. In the present case, this was happening with a degree of cruelty that he had not foreseen in 1877.

And the irony of this, Mikhailovsky pointed out, was that Marx himself did not agree with this madness. Here he could quote Marx's letter to the editorial board of *Otechestvennye zapiski*. Mikhailovsky summarized it as follows:

> Marx did not present his formula of the capitalist process as a 'passport of a historico-philosophical theory': he stated only that having embarked on this route, every country, including Russia, would have to submit to the laws of economic development he had formulated, and further, that the outcome in each individual case was determined by the particular historical conditions of the country concerned, and that he did not consider it at all obligatory for Russia to embark on the capitalist path. Even the expropriation of the people, which was the necessary condition for capitalist development, did not necessarily lead to that result; depending on the historical conditions, it might lead to something quite different. (Mikhailovskii 1909: 327)

Mikhailovsky was able to indicate that this was quite different from what many Marxists in Russia maintained, and he was not surprised to learn that Marx had not considered himself to be a 'Marxist'.

The Marxist that Mikhailovsky gave as an example of those who considered the development of capitalism in Russia inevitable because of the dictates of the Hegelian triad was Sieber. Here Mikhailovsky drew upon his personal reminiscences of the now deceased Sieber. He recalled:

> I became acquainted with Sieber at the beginning of 1878, when he paid a visit to St Petersburg. In any case, it was soon after the appearance of Zhukovsky's article on Marx and our own reply. An outstanding

specialist in his field, Sieber struck me as a complete novice in philosophy, to which he was attracted by Hegel via Marx and Engels. I remember, so to say, the passion with which he expounded the famous illustration of the threefold Hegelian formula, whose allure I had experienced myself in my youth: 'Take a grain of barley, sow it – the seed gives out a shoot, which is the negation of the seed, because it destroys it. But then the further development of this negation leads to the negation of the shoot in its turn, a negation which is, moreover, a return to the first stage: the stalk ends in an ear, a multiplicity, a collection of seeds'. And the same process, seemingly, took place in all spheres of existence, including that of human relations. (Mikhailovskii 1909: 323–4)

The illustration of the Hegelian triad by means of the seed of barley – as Mikhailovsky indicated elsewhere – was taken from Engels's book *Anti-Dühring*, which had been published in 1878. Mikhailovsky added that:

As a novice in Hegelianism he was relentless, and the history of the grain of barley, negating itself in the stalk, in order that this negation should be negated in the ear, was for him the archetype of Russian and every other kind of history. A decent man, probably never having knowingly harmed anyone in his life, he did not balk at the sufferings and miseries which accompanied the second stage of the Hegelian triad – they were inevitable and would be repaid a hundredfold at the dawn of the new era. 'Until the peasant is boiled down in the factory cauldron, we shall get nowhere', Sieber used to say. (Mikhailovskii 1909: 327)

As he was reviewing *Anti-Dühring* at this time, it is very likely that Sieber discussed it with Mikhailovsky. But it is wrong to attribute Sieber's conviction that capitalism was a universal system to the influence of Engels's book; this came from his general understanding of Marx's work, and statements to this effect predated the appearance of *Anti-Dühring*. He would, in any case, hardly be influenced by a book with which he was so unimpressed, especially in its treatment of dialectics. Moreover, while it is possible that Sieber made the remark about Russian peasants in private conversation, it is not to be found in his published writings.

One can understand why Mikhailovsky should concentrate his criticism of Russian Marxism on Sieber. Sieber was the most authoritative of all the followers of Marx in Russia, and therefore someone whose views it was important to discredit, even if these views had to be misrepresented for the sake of the polemic.

While making no specific reference to Plekhanov's attempt to class every writer who questioned the necessity of capitalist development in Russia as a '*narodnik*', Mikhailovsky made it quite clear that he himself did not accept the designation. In an article published in October 1893 he investigated the term in connection with those writers who considered themselves to be '*narodniki*'. He knew of only two such people. One was Vorontsov, and the other was the recently deceased Yuzov-Kablits. From a comparison of their writings, however, it emerged that by the term '*narodism*' each understood something entirely different.

On the suggestion that '*narodism*', whatever it might be, was derived from Slavophilism, Mikhailovsky denied that this was even true of Vorontsov.

> Mr. Vorontsov began with an analysis of economic facts, which led him to the conclusion ... that the path of economic development taken ... by Western Europe is not obligatory for Russia. This was the position of the Slavophiles, and later of a group of writers who had nothing in common with the Slavophiles except for this point. (Mikhailovskii 1909: 627)

It was on this point that Mikhailovsky found himself in agreement with Vorontsov, and on it he supported Vorontsov against the Russian Marxists. But he was adamant that: 'rejecting Marxism certainly does not mean declaring oneself a *narodnik*' and that it was 'not at all obligatory to choose between these two doctrines' (Mikhailovskii 1909: 683).

Mikhailovsky's offensive against Russian Marxism evoked an immediate and impassioned response. He received a great many letters in protest, and several pamphlets were published in defence of Marxism in 1894. These included Struve's *Critical Notes*, Lenin's *What the 'Friends of the People' Are and How They Fight against the Social Democrats* and Plekhanov's *The Development of the Monist View of History*.

Plekhanov's *The Development of the Monist View of History* was published in St Petersburg at the end of 1894 under the pseudonym of 'Beltov' (Plekhanov 1961). Unlike most of his previous works, this was a legal publication, so that both the name of the author and the title of the book had to meet the needs of the Russian censorship.

The *Monist View of History* was a kind of running battle with Mikhailovsky, and indeed, as appendices to the second edition show, it was a battle which continued after the book was published. Despite this polemical character of the work, it incorporated several ideas found in Plekhanov's earlier writings, and he obviously intended that it should give a systematic exposition of what he considered the Marxist viewpoint to be. The rather confused structure of the book, however, suggests that the two different purposes of the book came into conflict.

At the heart of the systematic part of the work was the contention that 'dialectical materialism' was the solution to the problem other philosophies had tackled unsuccessfully, namely, how to account for the interconnection of environmental factors and intellectual influences on the development of society. Metaphysical materialism in the eighteenth century and dialectical idealism in the form of German philosophy had made important contributions to solving the problem, but each had been one-sided in its own particular way. These shortcomings had been eliminated in 'dialectical materialism', which was the synthesis of metaphysical materialism and dialectical idealism:

> Holbach and Helvétius were metaphysical materialists. They fought against metaphysical idealism. Their materialism gave way to dialectical idealism, which in its turn was overcome by dialectical materialism. (Plekhanov 1961: 741)

The structure of this argument was reminiscent of that of *Socialism and the Political Struggle*, where it was shown that Plekhanov's point of view was the synthesis of two one-sided positions. This structure would have emerged more clearly in *The Monist View* if Plekhanov had limited himself to the three chapters: 'French Materialism of the Eighteenth Century', 'Idealist German Philosophy' and 'Modern Materialism'. But in addition to these, Plekhanov included two further chapters: 'French historians of the Restoration' and 'Utopian Socialists', thus giving five headings in all, and so obscuring the underlying tripartite structure.

The key to this sacrifice of symmetry is probably to be explained by the terms of the polemic with Mikhailovsky. Plekhanov's reaction to Mikhailovsky's criticism of the Hegelian triad was to say that the triad had no independent significance; that even Hegel's arguments did not depend on it; that it was simply the 'totality of experience'. Since Plekhanov took this view, it would not have been appropriate to reply to Mikhailovsky in a book with a tripartite structure. But Mikhailovsky did not raise his objection to the triad until January 1894, by which time the systematic element in Plekhanov's book would already have been conceived. As a result, *The Monist View* explicitly denies the importance of the tripartite form, but implicitly upholds it.

Probably as a result of Mikhailovsky's remarks on the subject, the term '*narodnik*' appears rather infrequently in *The Monist View*, and when it does it is usually in the phrase '*narodniki* and subjectivists'. 'Subjectivism', in fact, is the feature that *The Monist View* adds to Plekhanov's characterization of '*narodnichestvo*'. No doubt with Mikhailovsky's condemnation of the Marxists' attitude to the famine in mind, '*narodniki*' are held to be people who are unable to look on the historical process in an objective and dispassionate way, but judge it subjectively. Plekhanov's argument is that the idea that Russia might have a non-capitalist future is a manifestation of 'subjectivism', a subjectivism which did not wish to countenance reality as it existed.

As far as Marx's letter to *Otechestvennye zapiski* was concerned, Plekhanov interpreted this as Engels had done in his pamphlet *On Social Relations in Russia*. To Marx's proposition that if Russia continued to pursue the path it had done since the emancipation of the peasantry it would become a capitalist country, and subject to the same laws of capitalism 'as other profane peoples', Plekhanov asserted that there were no grounds for supposing that Russia would leave the course of capitalist development it had embarked upon in 1861. Those who thought that such grounds existed Plekhanov classed as 'subjectivists'.

On the subject of Sieber there was a significant exchange between Plekhanov and Mikhailovsky. In the first edition of *The Monist View* Plekhanov denied any knowledge of Sieber's preoccupation with dialectical development. Mikhailovsky in reply cited the passage from Sieber's 1879 article on *Anti-Dühring* in *Slovo* which gives Engels's book credit for explaining 'the practical application and the method of dialectical contradictions' and concluding that: 'It would probably be right to say that this is the first time in the lifetime of so-called dialectics that it is presented to the reader in such a real light'(Ziber 1900b: 718). Mikhailovsky ended his quotation at that point, but to refute him, Plekhanov in an appendix to the second edition of *The Monist View*, continued the quotation from Sieber as follows:

> However, we for our part shall refrain from passing judgement as to the applicability of this method to the various branches of science, and also as to whether it constitutes – as far as any real meaning can be attached to it – a simple variation or even prototype of the methods of the theory of evolution or universal development. It is in this latter sense that its author regards it; or at least he strives to indicate a confirmation of it with the help of those truths achieved by the theory of evolution. And it must be admitted that in a certain respect quite a considerable resemblance is revealed. (Plekhanov 1961: 800–1)

Sieber had quite correctly observed that in *Anti-Dühring* Engels was trying to reconcile the philosophical dimension of Marx's system with developments in modern science. Plekhanov, for his part, was eager to show that, even having read and translated portions of Engels's book, Sieber remained unable to distinguish Hegelian dialectics from Darwin's theory of evolution.

The passage from Sieber that Plekhanov quoted was to have far-reaching consequences for how the history of Marx's ideas in Russia was presented. For the construction later historians placed on it was that since he did not understand dialectics, Sieber could not have appreciated the revolutionary content of Marx's ideas, and so should not be considered a 'Marxist'. This conception was first voiced by V. V. Vorovsky in 1908, and repeated by most writers who mentioned Sieber since (Vorovskii 1919: 15–16). The effect has been to obscure the significance of Sieber as a pioneer of Marxism in Russia and to leave Plekhanov unchallenged as 'the father of Russian Marxism'.

Time and Russia's economic development were on Plekhanov's side. Under the Ministers of Finance Vyshnegradsky and Witte, the Russian government pursued a policy of attracting foreign capital into the country. The influx of foreign firms substantially increased the number of industrial workers, especially in the capital cities, the Baltic provinces and in the south of Russia. By the end of the 1880s the workers' revolution that Plekhanov had predicted in *Socialism and the Political Struggle* no longer seemed unrealistic. Accordingly, at the International Workers' Socialist Congress held in Paris in July 1889 Plekhanov could confidently predict that 'the revolutionary movement in Russia will triumph only as a working class movement or it will not triumph at all' (Plekhanov 1961: 454).

5

Lenin

Russian revolutionaries paid a high price for the assassination of Alexander II in 1881. People's Will, the organization to which the assassins belonged was almost completely eradicated by the tsarist authorities. Consequently, the 1880s saw a relatively uneventful period in the history of the Russian revolutionary movement. The most significant event of the time was the attempted assassination of Alexander III on 3 March 1887 by a group of young students, calling itself the 'Terrorist Fraction of People's Will', which included Lenin's elder brother Alexander. Through the incaution of one of the conspirators, the police were able to forestall the event and arrest those they thought were most closely involved. Fifteen people were brought to trial, five of whom, including Alexander, were eventually sentenced to death.

Apart from the relatively small number of people brought to trial the authorities made mass arrests of those they suspected of having any connection with the assassination attempt. By the autumn of 1887 the number of such arrests reached over 100. About 50 were sent to Siberia without trial, and the remainder given lesser penalties such as prison sentences, expulsion from the university or placement under police surveillance.

Those revolutionaries who had escaped arrest became increasingly convinced of the futility of terrorist action. It was not worth the risk of so many arrests and wasted lives. Thenceforth attention turned increasingly to peaceful propaganda in workers' study circles, which was an activity that the Russian government was inclined to treat more leniently. The tactic of terrorism was renounced, not through any principled decision, but for practical considerations of survival (White 1998).

Polish students, some of whom had been connected with the attempted assassination of Alexander III, were the first organizers of workers' circles in St Petersburg, which began to be formed in 1887. The successor to these Polish students was the Russian Mikhail Brusnev, in whose flat the bomb-making materials for the projected assassination of Alexander III had been secreted. A characteristic feature of the Brusnev organization was the amount of initiative taken by the workers themselves, and the point of principle made of this by the members of the intelligentsia involved in the workers' circles. It was understood by both workers and intelligentsia in the organization that the 'emancipation of the working class was the affair of the working class itself', and that the intelligentsia had no special part to play. Their role was to educate the workers and teach them the skills necessary to organize themselves, but when this was done the workers would have no further need of the intelligentsia. Brusnev recalled that the aim of the organization was:

> to emancipate the workers' movement from the leadership of the intelligentsia, an unreliable and inconstant leadership, frequently at odds with the ideology of the working class. The idea that the emancipation of the working class was the affair of the working class itself, was introduced by us into all of the workers' circles and was completely assimilated by our workers, even by those who were not in positions of leadership. (Brusnev 1923: 21)

In this respect the Brusnev organization showed continuity with previous revolutionary groups from Land and Liberty to Emancipation of Labour, in that it adhered to the International's '*narodnik*' principle of workers' self-emancipation.

In 1893 Lenin made contact with the circle of students, mainly from the St Petersburg Technological Institute, who were the successors to the Brusnev group, and with which his brother Alexander had had connections. The chief organizer of the group was the accomplished conspirator Stepan Radchenko, and its main theoretician was his fellow student at the Institute, Herman Krasin. Its membership included three young women teachers at evening and Sunday schools for workers: Zinaida Nevzorova, Appolinaria Yakubova and Lenin's future wife Nadezhda Krupskaya (Krupskaya 1970: 19–29).

As one of its subjects for discussion the group chose to examine the market question. The topic had an important contemporary ideological significance because V. P. Vorontsov, and more recently Danielson in his book on the Russian economy, had highlighted the lack of internal and external markets as an obstacle to the development of capitalism in Russia. Lenin acted as discussant to a paper on the subject by Herman Krasin and impressed the group with a lengthy refutation of Krasin's ideas, illustrated by mathematical formulae taken from the second volume of Marx's *Das Kapital*. The version of the paper published many years later with its precise definitions and its esoteric terminology might lead one to suppose that Lenin had a consummate mastery of the subject. But the paper could not possibly do what it purported to do, that is to demonstrate on the basis of *Das Kapital* volume two that capitalism in Russia would develop through expanded reproduction. It was unlikely that Lenin would succeed in doing what Marx had failed to do for over a decade (Lenin 1960a: 75–125).

Encouraged by his friends in the study group, in the spring of 1894, Lenin began to write a critique of Mikhailovsky and other critics of Russian Marxism which was published under the title, *What the 'Friends of the People' Are and How They Fight against the Social Democrats*. The term 'friends of the people' is used instead of '*narodniki*' in the light of Mikhailovsky's recent articles. In the three-part essay (of which only two sections are extant), as in Plekhanov's writings, the tone is sarcastic and concerned with scoring discrete debating points. Individual statements are taken from the opponent's work and ridiculed. In this process the overall argument of the opponent is never revealed and tackled head-on. The work was also meant to have a positive side, to expound Marx's ideas. But although Lenin was able to demonstrate considerable erudition in this regard, the exposition of Marx's ideas was diffuse and piecemeal.

This, however, had a certain advantage: two mutually contradictory stages in Marx's thought could be defended within the confines of a single essay. Thus, in the opening pages of the work Lenin set out the ideas Marx had elaborated in the 1850s and early 1860s, when he had believed that capitalism must inevitably become a universal system. These ideas included the conception that society should be understood in terms of 'natural laws', of 'historical necessity' and 'determinism'. In this connection Lenin reproduced the famous passage from *A Contribution to the Critique of Political Economy* in which Marx referred to the economic base and the legal and political superstructure of society, and designated the Asiatic, classical, feudal and capitalist modes of production as successive epochs in the economic formation of society (Lenin 1960a: 139).

But some pages later, with Marx's letter of 1877 to *Otechestvennye zapiski* in mind, Lenin denied vehemently that any Marxist had ever considered Marx's theory as an obligatory philosophical scheme of history. None could, he asserted, because Marx himself had denied having such a scheme. Lenin added that if Mikhailovsky had heard anyone doing so, he should not regard them as proper Marxists (Lenin 1960a: 192). One may surmise that Lenin was not entirely comfortable with Marx's declaration in the letter to *Otechestvennye zapiski*. Although he referred to it on two occasions, on neither of them did he mention that Marx had conceded that a non-capitalist course of development for Russia was possible.

The difficulty for Lenin was that to all appearances Marx had espoused a doctrine of historical necessity and of successive economic formations. This would seem to imply that all countries, Russia included, would pass through the capitalist stage. Marx himself had declared in his preface to *Das Kapital* that, 'The country that is more developed industrially only shows, to the less developed, the image of its own future' (Marx 1976: 91). But it was impossible to say that Marx's theory determined a capitalist future for Russia, because it was with regard to Russia that Marx had gone out of his way specifically to deny that he had any such theory. A systematic examination of Marx's ideas would have pointed up this contradiction and regarded it as a question to be investigated; but for the requirements of the polemic, both sides of the contradiction were incorporated into the exposition of Marx's ideas regardless.

The contradiction might have been got round by some reference to the 'dialectics' of the historical process, as Plekhanov had done, but it seems that at this time Lenin was not greatly familiar with the theoretical side of Plekhanov's writings. There is no mention in *Friends of the People* of 'dialectical materialism'. In fact there Lenin states – quite correctly – that Marx and Engels never used the term 'economic materialism', but referred to their world outlook simply as 'materialism' (Lenin 1960a: 151).

Since it was impossible to claim, on the basis of Marx's theories, that the development of capitalism in Russia was inevitable, an argument of another order had to be deployed. This was that empirically capitalism *had* developed in Russia. Plekhanov had already argued in this way, and Lenin had determined to follow his example. It was a method that required the painstaking accumulation of statistical evidence, an activity which would culminate in the publication of his major work *The Development of Capitalism in Russia*.

Lenin's *Friends of the People* was circulated in a small hectographed edition, in this way avoiding the problems of getting it past the censor. But the same year saw the legal publication of Peter Struve's *Critical Remarks on Russia's Economic Development*, a book written from a Marxist viewpoint against *narodism*. Struve took a completely different approach to Lenin on the question of why capitalism would develop in Russia. Struve had no doubt that Marx did indeed have a 'whole historico-philosophical theory' which embraced 'all possible changes in social forms, both in the past and in the future'; it was 'a bold attempt to explain the whole historical process from a single principle'. He denied lacking sympathy for the sufferings of the people, but believed that in the long run capitalism would be beneficial. With an implicit reference to Tikhomirov, Struve concluded his book with the call: 'Let us admit our lack of culture and go to the school of capitalism' (Struve 1894: 288).

Lenin welcomed Struve's attack on *narodism*, but he was irritated by Struve's patronizing attitude to Marx and Engels and by what Lenin considered to be the superficiality of Struve's critique of *narodism*. Nevertheless, Lenin joined forces with Struve in publishing a collection of articles criticising *narodnik* views. His own contribution to the collection was more concerned with demonstrating the alleged errors of Struve than those of his ostensible opponents. The publication was seized by the police and burnt, only 100 copies being saved.

Lenin was arrested in 1896 for his activities in workers' circles, and following a term of imprisonment was sentenced to three years exile in Siberia. There, in the village of Shushenskoe, in company with his wife Krupskaya, he worked on his book *The Development of Capitalism in Russia* (Lenin 1960b).

On the grounds of making the subject more manageable, in the Preface, Lenin set out four limitations which determined the parameters for his study: (1) the question of the development of capitalism in Russia was treated from the standpoint of the home market, leaving aside the problem of the foreign market and data on foreign trade; (2) the study was restricted entirely to the post-Reform period; (3) almost exclusively the interior, purely Russian, provinces of Russia were covered; (4) only the economic aspect of the subject was investigated (Lenin 1960b: 25). These limitations, when stated in the Preface, no doubt sounded reasonable enough, to be explained by the caution of a writer anxious to keep his project within feasible bounds. But in fact they are used to justify an approach which skews the study in the direction Lenin desired.

The Development of Capitalism in Russia consists of three main sections. The first is a theoretical section in which Lenin attempts to show that Russia is a capitalist country in Marx's sense of the term. In particular, he argues that a home market has been created for Russian commodities. The second section deals with the differentiation of the peasantry, and is an attempt to demonstrate that the inequalities among peasant families are leading to the formation of a peasant bourgeoisie on the one hand and a peasant proletariat on the other. The third section is concerned with Russian industry, and surveys the three main types of industry to be found in the country at the end of the nineteenth century. These are handicraft industries, manufacture industries, in which workers are brought together within a single establishment, and modern machine industry, where division of labour has taken place and industry has become finally separated from agriculture. The conclusion is that Russia has become a capitalist country, though one which is relatively little advanced.

As the timescale is restricted to the post-Reform period, Lenin's presentation of the Russian economy has the character of a snapshot. There is very little indication in it of temporal sequence, of what has always been there and what is new. Thus, when Lenin presents his reader with statistical tables showing inequalities among peasant families, the implication is that this inequality is a new phenomenon. But there are no data to show this is the case; there are no corresponding tables demonstrating that at a certain point of time in the past there had been greater equality among peasant families. In any case it would have been surprising if such equality had existed because the periodic redivisions of land within peasant communes presupposed an inequality among families.

As regards Russian industry, one might easily believe that Lenin's depiction of handicraft, manufacture and machine industry was a historical progression of types. In fact, all of these forms of industry existed simultaneously when Lenin was writing, and Russian industry was still overwhelmingly small-scale handicraft industry. If one supplies the historical dimension to Lenin's description of Russian industry, by comparing it with, say, Tengoborski's *Commentaries on the Productive Forces of Russia* published in 1855

(Tengoborski 1855), it would appear that not a great deal had changed in the post-Reform era. The same categories of industrial undertaking, for example, can be found.

The inclusion of a historical perspective would have raised an insoluble question for Lenin. It is that, since many of the phenomena he classifies as capitalist can be found in pre-Reform Russia, for example the production of goods for sale, it requires Lenin to determine at which point these phenomena acquired a capitalist character. In the case of the production of articles for sale, it requires Lenin to say when and why these goods took on the character of commodities. This was a conundrum Marx had avoided by restricting his investigation to societies in which the capitalist mode of production prevailed. This, however, was not a solution that Lenin could adopt.

Lenin's approach to the question is legalistic. It was sufficient for his purposes to show that the economic categories which Marx had used in his analysis of the capitalist system could be applied to Russia. Thus, all economic phenomena are interpreted as manifestations of capitalism; in particular all goods produced for sale are regarded as commodities. What is missing is some criterion for judging whether goods are or are not commodities. It is missing for good reason. The criterion of commodity production would be the context in which it occurred. Goods produced for sale would be commodities if production for the market were generalized, if commodity production were the system which prevailed. But at the time Lenin was writing not even he would have maintained that capitalism was the predominant economic system in Russia.

Lenin also focused his study on the question of the home market for polemical purposes, believing that on this question his opponents were particularly vulnerable. But the focus on exclusively internal economic developments had a bizarre consequence. It was that the question of foreign investment in Russia was left out of the reckoning almost entirely. In the whole lengthy work only two sentences refer to foreign capital. *The Development of Capitalism in Russia*, moreover, was written and published while Sergei Witte was Minister of Finance and when foreign investment was being encouraged by government policy. For Lenin to have discussed the question of foreign investment and the tariff policy which encouraged it at any length, would have meant conceding his opponents' case that the development of capitalism in Russia was artificially stimulated. Vorontsov, in *The Fate of Capitalism in Russia*, for example, had given the question of foreign investment in Russia considerable prominence. By avoiding mention of foreign investment, however, Lenin ignored one of the main sources of capitalist development in Russia at the time and underestimated the amount of modern machine industry in existence because that machine industry originated outside the country.

The most significant of all the limitations that Lenin mentioned in his Preface was the intention to deal 'exclusively with the economic aspect of the process'. This looked innocuous enough because Lenin did not spell out what it was that he was excluding by this particular restriction. By classifying the commune as a social or ethnographic phenomenon, it could be left out of all consideration of the treatment of the peasantry. This means that the commune, its dynamics, or how communal life influenced the economic situation of the peasantry in the post-Reform era are not discussed. From reading Lenin's book one would never guess that most Russian peasants continued to live in village communities.

Lenin's manoeuvre begs the question of capitalist relations in Russia, for it is tantamount to a refusal to recognize the existence of social institutions in which cooperation, mutual aid and the pooling of resources take place. With a stroke of a pen, Lenin, for purposes of his book, has abolished the peasant communes and has put atomized civil society in their place. The implication is that the structure of Russian society corresponds exactly to the statistical tables of land-ownership, horse-ownership and agricultural implement ownership which give such a scientific appearance to Lenin's argument. But the presupposition of these tables is that every proprietor of a horse, a plough, a morsel of food cleaves to his or her piece of property and resolutely refuses to share it with any living soul. One is required to believe that no borrowing or lending, no cooperation or pooling of resources takes place. But it was precisely mutual aid that was the characteristic feature of peasant life in the agrarian communities.

Lenin's notes for *The Development of Capitalism in Russia* show that he was unwilling to countenance the possibility that life in village communities might be any less egotistical than elsewhere. One of the authors Lenin consulted, S. Kapustin, had pointed out that commune members ploughed or harvested the land of those who were unable to do so themselves, provided horses for those who had none of their own, paid taxes for those who had become impoverished, took care of orphans and so on. In contrasting urban and rural society Kapustin remarked, '... among us nobody considers it his duty, for example, to feed the hungry and shelter the homeless'. Lenin in a marginal note enquired: 'And is it any different in the peasant commune? Where are the facts?' (Lenin 1970: 55). The facts were in almost every work written on the peasant commune from Haxthausen's onwards, none of which were cited in Lenin's book.

The Development of Capitalism in Russia has been called the fullest, best-documented and best-argued examination of the crucial period of the evolution of capitalism out of feudalism in the literature of Marxism (Harding 1981: 107). In relative terms this might well be the case, since there are rather few works of that particular genre. But in absolute terms it is a highly misleading work. It is a very poor guide to the social and economic situation in Russia at the time. It also gives a false idea of what Danielson and Vorontsov were arguing, and from what standpoint. It does not address squarely the problems they raised.

It is interesting to note that when Marx had examined the question of how capitalism developed in Russia in the 1870s, he had approached it in quite a different way. For Marx the question of how capitalism originated was identical to the question of how capital began to circulate. This involved establishing the links in the chain which made the circuits of capital possible. He found that these included the taxation policy of the government, the railways and the banks. Ironically, this approach, adopted by Marx, Danielson and Vorontsov, was the one condemned by Lenin as '*narodnik*'.

An essential element in the development of capitalism for Marx was the dissolution of traditional social bonds and their replacement by civil society, the fragmented aggregate of atomized individuals, and the subsequent grouping of these individuals into antagonistic classes. This dimension is absent from Lenin's thinking entirely. There is no investigation of whether, and in what ways, economic development in the post-Reform era has eroded the social cohesion that characterized peasant village life. Lenin never recognized that such social cohesion existed. For Lenin, the characteristic of capitalism is not the growth of individualism but the stratification of peasant society. The bulk of *The Development of Capitalism in Russia* consists of commentaries on tables of statistics showing the distribution of land, livestock and other resources between peasant families in various parts of the country. These purport to show the emergence, on the one hand, of a relatively wealthy group of peasants destined to form an agrarian bourgeoisie and, on the other, of a stratum of poor peasants, well on the way to becoming rural proletarians. Marx had noted the emergence of differences in economic status among the Russian peasantry, described, for example, in Flerovsky's book, but he had viewed this in the context of ways in which capital circulated in the country.

What Is To Be Done?

Lenin's chief theoretical work at the beginning of the twentieth century was *What Is To Be Done?* This work has attracted a great deal of commentary and is the one for which Lenin is most renowned. From the perspective of the history of Marxist thought in Russia, *What Is To Be Done?* is a major landmark. It brings to an end the principle upheld by all post-Reform revolutionary organizations that 'the emancipation of the working class must be the affair of the working class itself'. Lenin does not mention this principle in *What Is To Be Done?*, and after its publication it disappears from revolutionary discourse.

The removal of this founding principle of the First International is an important measure because it makes possible a political organization in which the radical intelligentsia do not play a subservient role to the workers. It allows them a leading role in the labour movement, and in *What Is To Be Done?* implies that this role is the essential one of bringing socialist theory to the workers, whose consciousness can rise no higher than the economic struggle.

It is obvious that the Marxist principle of workers' self-emancipation is incompatible with Lenin's arguments in *What Is To Be Done?* Lenin does not confront this problem. He does not try to demonstrate that the principle is wrong, or that it no longer applies. This would be extremely difficult, if not impossible, to do, because the danger of an intellectuals' domination over the workers was ever-present. It would also involve openly challenging the authority of Marx and Engels, something that Lenin would never do. Lenin's method was to avoid mentioning the principle, and instead to conduct a surrogate campaign against 'Economism', a term invented by Lenin.

An indication that the term 'Economists' meant people who held that 'the emancipation of the working class is the affair of the working class itself' comes from L. Martov's memoirs. There he conducts a tirade against the St Petersburg 'Economist' N. N. Lokhov, who interprets the slogan 'the emancipation of the working class is the affair of the working class itself' to mean that any proposal to form a workers' party is an un-social-democratic attempt by the intelligentsia to subordinate the working class to itself (Martov 2004: 292–3). It was the campaign against this kind of 'Economism' that gave legitimacy to the formation of the Russian Social-Democratic Labour Party (RSDLP).

Though it claims to have been written in some haste, *What Is To Be Done?* has a sophisticated structure that must have required careful planning on the part of its author. Of its five chapters, the first three are devoted to the polemic against Economism. Ostensibly, the fourth continues this polemic at a deeper level, being concerned with combating 'amateurism' (*kustarnichestvo*) in party organization, the contention being that Economism was but one manifestation of 'amateurism'. But in reality the chapter on 'amateurism' has no necessary connection with what has gone before, and could constitute a separate work. It is in this chapter that Lenin elaborates his ideas on how a revolutionary party should be constructed. The final chapter discusses the role of a newspaper in the party's organizational structure. *What Is To Be Done?* can be thought of as having two main sections, one against Economism and one against Amateurism.

On the face of it, the first chapter, 'Dogmatism and "Freedom of Criticism"', seems to approach the Economist issue in an indirect way by discussing the question of freedom of criticism. But in the context of the entire work, the first chapter is one which subtly foreshadows the conception of the party in chapter four, and in this way helps tie the two sections together. In Lenin's view, a social-democratic party cannot countenance the freedom of its members to indulge in questioning the principles on which it is based. That in practice meant 'the freedom to convert social-democracy into a democratic party of reform, the freedom to introduce bourgeois ideas and bourgeois elements into socialism'. The example of Bernstein's revisionism in the German Social-Democratic Party was held up as the kind of undesirable result of adhering to the principle of 'freedom of criticism'. People joined the party on a purely voluntary basis, and if they disagreed with its basic principles, there was nothing to prevent their leaving it and going elsewhere.

By developing the case against 'freedom of criticism' Lenin was able to equate Economism with Revisionism, using references to Bernstein to discredit his opponents. He also used the occasion to suggest that the party organization of the social democrats could not be democratic, and that the ideological foundations on which the party was based were all-important. Lenin then went on to stress the importance of theory for the party, laying down the maxim that 'Without revolutionary theory there can be no revolutionary movement' (Lenin 1973b: 369).

The second chapter of Lenin's pamphlet, 'The Spontaneity of the Masses and the Consciousness of the Social-Democrats', contains an account of the workers' movement in St Petersburg remarkable for the effrontery of its distorted presentation. The undisputed facts of the matter were that after the arrest of Lenin and his associates in December 1896, the Union of Struggle had continued to produce agitational leaflets for the workers; that the strike movement had reached unprecedented heights; and that the textile workers had shown extraordinary initiative and independence in the conduct of the strikes. Lenin, however, discounted these strikes as being 'simply trade-union struggles, but not yet social-democratic struggles' (Lenin 1973b: 375). The arrest of Lenin and his associates and their replacement by other veterans of Radchenko's group such as Yakubova as well as new recruits was depicted by Lenin as the substitution of orthodox social democrats by a young generation of 'Economists'. As Lenin put it: 'The overwhelming of consciousness by spontaneity ... occurred because an increasing number of "veteran" revolutionaries were "torn away" by the gendarmes and because increasing numbers of "youngsters" appeared on the scene'. These 'youngsters' then began to collaborate on *Rabochaia Mysl'* (Workers' Thought), which set about unconsciously carrying out the programme of the Economists (Lenin 1973b: 382).

This stylized version of events was contested by Yakubova and Takhtarev soon after the appearance of *What Is To Be Done?* (Takhtarev 1902: 68–70). The function of this version, as well as belittling the significance of the St Petersburg strikes and the activities of the Union of Struggle after 1895, was to create the impression that the opposition of the 'youngsters' to Plekhanov in Geneva and to Lenin in St Petersburg formed part of the same phenomenon – the emergence of Revisionism in Russian Social-Democracy (Frankel 1963).

The error of the Economists, Lenin contended, was that they bowed to the spontaneity of the workers' movement; they followed rather than led the workers. But the workers themselves could never attain a social-democratic consciousness; they could only develop a trade-union consciousness and struggle to improve their own economic situation. A socialist consciousness, on the other hand, could only be introduced into the workers' movement from outside, by the intellectuals (Lenin 1973b: 375). This, Lenin asserted, had been shown by the history of all countries. It followed that by bowing to spontaneity the Economists condemned the workers' movement to go no further than trade-union activities; the political assault on the autocracy could never be launched. Left to itself the working-class movement would become subordinated to bourgeois ideology.

Although the idea that a socialist consciousness had to be brought to the workers from outside originated with Paul Akselrod, the source Lenin cited for it was Karl Kautsky's article on the programme of the Austrian Social Democrats (Donald 1993: 30). This has given rise to the notion that Lenin derived his conception from Kautsky. The resemblance is, however, superficial. Kautsky did not believe that the workers' class consciousness was to be equated with their material interests. He stressed that class consciousness was the consciousness of solidarity of all proletarians, the consciousness of the individual's obligations with regard to the class as a whole. Kautsky saw the class struggle and class consciousness as ethical entities, and, as the proletariat could only achieve its own emancipation by eliminating all oppression and exploitation, it would protect all oppressed groups, providing the interests of these groups did not collide with social development. In this respect the proletariat accomplished tasks which went beyond its immediate class interests. The function of the social democrats was to furnish the workers' movement with an awareness of its general aim and, arising from this, to unite the workers in a single political party. But if socialism was not to remain utterly naive, and consequently politically impotent, it had to understand social relations. Scholarship, however, was still the preserve of the possessing classes, and consequently the proletariat was not capable of elaborating a viable socialism by itself; this would have to be done by people from the bourgeoisie who sided with the proletariat (Waldenberg 1972: 39).

In saying that socialist consciousness was something introduced into the proletarian class struggle from outside, Kautsky was doing no more than stating the historical fact that the individuals who had been socialist thinkers had come from the bourgeois intelligentsia. Socialist doctrines, consequently, required to be communicated to the workers, and this function, Kautsky believed, ought to be performed by the social democrats. But of course once the socialist consciousness had been communicated to the workers, the workers would then be in possession of that consciousness. Not so with Lenin; in his view, the socialist consciousness always remained outside the working class because the workers could never see beyond their narrow material class interests. Whereas Kautsky was stating a historical fact, Lenin was formulating a sociological law.

Much of Lars Lih's extensive commentary on *What Is To Be Done?* is devoted to refuting the idea of the historian Abraham Ascher that Lenin was 'worried about the workers' (Lih 2005: 13). If Lenin was worried about anything in *What Is To Be Done?*, it was about the intelligentsia because, in the opinion of Marx and Engels, they were superfluous to the emancipation of the workers.

The third chapter, 'Trade-Unionist Politics and Social Democratic Politics', concentrated on showing that the activities of the Russian Social Democrats to date, such as their publication of leaflets exposing the injustices and hazards of factory life, were only trade-union activities. The true function of social democrats, Lenin stressed, was not to represent the working class in relation to a given group of employers, but in relation to all classes in society and to the State. In Lenin's view the role of social democrats was to raise the level of working-class consciousness so that the workers were trained to respond to all instances of oppression, tyranny and injustice no matter what class in society was affected (Lenin 1973b: 412). It is interesting to note that this level of working-class consciousness, which for Lenin was only possible through the intervention of the intelligentsia, was for Kautsky something inherent in the class consciousness of the proletariat.

The premise of the fourth chapter, 'The Amateurishness of the Economists and the Organization of the Revolutionaries', is that if one is going to engage in revolution, one should not go about it in a haphazard way, but should do it properly, with all the necessary preparation and training. What was needed, Lenin believed, was a tightly-knit, conspiratorial, organization of professional revolutionaries capable of maintaining the energy, stability and continuity of the political struggle. Because these people were distinguished by their conspiratorial and organizational skills, it did not matter whether they belonged to the intelligentsia or the working class. Such distinctions, according to Lenin, were irrelevant in this connection (Lenin 1973b: 464).

The clandestine organization of professional revolutionaries Lenin advocated had little in common with a broad, open and democratic workers' organization. This he readily admitted, but argued that both types of organization had their place in the workers' movement. In Lenin's view, the existence of a party of experienced revolutionaries would greatly help the broader workers' organizations by centralizing those of their activities, such as the production of leaflets, which required an element of conspiracy. Lenin made no pretence that his revolutionary organization would be democratic. He believed that in this context democracy would be useless and harmful. It would only facilitate the work of the police in carrying out large-scale arrests, and serve to perpetuate amateurism within the revolutionary movement (Lenin 1973b: 479).

The fifth chapter of *What Is To Be Done?* on the plan for an all-Russian newspaper has attracted comparatively little attention, but in the light of subsequent events is one of the most important. In it Lenin argues that to give unity to the revolutionary party it is necessary to have a newspaper that would coordinate the activities of the scattered local committees. The newspaper would be a means of organizing the party, of ensuring its continuity in times when the revolutionary tide ebbed and preparing it for a nationwide armed insurrection. It was as the editor of such a newspaper that Lenin saw his role in the party, and it was one that he performed for most of his political career, and one which ensured that his opinions would be extremely influential. In fact at this time Lenin already edited such a newspaper, *Iskra* (The Spark), which, in preparation for the Second Congress of the Russian Social-Democratic Labour Party, was conducting an energetic campaign against Economism.

Lenin had intended that at the Second Congress in 1903 he could arrange it so that the party would be governed not only by a Central Committee but also by the Central Organ, at that time the newspaper *Iskra*. A Party Council would mediate between these two bodies. As one of the three proposed editors of *Iskra* (the other two being Martov and Plekhanov) Lenin would have a dominant position in the party. The Congress duly adopted this rather complex organizational structure, but otherwise things did not go according to Lenin's plan. Three of the existing six editors objected to being ousted by Lenin, and Martov refused to serve on the reconstituted editorial board. Lenin himself was forced to resign as an editor, so that in the aftermath of the Second Congress Lenin was left isolated politically and without a newspaper he could control. (Trotsky 1980: 23–30)

Lenin's political career might have ended at that point had it not been for the appearance in Geneva of Alexander Bogdanov, who had recently returned from exile in Vologda. Bogdanov was already the author of a textbook on Marx's political economy and two philosophical works. Through his friendship with Maxim Gorky, Bogdanov had access to enough finance to support a newspaper, and his connections with such people as Vladimir Bazarov, Anatolii Lunacharsky and I. I. Skvortsov-Stepanov would provide the kind of contributors the newspaper needed. By the end of 1904 the newspaper *Vpered* (Forward) was launched with Lenin as its editor (Valentinov 1968: 231–5).

Lenin's alliance with Bogdanov, however, was too fragile to last; too many serious differences divided the two men. Bogdanov did not subscribe to the idea in *What Is To Be Done?* that the socialist consciousness had to be brought to the workers from outside; he continued to believe that the intelligentsia had only a subsidiary role in the labour movement. There was also disagreement on what the relationship should be between the Social-Democrat deputies in the State Duma and the party to which they belonged. Bogdanov thought that the deputies should be answerable to the party, and in cases where they did not follow party policy, they should be given an ultimatum, and, in the last instance, be recalled. Lenin, on the other hand, did not believe that Duma deputies should be recalled, even though they flouted policies democratically agreed upon by the party. There was also conflict over money matters. Bogdanov was one of the small circle of people who controlled the finances of the Bolshevik fraction, so that Lenin was not able to dispense funds as he thought fit. The most serious disagreement between Bogdanov and Lenin was on philosophy. Lenin was a follower of Plekhanov, whose conception of 'dialectical materialism' he considered to be Marxist orthodoxy, and consequently thought of Bogdanov's ideas as heretical. Bogdanov, on the other hand, considered Plekhanov a charlatan in philosophy and intellectually dishonest as a person.

There had been tension between Bogdanov and Plekhanov since 1899 when Bogdanov's first philosophical work had been published. Bogdanov's strictures on Hegelian dialectics Plekhanov had denounced as a betrayal of materialism. Although repeatedly challenged to do so by Bogdanov, Plekhanov had never provided any systematic refutation of Bogdanov's arguments, but simply made disparaging remarks about Bogdanov's abilities. The nearest Plekhanov ever came to refuting Bogdanov's ideas was in a series of three letters entitled *Materialismus Militans* published in 1908, which denied that Bogdanov belonged to the camp of materialists, on the grounds that he had been influenced by Ernst Mach, who in turn had been influenced by Bishop Berkeley. And since Berkeley was a philosophical idealist, it followed that Bogdanov too was an idealist.

In a pamphlet entitled *Adventures of One Philosophical School* and in a collection of essays entitled *Studies in the Philosophy of Marxism*, both published in 1908, Bogdanov mounted an attack on Plekhanov's philosophical writings. He pointed out that as a 'materialist' Plekhanov was unable to define what 'matter' was. He could only say that it was something that acted on our sensations. To the question, What was it that acted upon our sensations?, Plekhanov's answer was:

> To that I reply, together with Kant: things-in-themselves. Consequently, matter is nothing but the totality of things-in-themselves, in so far as the latter are the sources of our sensations. (Bogdanov 1908: 7–8)

Not only was this a vague and elusive concept of 'matter', but in identifying himself with Kant's philosophy Plekhanov had also made a gaffe that Bogdanov was to return to repeatedly. Moreover, in order to justify his Kantian theory of knowledge, Plekhanov had deliberately mistranslated one of Marx's 'Theses on Feuerbach', a ploy which Bogdanov exposed with textual evidence. In Lenin's judgement Plekhanov had been singularly ineffective in his polemic with Bogdanov. Consequently, he took it upon himself to come to Plekhanov's aid with the publication of the book *Materialism and Empiriocriticism* (Lenin 1962).

Materialism and Empiriocriticism

It is Lenin's silence on Bogdanov's critique of Plekhanov that makes *Materialism and Empiriocriticism* such an enigmatic work. However, placed in context, it is clear that Lenin's real concern is to defend Plekhanov against the attacks of Bogdanov and his associates in *Studies in the Philosophy of Marxism* (1908). In particular, he wants somehow to rescue Plekhanov from the gaffe of having stated that he agreed with Kant on the question of 'things-in-themselves'. Lenin, however, never states this aim explicitly, and never in the course of the entire work does he quote what Plekhanov actually said. The implication is that to have done so would have been detrimental to the case Lenin wished to make. Instead, he refers, when necessary, to Plekhanov's statement obliquely, as when he says, for example:

> Our Machists have written so much about the 'thing-in-itself' that if all their writings were to be collected it would result in mountains of printed matter. The 'thing-in-itself' is a veritable *bête noire* for Bogdanov and Valentinov, Bazarov and Chernov, Berman and Yushkevich. There is no abuse they have not hurled at it, there is no ridicule they have not showered on it ... All the would-be Marxists among the Machists are combatting Plekhanov's 'thing-in-itself'; they accuse Plekhanov of having become entangled and straying into Kantianism, and of having forsaken Engels. (Lenin 1962: 98)

The implication is that the preoccupation with the 'thing-in-itself' is an irrational obsession on the part of Plekhanov's opponents, rather than a devastating piece of evidence against him.

Lenin had to deploy a good deal of ingenuity to counter these attacks on Plekhanov. Accordingly, he resorted to two types of argument. The first of these was that Bogdanov, Bazarov and the others had only seized upon Plekhanov as a tactic; that what they wanted to attack, but were afraid to do so, was Engels and his materialist standpoint. Thus, according to Lenin:

> Machist would-be Marxists have diplomatically set Engels aside, have completely ignored Feuerbach and are circling exclusively around Plekhanov. It is indeed circling around one spot, tedious and petty pecking and cavilling at a disciple of Engels, while a frank examination of the views of the teacher himself is cravenly avoided. (Lenin 1962: 99)

The other argument Lenin deployed was more convoluted, and was, in its way, a kind of justification for Plekhanov's espousal of Kant's 'thing-in-itself'. According to Lenin, the principal feature of Kant's philosophy was the reconciliation of materialism with idealism, a compromise between the two opposing currents. Thus, when Kant assumed that something outside us, a 'thing-in-itself', corresponded to our ideas, he was a materialist; when he declared this 'thing-in-itself' to be unknowable, he was an idealist. It was Lenin's contention that the 'Machists' criticized Kant for being too much of a materialist, while Marxists like Plekhanov criticized him for not being materialist enough. The 'Machists' criticized Kant from the right, the materialists from the left. In this way Lenin could argue that there was a materialist 'thing-in-itself' that Plekhanov was quite right to uphold, a reality that existed independently of our senses, something that Lenin accused the 'Machists' of denying.

Like Plekhanov's '*Materialismus Militans*' Lenin's *Materialism and Empiriocriticism* did not undertake a systematic examination or refutation of Bogdanov's ideas or those of the other contributors to *Studies in the Philosophy of Marxism*, whom he insisted in referring to indiscriminately as 'Machists'. Lenin's strategy was not to refute the ideas of his opponents, but to discredit them by attaching to them the label 'idealist'. Here, Lenin took up Plekhanov's ploy of claiming that the ideas of Bogdanov and other contributors to the collection were simply variants of Bishop Berkeley's philosophy, and that they were inconsistent with the propositions Engels had enunciated in *Ludwig Feuerbach* and *Anti-Dühring*. For this purpose it was enough for Lenin to reproduce those fragments of the writings of his opponents that he could claim were evidence of idealism or that he could in some way hold up to ridicule.

In response to Bogdanov's accusation that Plekhanov had deliberately mis-translated Marx's thesis on Feuerbach so that it would conform with his own conception of 'hieroglyphics' and 'things-in-themselves', Lenin asserted, rather lamely, that the passage in question was not a translation, but a 'free paraphrase' (Lenin 1962: 105). Nevertheless, he made clear that he did not agree with Plekhanov's conception of 'hieroglyphics', since it was not endorsed by Engels, who had spoken neither of symbols nor of hieroglyphs, but of 'copies', 'photographs', 'images' and 'mirror-reflections' of things (Lenin 1962: 232). Suspecting that Bogdanov might dismiss the procedure of using Engels's utterances as a criterion of truth to be 'authoritarian thinking', Lenin cautioned:

> And do not complain, Machist gentlemen, that I refer to 'authorities'; your outcry against the authorities is simply a screen for the fact that for the socialist authorities (Marx, Engels, Lafargue, Mehring, Kautsky) you are substituting bourgeois authorities (Mach, Petzoldt, Avenarius and the immanentists). You would do better not to raise the question of 'authorities' and 'authoritarianism'! (Lenin 1962: 232)

Bogdanov's reply to *Materialism and Empiriocriticism* was the book *The Fall of the Great Fetish* published in 1910. Much of Bogdanov's book was devoted to correcting the misapprehensions and distortions contained in *Materialism and Empiriocriticism* concerning the philosophical ideas of the contributors to *Studies in the Philosophy of Marxism*. As Lenin had anticipated, Bogdanov maintained that Lenin's attitude to Marx and Engels showed his authoritarian mode of thinking. In Bogdanov's view, Lenin regarded Marx and Engels as prophets of absolute truth, whose pronouncements were not subject to doubt or question. What Lenin's book demanded was that one should *believe* in Marx and Engels, an attitude that Bogdanov considered as more appropriate to religious than to socialist thinking (Bogdanov 1910b: 160).

Lenin did not reply to *The Fall of the Great Fetish*, and may have been discouraged from doing so by the poor reception *Materialism and Empiriocriticism* was given. According to N. V. Valentinov, 'it caused neither uproar nor debate, in fact, it did not arouse much interest at all' (Valentinov 1968: 250). For his part, following his brush with Lenin, Bogdanov turned his attention to recasting his philosophical ideas in the form of a major work on the 'universal science of organization', or *Tectology*. So that, although Lenin might have expected it, no new work by the 'Machists' appeared that required his denunciation.

The Marx and Engels correspondence

In 1913 the Dietz publishing house issued a four-volume collection of the correspondence between Marx and Engels entitled *Der Briefwechsel zwischen Friedrich Engels und Karl Marx 1844 bis 1883* (hereafter *Briefwechsel*). The collection was edited by Engels's literary executors, the German Social Democrats August Bebel and Eduard Bernstein. In a letter written on 13 or 14 November 1913 to his sister Mariia, Lenin remarked: 'I have just finished reading the four volumes of Marx's correspondence with Engels. I want to write about it in *Prosveshchenie* (Enlightenment). There is much of interest' (Lenin 1967: 504). Lenin did in fact begin a review article on the Marx–Engels correspondence for the journal *Prosveshchenie* at that time, though he did not complete it. The unfinished review article is interesting because it is where Lenin gave his overall assessment of the Marx–Engels correspondence, and indicated which of its aspects he found most significant.

In Lenin's opinion, what was central to the whole correspondence was the concept of 'dialectics'. He believed that what interested Marx and Engels most of all was 'the application of materialist dialectics to the re-shaping of political economy, to the study of history, natural science, philosophy, and to the policy and tactics of the working class. This was the original contribution they had made to the history of revolutionary thought'(Lenin 1963: 554).

On acquiring the Marx and Engels correspondence, Lenin got down to reading and annotating the volumes, copying extracts from the letters into a notebook. In 1959 the Institute of Marxism-Leninism published Lenin's annotations and notes on the correspondence under the title, *V. I. Lenin. Konspekt 'Perepiski K. Marksa i F. Engel'sa 1844–1883 gg'* (hereafter *Konspekt*). In 1968, a second edition of the work was issued as a supplementary volume to Lenin's *Complete Works* (Lenin 1968: xxiii). Despite this high status accorded to the publication it was not utilized as a source by Lenin's biographers, though it has an important bearing on the interpretation of Lenin as a philosopher and political thinker. There is a

strong element of continuity between the *Konspekt* and the more famous
'Philosophical Notebooks'. What links the two is that where Marx or Engels
expresses an opinion on an author in their correspondence, their judgement
is noted by Lenin in his *Konspekt*. When the opportunity arises, Lenin reads
the author mentioned in the correspondence, makes notes from the work
in question, and reproduces in these notes the opinions he has found in the
Briefwechsel.

Thus, Lenin noted Marx's admiration for Leibnitz and Engels's high
opinion of Clausewitz in his letter of 7 January 1858, where he remarked:

I am reading, *inter alia*, Clausewitz's *Vom Kriege*. An odd way of
philosophising, but *per se* very good. On the question as to whether
one should speak of the art or the science of war, he says that, more
than anything else, war resembles commerce. Combat is to war what
cash payment is to commerce; however seldom it need happen in reality,
everything is directed towards it and ultimately it is bound to occur and
proves decisive.

Lenin annotated this passage as, 'War=commerce=cash payment' (Lenin
1968: 35–6).

In his letter of 1 February 1858 Marx gave a lengthy critical analysis
of Ferdinand Lasalle's book on Heraclitus the Dark, commencing with the
following observation:

Heraclitus, The Dark Philosopher by Lassalle the Luminous One is, *au
fond* a very silly concoction. Every time Heraclitus uses an image to
demonstrate the unity of affirmation and negation – and this is often – in
steps Lassalle and makes the most of the occasion by treating us to some
passage from Hegel's *Logic* which is hardly improved in the process;
always at great length too, like a schoolboy who must show in his essay
that he has thoroughly understood his 'essence' and 'appearance' as well
as the 'dialectical process'.

On this Lenin's annotation was: 'Lassalle' Heraclitus – a schoolboy affair.
No critique of the concept of dialectics' (Lenin 1968: 35–6).

One feature of Lenin's notes is that he carefully records what either Marx
or Engels says on the subject of dialectics. A key passage in this respect was
contained in the letter of 14 January 1858, where Marx stated:

Incidentally, things are developing quite nicely for me. E.g. I have
completely demolished the theory of profit as hitherto propounded. What
was of great use to me as regards method of treatment was Hegel's *Logic*
which I had leafed through once again by mere accident, Freiligrath having
found and made me a present of several volumes of Hegel, originally the
property of Bakunin. If ever the time comes when such work is again

possible, I should very much like to write 2 or 3 printer's sheets making accessible to the common reader the rational aspect of the method which Hegel discovered but at the same time mystified. (Lenin 1968: 35)

Here Lenin noted: 'The rational in Hegel's Logic, in his method. Marx in 1858: once again leafed through Hegel's Logic and would have liked in 2–3 printer's sheets to have expounded what was rational in it. Minus his, Hegel's, "mystification"' (Lenin 1968: 35). From this letter Lenin would know for certain that Marx had made use of Hegelian philosophy in *Das Kapital*.

There was one passage in a letter from Marx dated 25 March 1868 concerning dialectics that Lenin obviously thought important, because he not only annotated it but also copied it into his notebook. It was:

But what would Hegel say if in the next world he was to learn that the Universal [*Allgemeine*] in Old German and Old Norse means nothing but the common land, and the Particular [*Sundre, Besondere*] nothing but the separate property divided off from the common land? So the logical categories are coming damn well out of 'our intercourse' after all.

Lenin interpreted this as meaning: 'Hegel did not see how the abstract concepts arise out of our circulation (intercourse)'. And he added: 'Hegel and his shortcomings' (Lenin 1968: 65, 435–6).

The irony here is that Lenin was eager to find in their correspondence any indication of how Marx and Engels understood dialectics. In this passage the manner in which Marx used Hegel's dialectics was staring him in the face. But Lenin could not recognize it because his idea of what constituted dialectics had been conditioned by the writings of Engels and Plekhanov.

In the second half of 1914 Lenin drew heavily on the Marx–Engels correspondence to write the article on Marx for the Granat encyclopedia. In the section of the article dealing with the tactics of the proletarian class struggle Lenin made explicit reference to the *Briefwechsel*. He said, 'An immense amount of material on this is contained in all the works of Marx, particularly in the four volumes of his correspondence with Engels, published in 1913' (Lenin 1964a: 74–5).

The 'Philosophical Notebooks'

When he moved from Poronin to Berne in August/September of 1914 Lenin made use of the library there to read the books that had been mentioned by Marx and Engels in their letters. The notes on these books went to constitute the 'Philosophical Notebooks'. Comparing Lenin's notes on the *Briefwechsel* with the original version of 'Philosophical Notebooks' that was published in *Leninskii sbornik* in 1929 and 1930, one can see a close correspondence between them. The books mentioned in the *Konspekt* are the chief ones summarized in the 'Philosophical Notebooks': those of Leibnitz, Clausewitz, Lassalle and Hegel.

In the case of Clausewitz, Lenin noted that he employed a 'dialectical method', and among the passages copied out from Clausewitz's *Vom Kriege* was the one Engels had mentioned comparing war to commerce (Lenin 1930: 392, 402). Having summarized Lassalle's book on Heraclitus, Lenin observed, 'One can understand why Marx called this work of Lassalle's "school-boyish" (see letter to Engels ...)', a letter which was included in the notes taken from the *Briefwechsel*.

On reading Lenin's notes on Hegel's *Logic*, it is clear that his two teachers in this sphere are Engels and Plekhanov. Lenin says, for example, that he is trying to read Hegel 'materialistically', and refers to Engels's *Ludwig Feuerbach* where the author states that 'Hegel is materialism that has been stood on its head' (Lenin 1961: 104). He copied out at length the section in *Logic* where Hegel speaks of the transition from Quantity to Quality in which Plekhanov had seen the essence of dialectics, and noted in the margin 'Leaps!, leaps!, leaps!' (Lenin 1961: 123).

Throughout his notes on Hegel's *Logic* Lenin reflects on the bearing his reading has on his campaign against the 'Machists', and from this one may deduce that this was the purpose Lenin had in mind in his Hegelian studies. In fact, he criticizes Plekhanov for not deploying Hegel against the Machists as well as the Kantians and agnostics in general (Lenin 1961: 179). The implication was that in a future debate with Bogdanov and his associates Lenin would argue from a point of view influenced by Hegel.

As one might expect from the exchanges which had preceded Lenin's philosophical studies in 1914, much of Lenin's attention in reading Hegel was devoted to the question of knowledge, and in particular to the subject of Kant's 'things-in-themselves'. Hegel's *Logic* was extremely instructive in this respect because it incorporated a thoroughgoing refutation of Kant's argument in *Critique of Pure Reason*. Hegel used the deduction of the philosophical categories to show that the movement of the Concept (which is the meaning Hegel gives to the term 'dialectics') has objective as well as subjective moments, that it incorporates both Being and Essence. The implication is that what is conveyed to the human Understanding may not be the whole of existence, but will be what is Essential in that existence. Lenin was clearly convinced by this argument, and he noted his discovery that, 'Dialectics is the theory of knowledge of (Hegel and) Marxism', adding that this was something that Plekhanov, not to mention other Marxists, had paid no attention to (Lenin 1961: 362). This statement was tantamount to an admission that the defence of Plekhanov he had mounted in *Materialism and Empiriocriticism* was mistaken.

Another discovery Lenin made through reading the *Logic* was incorporated in his much-quoted 'Aphorism':

It is impossible completely to understand Marx's *Das Kapital*, and especially its first chapter, without having thoroughly studied and understood the whole of Hegel's Logic. Consequently, after half a century none of the Marxists understood Marx! (Lenin 1961: 180)

Despite the extraordinary powers of perspicacity commentators have attributed to Lenin for this insight into Marx's thinking, there is really nothing remarkable about it. It is simply a restatement of what Marx had told Engels in his letter of 14 January 1858.

Several commentators have seen the development of Lenin's philosophical ideas as a progression from the mechanical materialism of his *Materialism and Empiriocriticism* published in 1909 to the Hegelian humanism of the 'Philosophical Notebooks' that he worked on in 1914. According to this interpretation, Lenin's conversion took place at the start of the war when, dismayed by the failure of social democrats throughout Europe to oppose the war and the consequent collapse of the Second International, he turned to the writings of Hegel in order to revive the revolutionary spirit of Marxism. Lenin's reading of Hegel's *Science of Logic*, the argument goes, enabled him to rediscover the dialectical essence of Marxism that had been neglected by the theoreticians of the Second International.

The evidence provided by the *Konspekt*, however, shows that the collapse of the Second International had nothing to do with Lenin's study of Hegel's *Logic*. This was stimulated by the appearance of the Marx–Engels correspondence in 1913 and sustained by the ongoing campaign against Bogdanov and the 'Machists'. Moreover, if one takes the *Konspekt* and the 'Philosophical Notebooks' together, it strongly suggests that, far from being an innovator in Marxist ideas, Lenin sought to conform with the opinions of Marx and Engels and to adhere to Marxist doctrine, or at least with that doctrine as Plekhanov presented it. This attitude to the works of Marx and Engels was one that Bogdanov classed as 'authoritarian thinking'.

6

Bogdanov

Bogdanov, whose real name was Alexander Alexandrovich Malinovsky, was born in Sokolka, a small town in the province of Grodno in 1873. Like Lenin, he was the son of a schoolteacher who became a school inspector. He was educated at the *gimnaziia* in Tula and entered the natural science faculty of Moscow University in 1892. In 1894 he was arrested and sentenced to internal exile in Tula for his part in a student disturbance. Unable to continue his studies at Moscow, he enrolled in the medical faculty at Kharkov University and qualified as a doctor of psychiatric medicine in 1899 (Bogdanov 1995: 18–21).

Bogdanov's revolutionary career began during his Tula exile when, along with his friends Vladimir Bazarov and Ivan Skvortsov-Stepanov, he began to teach in a workers' study circle that had been established by former members of the Brusnev organization. It was during this time that Bogdanov wrote his influential textbook, *A Short Course of Economic Science*, which was based on the lectures he gave to the workers in Tula.

Although Bogdanov's *Short Course* does not say so explicitly for censorship reasons, it is an exposition of Marx's economic doctrines. To make the subject accessible to a worker audience, Bogdanov does not follow the abstract approach that Marx takes in *Das Kapital*. Instead, the method adopted in the *Short Course* is historical: it shows how the disintegration of primitive human communities gives rise to increasingly complex forms of social and economic organization, culminating in the modern capitalist system. Bogdanov's historical approach carries on the tradition initiated by Sieber of showing how the characteristic features of capitalism emerged in the course of historical development.

The historical treatment of economics allows Bogdanov to discuss the succeeding types of social organization, the patriarchal clan, the feudal, merchant capitalist and industrial capitalist. A fundamental distinction that Bogdanov sees emerging as early as in the clan system is that between those who gave orders and those who carried them out. He viewed this distinction as one that would be eradicated only in a socialist society.

A characteristic feature of Bogdanov's approach is his interest in the way in which people's perception of the world changed in the course of history. In the earliest times, to understand the world, people attributed human characteristics to natural phenomena. Their outlook could be described as 'natural fetishism'. With the emergence of commodity exchange, fetishism manifested itself in the practice of isolated individuals to attribute exchange value to things, instead of seeing value as a relationship between people in society. Bogdanov was one of the few people in his day to pick up on the philosophical implications of Marx's concept of 'commodity fetishism' and to appreciate how the fragmentation of capitalist society gave rise to a distorted picture of reality, a process that Hegel and Marx had referred to as 'Reflection'.

More of Bogdanov's philosophical ideas appeared in the later editions of the *Short Course*. The first edition, published in 1897, was reviewed favourably by Lenin in the following year in the journal *Mir Bozhii* (God's World). In Lenin's judgement, of all the guides that were available on the subject of political economy, this was the best. He praised the clarity of the book's exposition, and admired the way in which the author had arranged his material chronologically, characterizing the periods of economic development in their proper sequence: primitive clan communism, feudalism, guilds and, finally, capitalism. This, Lenin declared, was exactly how one ought to expound political economy (Lenin 1960c: 46–54).

In 1899 Bogdanov published his first philosophical work, *Basic Elements in the Historical View of Nature*. The main influences in it were the two scientific discoveries of recent times that Bogdanov believed could explain much in the natural world, human perception and society. These were Darwin's theory of natural selection and the principle of the conservation of energy. In this Bogdanov was largely in agreement with Engels, but drew very different implications. He was looking for a method that would be universally applicable, that would be 'monist', and dialectics did not conform to this criterion. As he explained: 'The word "dialectics" suggests facts of development which are characteristic ... only of living nature ... plus the fact that it indicates precisely "development in contradictions", which is even less a universal fact' (Bogdanov 1899: 18). The approach adopted in *Basic Elements* was to argue that nothing was static, but in a constant state of flux, interacting with its environment. What passed for stability or immobility was in fact the resultant of a moving equilibrium of countervailing forces. This phenomenon of the 'moving equilibrium' could be observed in all spheres of existence, and was, Bogdanov explained, why he had called this approach to reality 'historical' rather than 'dialectical'.

While he was studying medicine at Kharkov, Bogdanov joined a local social-democratic group which was led by the future prominent Menshevik P. Nezhdanov-Cherevanin. At the time the group was formed, Marxists were coming under attack by Mikhailovsky for insisting that Russia must undergo a capitalist stage. To Mikhailovsky this showed that they connived at the development of capitalism and were indifferent to the plight of the victims of the capitalist system. This was the reproach to Marxists that occasioned responses from Plekhanov, Lenin and Struve. In Kharkov Nezhdanov and his friends were indignant at Mikhailovsky's accusations and wrote two letters in reply, one in 1893 and one in 1894. The letters denied that the intelligentsia were in any position to halt the inevitable course of economic development, but they did not accept that they were indifferent to people's sufferings or that their doctrine of 'economic materialism' lacked a moral dimension. Nezhdanov in fact argued this point at length in a book entitled *Morality* which was published in 1898. Bogdanov took no part in this campaign against Mikhailovsky, or discussions on morality, because he believed that people should not be governed by formal codes of behaviour, but act out of sympathy and consideration for each other. For this attitude he narrowly escaped being 'expelled for immorality' from Nezhdanov's group (Bogdanov 1911: 81–2).

Bogdanov was arrested in November 1899 for conducting socialist propaganda in Tula. After spending six months in prison he was released in May 1900 and sent to Kaluga to await his final sentence. It was in Kaluga that he met Lunacharsky, a fellow exile, who was to become one of his closest associates. Lunacharsky had studied in Berne with the philosopher Richard Avenarius, and at that time was a follower of Avenarius's philosophy of Empiriocriticism. Avenarius's *Critique of Pure Experience* was the polar opposite of Emmanuel Kant's *Critique of Pure Reason*. Whereas Kant had regarded *a priori* knowledge to be more reliable than empirical data, Avenarius sought to eliminate from human perception any elements that did not have their roots in experience. Encouraged by Lunacharsky, Bogdanov made a study of Avenarius's work, and also that of Ernst Mach, who shared some of Avenarius's ideas, but expressed them in more accessible language.

In the light of Bogdanov's preoccupations in *Basic Elements*, one can understand what the attraction of Avenarius for him would have been. Avenarius treated human perception as the interaction of the human central nervous system (System C) with the environment, how it adapted itself to its surroundings and how it acted best to conserve energy. In other words, Avenarius's ideas in effect were an extension of Bogdanov's existing line of thought. However, his acceptance of Avenarius's ideas was much less unreserved than Lunacharsky's. A significant point of difference concerned the respective attitudes of the two men to Avenarius's concept of the 'perfect constant'. This was the point at which the adaptation of System C to the environment and the adaptation of the environment to System C had reached complete equilibrium. This, in Lunacharsky's opinion, was the ultimate ideal of human society. Bogdanov, on the other hand, thought this ideal not at all desirable, as it was a static one that stifled further development (Avenarius 1905: 61–2).

Vologda

In February 1901 Bogdanov left Kaluga to begin his three-year term of exile in the provincial town of Vologda. Because it had very little industry and no institutions of higher education, and consequently few workers or students to propagandize, Vologda had become a traditional place of residence for political exiles. On the other hand, the presence of so many like-minded people made the town a desirable place to be exiled to. Soon after his arrival there, Bogdanov was joined by Lunacharsky and a number of other former members of the Kiev Social-Democratic organization, among them the philosopher Nikolai Berdyaev.

Berdyaev was one of the group of people whom Lenin termed 'Legal Marxists', whose leading figure was Peter Struve. After the publication of his *Critical Notes* (1894), Struve had begun to appreciate the force of Mikhailovsky's critique of Marxism, that the doctrine of 'dialectical materialism' had no moral dimension. When Bogdanov met him, Berdyaev was in the process of abandoning Marxism in favour of the idealist philosophy of Immanuel Kant. Berdyaev's critique of Marxism prompted Bogdanov, Lunacharsky and other exiles to engage with him in passionate debates.

In the philosophical works written by Berdyaev while in his Vologda exile, one can observe what his criticisms of Marxism were. He found unconvincing the idea that in the wake of a single social cataclysm, a revolution, a new social order could be formed. He thought too that the socialist order which would emerge from this revolution would be as self-satisfied, complacent and philistine as the society it replaced. Berdyaev further questioned the Marxist conception of the economic 'base' of society giving rise to its ideological 'superstructure'. 'How can', he asked, 'this economic development create ideological development? ... What internal causal link is possible between the economy ... and ideology, whether it be the discovery of a scientific law, the construction of a metaphysical system, the experience of moral ideals or an artistic creation?' (Berdyaev 1901: 1–26).

In replying to Berdyaev's strictures on Marxism, Bogdanov did not try to defend the doctrines that Berdyaev rejected, but reformulated them in such a way as to take Berdyaev's arguments into account. It was in this way that Bogdanov elaborated some of the most characteristic features of his philosophical outlook.

In agreement with Berdyaev, Bogdanov did not attach any importance to the suddenness with which any social transformation came about; what was important for him was the change that took place, not the speed with which it occurred. This was an approach that Bogdanov would display in his conception of proletarian culture, and also in his views on changes in the material world that he discussed in his main work, *Tectology*.

The encounter with Berdyaev also influenced Bogdanov's conception of a socialist society. For Bogdanov, the socialist society should not be self-satisfied or complacent; it should not be static. Such a society would always be developing, always facing new challenges to overcome. This is the vision of the socialist society that one finds in Bogdanov's economic writings and most prominently in his novel *Red Star*.

As for Berdyaev's objection to Marx's conception of the 'base' and 'superstructure' of society, Bogdanov conceded that, although this formulation was still essentially valid, the concepts Marx had used lacked precision: since the time Marx wrote evolutionary theory had made great strides, so that the relationship between economics and ideology could be expressed in terms of adaptation to the environment.

Bogdanov's argument was that in their struggle for existence, people could not pool their efforts without consciousness. Without consciousness, without perception, there could be no coming together in society. In this way the social instinct was inseparable from consciousness, so that, in Bogdanov's words: 'Social being and social consciousness in the exact sense of these words is identical.' He then went on to show how on the basis of technical progress there developed the complex system of social being, with its varied elements and united whole (Bogdanov 1906a: 64).

In showing that even at the most rudimentary level a system of social labour implied communication, Bogdanov was supported by the research of Ludwig Noiré on the origins of language. Noiré had found that words emerged from technical processes, the sounds people made in coordinating their efforts. This allowed Bogdanov to argue that even at the most rudimentary levels of social production some ideological element was involved. This ideological element was organizing adaptation in the social-labour struggle for existence (Bogdanov 1906a: 70).

While in Vologda Bogdanov published the philosophical treatise *Perception from the Historical Point of View*, which carried on the polemic with Berdyaev, and also sketched out what would be key ideas in Bogdanov's system. These were 'general methods', which would overcome the divisions of society caused by specialization and the division of labour, and 'synthetic cooperation', which would be a feature of a society or an organization in which the division into people that gave orders and those who carried them out had been overcome.

Another project in which Bogdanov was involved during his Vologda exile was the publication of the volume of essays entitled *Studies in the Realistic Outlook*. This was a volume that was conceived as a reply to *Problems of Idealism*, a collection of essays published in Moscow in 1902 (Poole 2003) reflecting the growing attraction of idealist philosophy in intellectual circles, and also the disillusionment in those circles with Marxist and positivist theory. Prominent among the contributors to the volume were figures who had made the transition 'from Marxism to idealism': Sergei Bulgakov, Berdyaev and Struve. Bogdanov contributed two essays to *Studies in the Realistic Outlook*, one on Rudolf Stammler's critique of Marxism, and one on the process of distribution in capitalist society and the way in which the expansion of the economy required the balanced growth of its various sectors. This was a subject that Bogdanov would later develop in his writings on the socialist planned economy.

It was while in Vologda that Bogdanov wrote the first and most important articles that would go to form the three-volume collection of essays entitled *Empiriomonism*. In *Empiriomonism* Bogdanov gives credit to Mach and Avenarius for seeking to purge perception of elements which do not properly belong to experience, and for the attempt to construct a monist system that would eliminate the distinction between subjectivity and objectivity. However, Bogdanov did not think that Empiriocriticism had succeeded in this endeavour, and it was the aim of arriving at a truly monist system that Bogdanov took up in his *Empiriomonism*.

To this end Bogdanov began by defining the characteristics of the physical and the psychic as 'objective' and 'subjective' respectively. The conclusion Bogdanov arrived at was that the criterion of objectivity could not be in individual experience but had to lie in the sphere of collective experience. For him, what counted as objective were those data of experience which have an identical vital significance for ourselves and for other people. The objective character of the physical world consisted in the fact that it exists not only for me personally, but for everyone, and also has the same particular significance for everyone. The objectivity of the physical series was its universal validity. Subjective experience, on the other hand, was that which lacked universal validity; it had significance only for one or a number of individuals (Bogdanov 2003: 15). Bogdanov was encouraged to find that the criterion of universal or social validity was one Marx had used for objectivity in *Das Kapital* (Bogdanov 1910b: 188–9).

Pravda

Bogdanov's exile in Vologda ended at the beginning of 1904. He was immediately invited to contribute articles to a new journal of 'literature and social life' entitled *Pravda* (Truth); other contributors to the journal included Lunacharsky, Skvortsov-Stepanov and the historians M. N. Pokrovsky and N. A. Rozhkov. To some degree *Pravda* was a continuation of *Studies in the Realistic Outlook*, in that it carried on the polemic against *Problems of Idealism*. Bogdanov's main contribution to the journal, the essay 'The Integration of Mankind', however, was not of a polemical kind. It was a work which argued that the point of view of the isolated individual in civil society gave a distorted view of the world and of mankind's place in it; that for such a distorted view to be overcome, it required that the fragmentation of human society should be surmounted and humanity become an integral whole (Bogdanov 1990: 28–46). 'The Integration of Mankind' was an essay in the tradition of Friedrich Schiller's 'Historical Letters' and Mikhailovsky's

'On Progress', and, though it was unknown to Bogdanov at the time, also of Marx's 'Economic and Political Manuscripts of 1844'.

In the spring of 1904 Bogdanov travelled to Geneva to meet Lenin, with whom he had corresponded while he was still in Vologda. Lenin was at this time in desperate straits as Martov and his supporters extended their control over the institutions of the party. Lenin was particularly irked that he did not have a newspaper with which to exert his influence. Bogdanov's support at this juncture was crucial for Lenin. As Valentinov explained, Bogdanov at that time was already established as a writer; he was very well known among Social Democrats, and had good literary contacts in St Petersburg and Moscow, in particular with Gorky (Valentinov 1968: 235).

For his part, Bogdanov believed that the split in the RSDLP was regrettable and unnecessary, but he sympathized with the Lenin camp because it seemed to him that Martov and his group were acting in defiance of democratic decisions that had been made by the Second Congress. Bogdanov certainly did not subscribe to the idea of *What Is To Be Done?* that the socialist consciousness had to be brought to the working class from outside, and while collaborating with Bogdanov Lenin did not repeat it. Symptomatically, *One Step Forward, Two Steps Back*, the pamphlet Lenin wrote to justify his stance at the Second Congress, makes no mention of the idea, but instead advances Bogdanov's conception that the workers' experience of industrial action has made them disciplined, whereas the intelligentsia are much more individualistic and unruly. When, at the instigation of Martov and the editors of *Iskra*, Rosa Luxemburg wrote an article criticizing this idea, she was answered not by Lenin but by Bogdanov (Bogdanov 1925).

Despite Lenin's rejection of Bogdanov's philosophical views, he was prepared to form a political alliance with Bogdanov. The two men agreed to campaign for the convocation of a third party congress, which would resolve the conflicts created by the Second Congress. They would establish a newspaper, which would promote the point of view of the Majority group in the RSDLP. The newspaper *Vpered* (Forward) duly appeared in Geneva in 1904 edited by Lenin.

Democratic centralism

While Lenin remained in Geneva until November 1905, Bogdanov returned to Russia to prepare for a third congress of the RSDLP which, he expected, would restore unity to the party. He was in St Petersburg on 'Bloody Sunday', when tsarist troops opened fire on a peaceful demonstration, inciting a wave of strikes that would be the beginning of the 1905 revolution. As the most senior Bolshevik in Russia, it fell to Bogdanov to provide leadership to the party at this crucial juncture. It is symptomatic of how completely Bogdanov's name has been erased from the historical record that in works on the 1905 revolution Bogdanov is rarely, if ever, mentioned.

How Bogdanov exercised his leadership in the 1905 revolution can be seen from the numerous leaflets and pamphlets that he wrote at the time. His political thinking was rooted in the anti-authoritarian spirit that suffused his philosophical writings. His ideal state was 'synthetic cooperation' in which the distinction between those who gave orders and those who executed them would be eliminated. This, however, was not possible in a revolutionary situation when quick decisions had to be made. Bogdanov was convinced that it was possible to construct the party organizations in such a way that, without diluting the obligation to follow the decisions of the party centres, these decisions would correspond with the will of the majority of the party. The way to achieve this, Bogdanov argued, was by three types of mechanism: (1) the elective principle; (2) short terms of office; (3) wide transparency (*glasnost'*) in party matters. With these mechanisms in place, Bogdanov thought that the leaders would be made answerable to the membership of the party. Openness would ensure that leaders' mistakes were visible, and limited terms of office could see them replaced within a comparatively short time (*Listovki bol'shevistskikh organizatsii v pervoi russkoi revoliutsii 1905–1907 gg.*, 1965: 98–104). During the 1905 revolution, it was on Bogdanov's principle of 'democratic centralism' that the Bolshevik party was organized, not on Lenin's conception of party organization.

In the wake of the defeat of the 1905 revolution many of the intellectuals who had joined the Social-Democratic Party during the revolutionary upsurge now deserted it. Their departure created difficulties for the party organizations which had now lost the people who had performed the important functions of secretaries, propagandists, agitators, organizers and authors of leaflets and pamphlets. To some extent the workers had taken on these functions, but increasingly they felt the need for training in the skills that would enable them to perform their party functions better, and ensure that the party was prepared for the next revolutionary upsurge. It was in order to provide such workers with the necessary knowledge and training that Bogdanov and Gorky organized party schools, first on Capri in 1909 and then in Bologna in 1910–11 (Bogdanov 1910a: 1).

Socialist society

As a member of the Executive Committee of the St Petersburg Soviet, Bogdanov was arrested and imprisoned in December 1905 and released only in May of the following year. He took advantage of his term in prison to write the third volume of *Empiriomonism* and a chapter on 'Socialist Society' for his *Short Course of Economic Science*. In this chapter Bogdanov looked forward to a time when industrial production would become fully automated, when the role of workers would be reduced to overseeing the functioning of machines. Work at the machine would become much more of an organizing function, and increasingly of an intellectual rather than of a physical nature. The division of labour would no longer imply specialization which narrowed and impoverished the psyche of the worker. Now specialization would be transferred from the workers to the machines. This would also break down the barriers of communication between people that specialization had brought about; contacts between people would be broadened and deepened furthering cooperation and mutual understanding.

The age-old division into organizers and executives would be overcome, and labour groupings would become increasingly fluid. Workers would be able to change jobs easily, going from one machine to another, sometimes in an 'organizer' role and sometimes as an 'executive'. This would be possible because the anarchy of the market and competition would be eliminated and production would be organized by society, consciously and in a planned way (Bogdanov 1906b: 277–81).

The distribution of products would take place in a rational fashion. There would be social ownership of the means of production, but each person would be entitled to 'individual property' and receive sufficient consumer goods to satisfy his or her needs. Bogdanov conceded that this operation would be of enormous complexity, and that the statistical apparatus and information technology required was far in advance of anything that existed at the present time (Bogdanov 1906b: 282).

In terms of social psychology, the socialist society, free of the individualism engendered by the market and competition, would foster the growth of mutual sympathy and mutual understanding. From society's mastery over external nature and its own nature would come the end of all kinds of fetishism. People's perception would be pure and clear, free of any mysticism or metaphysics. Both natural fetishism and commodity fetishism would disappear.

The combination of mutual understanding and the absence of fetishism would create a third element in the psychology of a socialist society: this was the progressive elimination of the remnants of compulsion in social life. These include what Bogdanov referred to as the 'compulsory norms', the systems of customs, laws or ethics governing the behaviour of people in society. Since these were designed to regulate the conflicts which arose between individuals, groups or classes, the absence of these conflicts would render 'compulsory norms' redundant in a socialist society (Bogdanov 1906b: 283–4).

Bogdanov concluded by arguing that the retention in socialist society of a State structure and a legal framework was unnecessary, even to ensure that every person ought to perform a certain amount of labour for the social good. He pointed out that every State structure was an organization of class domination, and that it would be unnecessary where there were no classes. He believed that the prevalence of the social sentiment that connected people would be sufficient to ensure that every individual would do what they could for the benefit of all. Only in the transition period, when traces of the class divisions of the past remained, was the State form conceivable in the new society. But even this State would be one of class domination, this time the domination of the proletariat, the class which eliminates the division of society into classes. With the elimination of that division would come the elimination of the State as well (Bogdanov 1906b: 284).

In 1908 Bogdanov put his ideas on what the future collectivist society would be like in literary form in the novel *Red Star*. Bogdanov calls *Red Star* a 'utopian' novel, but since its purpose is to set out his conception of an actual socialist society, it is more accurate to describe it as an 'Aesopian' novel. The story is set in Russia in the aftermath of the 1905 revolution, when the hero, Leonid, a left-wing Social Democrat, is befriended by Menni, a visitor from Mars, and is taken by him to visit the red planet. The Martians have already established a collectivist society, and the description of its features forms the substance of the novel.

The Martians have been able to overcome the difficulty of creating the statistical apparatus and information technology required for a rational system of production and distribution. Thus:

> The Institute of Statistics has agencies everywhere which keep track of the flow of goods into and out of the stockpiles and monitor the productivity of all enterprises and the changes in the number of workers in them. In that way it can be calculated what and how much must be produced for any given period and the number of man hours required for the task. It then remains for the Institute to calculate the difference between what there is and what there should be, and to make this known to everyone. A flow of volunteers then re-establishes the equilibrium.
>
> To Leonid's inquiry if there was any restriction on the consumption of goods, Menni informed him that there was none; everyone took whatever was needed in whatever quantities they desired. There was no need for money, documentation or any form of compulsion; all labour was voluntary. (Bogdanov 1984: 66)

The Martian economic planning system had the necessary flexibility to respond to changed circumstances. As Menni explained, the Institute of Statistics had to be alert to new inventions and changes in environmental conditions that might affect industry. Labour might have to be transferred to different branches of industry, necessitating a recalculation taking the new factors into account, if not with absolute precision, then at least with an adequate degree of approximation (Bogdanov 1984: 67).

In keeping with Bogdanov's conception that the socialist ideal was not static, but dynamic, that there would always be difficulties to overcome, that the struggle against nature would never cease, Mars has to contend with the problem of diminishing natural resources. One possible solution would be the colonization of Earth. In this context Bogdanov uses the speech by the

Martian Sterni on the prospects for a socialist revolution on Earth to voice some apprehensions of his own.

Because the topography of Mars was more homogeneous than that of Earth, the people were much less divided into separate races, nationalities and linguistic groups than the inhabitants of Earth. As a result, the socialist revolution on Mars had been a relatively peaceful affair. Earth, on the other hand, was riven by political and social divisions, which meant that instead of following a single uniform pattern of development, one had to expect not one but a number of revolutions taking place in different countries at different times. Sterni could imagine that the individual advanced countries where socialism had triumphed would be like islands in a hostile capitalist and even pre-capitalist sea. In those circumstances, where socialism survived, its character was likely to be distorted by the years of encirclement. In a passage, strikingly prophetic of the phenomena associated with 'socialism in one country', Bogdanov puts into the mouth of Sterni the remark: 'We do not know how much barbarity and narrow-mindedness the socialists of Earth will bring with them into their new society' (Bogdanov 1984: 115).

On Mars the problem of the fragmentation of society through specialization has been overcome by the universal acquisition of general methods which are applicable to a wide range of industrial processes. In the novel, Leonid undergoes training in such general methods when he goes to work at a Martian clothing factory. He had to study the established scientific principles of industrial organization as well as the structure of the factory in which he was employed. He had to acquire a general notion of all the machines in use there, and know in detail the one with which he would be working (Bogdanov 1984: 96). Leonid worked by turns in all sections of the factory, supervising the operation of the various machines. By the time Bogdanov had published his second novel, *Engineer Menni*, in 1912, he had begun to elaborate his science of general methods, to which he had given the name 'Tectology'. In *Engineer Menni*, tectology is introduced in a context of overcoming the specialisms engendered in individualist society that obstructed mutual understanding.

Conflict with Lenin

Although the Russian government was eventually able to gain the upper hand in 1905, in Bogdanov's view, all the factors that had caused the upheaval were still in operation and it was only a matter of time before a new revolutionary wave would appear. The task of the Social Democrats, consequently, would be to prepare the working class for the coming revolution. Lenin's perspectives were quite different. He saw the crushing of the uprising in December 1905 as the end of the revolutionary era. He believed that the only tactic open to Social Democrats was the parliamentary one, and he defended the Social-Democratic Duma group against all criticism.

Bogdanov suspected Lenin of wanting 'parliamentarianism at any price', whereas Lenin equated Bogdanov's insistence that the group be answerable to the party as a whole with the desire to withdraw the Social-Democrat group from the Duma altogether. This difference in perspective along with philosophical disagreements led to Bogdanov's expulsion from the informal Bolshevik Centre in 1909. The reason given for Bogdanov's expulsion was that Bolshevism was an ideological current, and to be a member one must subscribe to Bolshevik ideology.

The ground for Bogdanov's expulsion had been prepared by the publication of Lenin's *Materialism and Empiriocriticism*. With the elevation of this work in Soviet times to the status of a key work of philosophy, and with the corresponding suppression of Bogdanov's writings, it was Lenin's book that became for many years the main source for Bogdanov's ideas. In this way it came to be accepted that Bogdanv was a follower of Mach, and that his philosophy, which had its roots in the idealism of Bishop Berkeley, led ultimately to solipsism. Even the most superficial acquaintance with Bogdanov's writings would show this characterization to be fictitious. Nevertheless, Lenin's misrepresentations served their purpose.

Bogdanov's position was undermined by his association with Lunacharsky, whose book *Socialism and Religion* was an easy target for distortion. Lenin asserted that in it Lunacharsky was preaching 'the union of scientific socialism with religion'. In fact the book did nothing of the kind. Lunacharsky's approach to religion had grown out of his interest in aesthetics, which he had come to view as a particular manifestation of the more general human impulse of evaluation. It was evaluation together with cognition, Lunacharsky believed, which made action possible. Through evaluation one became aware of the difference between what the world was and what it ought to be, between reality and ideals. According to Lunacharsky, the elemental approach to resolving this contrast was religious, and this provided him with his definition of religion: 'Religion is that thinking about the world and that world-sensation which psychologically tries to resolve the contrast between the laws of life and the laws of nature' (Lunacharskii 1908: 40).

Religion, however, in Lunacharsky's view, was not capable of satisfactorily resolving the contradiction. This would only be accomplished by scientific socialism, by means of knowledge and labour, science and technology. In sum, what Lunacharsky's book set out to do was to place modern socialism in the context of earlier systems which were concerned with human ethical ideals, and to demonstrate that socialism was the answer to mankind's earliest and most fundamental aspirations.

Lunacharsky's book was a serious and stimulating investigation into the relationship between religion and modern socialism. Its argument advocated the rejection of religion in favour of socialism. Lenin's impression of the book was clearly not derived from actually reading it. More likely, what he had read was Plekhanov's review of it, which distorted Lunacharsky's meaning to give the impression that Lunacharsky was propounding a new socialist religion without God. In the second volume of his book Lunacharsky drew the attention of his readers to the way Plekhanov had read into the book only what he wished to find (Lunacharskii 1911: 395–7). These protests were to be of no avail; Lunacharsky's 'religious seekings' were to be held up by both Plekhanov and Lenin as an indication of where Machist philosophy might lead.

Bogdanov's reply to *Materialism and Empiriocriticism*, *The Fall of the Great Fetish*, came out in 1910, after he had been expelled from the Bolshevik Centre, and so had no influence on events. The tone of the two works was completely different. Whereas Lenin's book was a tirade against his opponents, filled with personal abuse, Bogdanov's was an almost abstract disquisition on the danger of authoritarianism in the leadership of the workers' movement. Clearly, Bogdanov has Lenin in mind, though this is not stated explicitly.

In an organization in which the sense of collectivity was poorly developed, there was a strong likelihood that ideological leaders would be looked up to as 'authorities' in the traditional sense, and regarded as people of a higher type, whose words always had the force of truth. It was easy, moreover, for leaders from outside the working class, who were to a lesser degree than the workers imbued with a sense of comradely relations, to think of themselves as innately superior to the workers, as they carried this attitude with them from their former way of life.

Bogdanov went on to say that at the present time more and more leader-ideologues were emerging from among the workers themselves. Although these people were less prone to authoritarian tendencies than their colleagues from the 'intelligentsia', they were by no means immune. Bogdanov had encountered working-class leaders who had come to the fore during the revolutionary upsurge of 1905–06, and he had been struck by how spoilt they were by authoritarian conceit and ambition.

Bogdanov agreed that the intelligentsia played an important part in the workers' movement. He recalled that the very basis of proletarian thought and proletarian ideals were originally formulated by intellectuals. They were able to do this better than the working classes themselves because they had better access to all the earlier discoveries of science and culture, on which the development of a higher type of ideology had to rely. They were also able to devote a greater amount of time to intellectual activities than workers who were engaged in production.

In the only explicit reference to Lenin's *What Is To Be Done?* Bogdanov observes:

Once Lenin in *What Is To Be Done?* made a slip of the tongue, saying that the working class was incapable, independently, without the help of the socialist intelligentsia, to raise themselves above the ideas of trade-unionism and come to the socialist ideal. The phrase was uttered quite by chance in the heat of a polemic with the 'economists,' and had no connection with the basic views of the author. (Bogdanov 1910b: 193)

It is unlikely that Bogdanov really believed that Lenin's pronouncement was a 'slip of the tongue', but by saying it was he registered his own opinion that the idea was too absurd to be taken seriously.

Proletarian culture

Experience in the 1905 revolution had demonstrated clearly to Bogdanov that even the most militant worker leaders were not immune from authoritarian attitudes, not only in the political sphere but also in their everyday and family lives. These attitudes in Bogdanov's view were a serious obstacle to the emergence of a socialist society. For Bogdanov a socialist society was one in which the whole of production was organized on the basis of comradely cooperation, and from this flowed all the other features of socialism, such as the abolition of private property, the elimination of classes and a distribution of products such that every person would be able to achieve their full potential in following their vocation. But this would only be possible when the working class had finally achieved its victory and had the opportunity to organize the whole of society. But until that time there could be no gradual elimination of classes, no gradual transition to social property of the means of production, or no planned distribution of the social product. But the element of socialism that could develop within the existing capitalist society was socialism's most essential element – comradely cooperation. In Bogdanov's view, this was the prototype of socialism, its real beginning. The more it grew and developed within the narrow confines of the old society the more acute would be its contradictions with them. These contradictions would culminate in a series of revolutions that would lead to the establishment of a socialist society.

It was completely natural that the proletariat would want to live in its own way and not in the manner that the old society had imposed upon it, that it would want to develop its own forms of human relations and express them in its own social ideal. This being the case, it followed that the struggle for socialism would not be reduced simply to the war against capitalism; it would also be for the creation of newer and newer elements of socialism in the proletariat itself, in its internal relations, in its everyday living conditions, that is, it would be the elaboration of a socialist proletarian culture (Bogdanov 1990: 99–103).

For Bogdanov, therefore, the campaign to foster a proletarian culture, to cultivate comradely cooperation, was a means of laying the foundations of a socialist society within the confines of the existing capitalist system. In this way, the ideal of socialism became the means of achieving it; comradely cooperation was the form of organization characteristic of the proletariat.

Bogdanov called upon socialists to further the development of genuinely comradely relations in all the everyday practice of the proletariat. This was essential since even in proletarian organizations one could observe the continued existence of relations between people which had nothing in common with socialism: the struggle of ambitions, the authoritarian pretensions of 'leaders', the unconscious deference of their followers, the resistance to comradely discipline and the intrusion of personal interests and motives into the collective cause and so on. All these phenomena were unavoidable in the initial stages of the workers' movement, considering that the proletariat had not come into the world as a well-established class, but had been composed from the urban poor, the peasantry and small proprietors, all of whom were accustomed to living by private, individual, interests and subordinating themselves to despotic authorities.

Bogdanov drew attention to the urgent need for change in the family life of the proletariat. There, the despotic relationship of the husband to the wife, the demand for unquestioning obedience of the children to the parents, were attributes of the traditional structure of the family. He considered that the slavery of women impeded the power of the working class by depriving its ranks of female comrades, while the slavery of children harmed the socialist upbringing of future activists. It consequently behoved socialists to campaign energetically, by word and by example, against any remnants of family slavery, and not to think them unimportant or relegate them to the status of private affairs (Bogdanov 1990: 102).

As a means of promoting proletarian culture Bogdanov advocated the establishment of a Proletarian University. Its aim would be, within the existing society, to prepare cadres of conscious and integrated representatives of the society of the future, people who would be equipped to bring about the great transformations to come. The new university would not be for young people fresh from school but for mature workers with experience in the sphere of labour and social struggle. The teaching in the university would not be run on the authoritarian lines of conventional universities but on the principle of comradely cooperation; the students would be the comrades of their teachers, and would not learn passively but would continually question what they were being taught. Bogdanov had had experience of this kind of teaching in the workers' circles in Tula and in the party schools which were held on Capri and in Bologna in 1909–11.

Bogdanov also urged the compilation of a Proletarian Encyclopedia. The precedent for such an encyclopedia was the one compiled in France in the eighteenth century by Diderot and d'Alembert, which had reflected the individualist culture of bourgeois society. Whereas the entries of this and other existing encyclopedias were written by individual scholars within their particular disciplines without any regard for the overall coherence of the work, the new Proletarian Encyclopedia would integrate knowledge and break down the barriers between disciplines. Subjects would be treated in their historical and social context and in relation to each other. Though it would appear that Bogdanov never produced a Proletarian Encyclopedia, he did produce a work which ordered its material in exactly the manner in which the Proletarian Encyclopedia was supposed to do. This was *Tectology, the Universal Science of Organisation*.

The need for elaborating a proletarian culture, in Bogdanov's view, became a matter of urgency with the onset of the First World War. He believed that the collapse of the Second International and the upsurge of nationalism throughout Europe was attributable to the fact that proletarian culture was still in its infancy, whereas the culture of the bourgeoisie was well developed and universally pervasive. In these circumstances, the workers had adopted the attitudes of their national bourgeoisie and succumbed to the nationalist war fever.

Tectology

The premise upon which Bogdanov's Universal Science of Organization (*Tectology*) is based is that organization is an activity that can be applied not only to living beings but to inanimate objects as well; that everything 'organizes'. Bogdanov shows this by presenting a number of parallel cases where human practice has in some way emulated nature. He cites the case of a sail, designed to propel sailing vessels by harnessing the power of the wind and the same mechanism applied by airborne seeds. In nature one found numerous examples of the protection of delicate living fibres, fluids or semi-fluids, using the method of an external skeleton. These included the shell on a snail, the skin on mammals, and above all, the skull to protect the brain. This was in essence the method used by people when they made different vessels, crockery, boxes and the like. The societies of humans and ants both engaged in herding: the humans of cows and the ants of aphids. The sexual organs of a flower and a woman had many parallels in their respective structures.

These coincidences, Bogdanov argued, could not be explained by imitation or with reference to a common origin. What united them was the organizing activity, something common to both living and nonliving things. The definition that he gave of organization was: 'a whole that is greater than the sum of its parts'. Organizing activity was always directed towards formation of some kind of system from parts or elements. Whatever any particular case might be, one characteristic always remained the same: that what was being organized was a given activity, a given resistance.

Bogdanov went on to explain that a resistance was simply an activity from another point of view. If one fought against an enemy, the enemy was the resistance to be overcome; from the point of view of the enemy it was the other way round. Activity and resistance were not two entities but two interrelated sides of the same phenomenon. Everything that was accessible to our experience, to our efforts and to our perception, was activity-resistance.

If something else existed that did not have this character, it would not produce any effect on our senses, would not offer any resistance to our movements. Consequently, it could not enter into our experience and would forever remain unknown and inaccessible to us.

If one approached the question of organization in this way, Bogdanov argued, then the concept was universally applicable at all levels of being, not simply in the sphere of life: everywhere there were combinations of activities and resistances. It followed that absolute non-organization was impossible in experience; for if it existed we could know nothing of it. The entire world consisted of an organizing process, an infinitely developing series of complexes of different forms and levels of organization in their mutual relations, in their struggle or their unification. All of these, however remote from each other they were qualitatively and quantitatively, could be subsumed under the same organizational methods, the same organizational forms.

In an echo of Mach and Avenarius's usage, Bogdanov called a unit of organization a 'complex', and its component parts 'elements'. Depending on what was the subject of study anything might be a complex or an element. In an almost poetic passage, Bogdanov illustrated the relativity of his terms and simultaneously the breadth of vision of tectology:

> Gigantic suns and nebulae have to be taken as elements of star systems; enterprises or people as elements of society; cells as elements of an organism; molecules or atoms or electrons as elements of a physical body, depending on the question at hand; ideas and concepts as elements of theoretical systems; representations and voluntary impulses as elements of psychic associations, etc. (Bogdanov 1989: 119–20)

Bogdanov gave as his definition of organization a complex which was greater than the sum of its elements; conversely, a complex which was less than the sum of its elements was disorganized. Neutral complexes were those which occupied an intermediate position between these two states, the point of equilibrium between organization and disorganization. The elements which constituted the complexes were activity-resistance of all possible types, so that the theme of activity-resistance pervaded the whole of the work (Bogdanov 1989: 125).

With its examples taken from a great variety of sciences, *Tectology* was a work that could only have been written by a person with Bogdanov's breadth of knowledge. One finds in it references to physics, chemistry, mathematics, psychology, sociology, mechanics, linguistics, medicine, theology, geology and so on. Some of the examples are autobiographical, taken from Bogdanov's experiences in the Bolshevik fraction of the RSDLP. There are also many references to military affairs, suggesting that his experience in the army during the First World War was an instructive as well as a traumatic one for him.

Despite *Tectology*'s claims to be a science rather than a philosophy, there is considerable continuity in it with Bogdanov's earlier philosophical works. One element of continuity is the theme of the interchange between a complex and its environment: how adaptation of the one to the other takes place through positive or negative selection, and how there can be no real conservation of forms, since everything is in a state of dynamic equilibrium.

Although Bogdanov elaborates many organizational forms in *Tectology*, the one that had the widest application in the political sphere was the so-called 'law of the leasts'. An example Bogdanov gave of this was of a chain from which a weight was suspended. When the weight was increased beyond a certain point the chain would break at its weakest link. The structural stability of the whole was determined by the least stable of its parts. This scheme applied not only to mechanical systems but to all systems, physical, psychic and social and the like. The law of the leasts had a great number of important practical consequences. A squadron could only sail as fast as its slowest ship; a military detachment consisting of infantry and cavalry would break up if the cavalry did not limit itself to the speed of the infantry. If there was a political party consisting of a bloc of two fractions, one progressive and one conservative, the party programme and tactics would be decided by the conservative fraction (Bogdanov 1989: 216–22).

In *Tectology* Bogdanov returned to the critique of dialectics that he had first made in 1899 in his *Basic Elements of the Historical View of Nature*, where he had objected that dialectics was only applicable to living nature and that 'development in contradictions' also had a limited application. Now, from the point of view of tectology, he was able to present a more detailed examination of the limitations of the dialectics of the kind that Engels and Plekhanov propounded.

He did this by taking the illustration that Engels had given with the grain of barley, which negated itself through germination and producing a whole plant, which in turn 'negated' itself by the creation of seeds, and passed into a synthesis, formally similar to the thesis, but enriched in content, the end result being a plurality of barley grains. Bogdanov then demonstrated how these events were interpreted tectologically, in terms of the dynamic equilibrium of the grain of barley with its environment. Such a scheme, Bogdanov argued, was universal, and, in contrast to the old dialectical triad, could explain the processes at work to the smallest detail.

7

Trotsky and permanent revolution

Lev Davydovich Bronstein, whose pseudonym was Leon Trotsky, was born on 25 October 1879 in Kherson in the Ukraine. In Nikolaev, where Trotsky spent his final school year, he joined the Southern Russian Workers' Union and carried on propaganda and educational activities among the local workers. On his outlook at that time, he wrote in 1922 to the historian V. I. Nevsky: 'In 1896–97 I considered myself an opponent of Marx, whose books, it is true, I had never read. I judged Marxism from Mikhailovsky's perspective'. His first wife Alexandra Sokolovskaya recalls that Trotsky and his friends were furious with Plekhanov for what they considered to be unwarranted attacks on Mikhailovsky. At the New Year's Eve celebration of 1897 Trotsky proposed the toast: 'A curse on all Marxists and all who bring aridity and cruelty into all walks of life' (Vasetskii 1992: 15). The signs are that in this early period of his career Trotsky shared Mikhailovsky's opinion that the Marxists were indifferent to people's suffering in face of the inevitable development of a capitalist economy.

In 1898 the members of the Southern Russian Workers' Union were arrested and Trotsky spent two years in Odessa prison, where he espoused Marxism and adopted the name of one of the warders as his pseudonym. He was sentenced to four years exile in Eastern Siberia, but in 1902 he managed to escape and make his way to London where he made contact with Lenin. Trotsky had already demonstrated outstanding literary talent, earning him the soubriquet 'The Pen'. Accordingly, Lenin invited him to contribute to *Iskra* and even to join the paper's editorial board. This invitation, however, was vetoed by Plekhanov, who suspected Lenin of trying to take control of the editorial board by ensuring the predominance of his supporters.

In his reminiscences of Lenin published in 1924 Trotsky recalls discussing Bogdanov's writings. He gives an interesting insight into how they were viewed by Lenin and himself before Bogdanov's conflict with Plekhanov had escalated. He writes:

> I also told him how we had read Bogdanov's first philosophical books with great interest. I remember very clearly the import of Vladimir Il'ich's remark: he too thought that the book on *The Historical View of Nature* seemed very valuable, but Plekhanov did not agree with it, saying it was not materialist. At that time Vladimir Il'ich had no views of his own on this question and only repeated Plekhanov's opinion, with respect for his philosophical authority, but also with some perplexity. I too was very surprised then by Plekhanov's verdict. (Lunacharskii, Radek and Trotsky 1991: 11)

As a delegate from the Siberian Social-Democratic Union, Trotsky attended the Second Congress of the RSDLP. At the Congress Trotsky initially supported Lenin, but in the course of discussing the first clause of the party programme on the definition of a party member Trotsky abruptly changed sides and took the part of Martov. He noted the emergence of two ideological currents at the Congress: Lenin and his supporters were the 'hard *Iskraists*', while he himself and the Siberian delegation belonged to the 'soft *Iskraists*'. He was struck by the 'lust for power' which guided Lenin's actions at the Congress, in particular, his efforts to ensure the independence of the *Iskra*, the 'Central Organ', against possible pressures from the Central Committee. In order to do this, Trotsky reasoned, Lenin had to eject from *Iskra*'s editorial board those members of it who recognized the preponderance of the Central Committee. This episode was the one in which Lenin overplayed his hand and precipitated the split in the RSDLP into two rival fractions (Trotsky 1980: 22–6).

Trotsky's contemporary observations on Lenin's behaviour at the Second Congress are instructive about what the issues at stake at the Congress were and, in particular, about where Lenin's priorities lay. Trotsky has no doubt that Lenin's intention was to control the party from his power base in the party newspaper. This is consistent with the importance Lenin attached to the role of a party newspaper in *What Is To Be Done?* and with his later predilection for the position of editor in party newspapers.

In 1904 Trotsky returned to the theme of Lenin's political theory and practice in a lengthy critique entitled *Our Political Tasks* (1979). This is a remarkable document for the insight it has into the manner in which *What Is To Be Done?* departed from the principle of the First International that the emancipation of the working class is the affair of the working class itself. Trotsky does not refer explicitly to this principle, and it is possible that he did not know it, as his familiarity with Marx's writings in this period was limited. But what he says is Marx's thinking expressed in different words.

In *Our Political Tasks* Trotsky explains that his intention is to draw attention to the difference in principle which separates two opposing approaches to party organization: 'In the one case we have a party which *thinks* for the proletariat, which *substitutes itself* politically for it, and on the other we have a party which politically *educates* and *mobilises* the proletariat to exercise rational pressure on the will of all political groups and parties.' Trotsky's second type of party could describe all the organizations from Land and Liberty down to the Brusnev group, which saw themselves as subsidiary to the labour movement. His first type of party describes the kind of organization that Lenin advocated in *What Is To Be Done?* It was one which claimed to know what the workers' interests were better than the workers themselves. In a remarkably prophetic passage Trotsky showed what the outcome of 'substitutionism' would be: 'In the internal politics of the party these methods lead ... to the party organisation "substituting" itself for the party, the Central Committee substituting itself for the party organisation, and finally the dictator substituting himself for the Central Committee' (Trotsky 1979: 77).

From his exile in Geneva Trotsky watched events leading to the 1905 revolution unfold. At the end of 1904 he wrote a number of articles which were published in 1905 under the title, *Before 9 January*. In this pamphlet one can discern the beginnings of what later would become the theory of permanent revolution. Trotsky said that what inspired him was Plekhanov's dictum that the 'Russian revolution would triumph as a workers' revolution or it would not triumph at all' (Trotsky 1925: 521). And in fact there is an echo of Plekhanov's words in Trotsky's declaration that 'Russian democracy can only be revolutionary democracy, or it can be no democracy at all' (Trotsky 1905: 28). The context in which this idea occurs is an analysis of the weakness and timidity of Russian liberalism, and its inclination to come to terms with the autocracy rather than to strive for its elimination.

Trotsky's argument was that in Russia democracy could only be revolutionary because the country had no official institutions from which a democratic Russia could trace its ancestry. Russia had only two types of political institutions: on the one hand there was the monarchy, supported by a colossal multi-branched bureaucratic apparatus; and on the other hand there were the so-called organs of local self-government: the zemstvos in the countryside and the dumas in the towns. The liberals intended to build the future Russia on these two historic institutions. Constitutional Russia must, according to them, arise out of a contract between the autocracy and the institutions of local self-government.

But, according to Trotsky, this kind of compromise would deprive Russian democracy of the possibility to be based on national traditions; it would be called into being by a simple decree from above. Democracy could not be based on the zemstvos because the zemstvos were not democratic; they were composed of the upper social strata and required the ownership of property to be a member. Democracy worthy of the name must recognize popular sovereignty, so that any attempt by the zemstvos to speak on behalf of the people and form pacts with the autocracy must be branded as political imposture.

But the people had no legal forms to express their sovereign will. These could only be created by revolutionary means. The demand for a national Constituent Assembly was a break with all the official tradition of Russian history. By calling the sovereign people on to the historical stage, democracy was driving the wedge of revolution into Russian legal history. The inference Trotsky drew was that:

> We have no democratic traditions; we have to create them. It is only possible to do this by revolution. A party of democracy can only be a party of revolution. This idea should penetrate the general consciousness, must fill our political atmosphere, the very word democracy must be suffused with the content of revolution, so that by coming into contact with it, it cruelly burns the fingers of the liberal opportunists who try to assure their friends and enemies that they became democrats as soon as they were called by this name. (Trotsky 1905: 29)

Whereas in the first articles in the *Before 9 January* collection Trotsky emphasized the incapability of the Russian liberals to take the lead in overthrowing the autocracy and establishing a democratic regime, in the article 'The Proletariat and Revolution' he predicted the leading role of the working class in the coming revolution. He did this on the evidence of a number of strikes that had taken place in the course of 1903 in response to the hardship and deprivation caused by the war against Japan. At the moment it was the liberals who were making the running as the force opposed to the tsarist autocracy, but, Trotsky believed, the liberals ought to step aside and allow a workers' revolution to take place (Trotsky 1905: 44).

Trotsky tried to have his pamphlet published by the Mensheviks' printing press, but the Mensheviks were riven by internal conflicts, some favouring and some opposing an alliance with the liberals, with the result that the publication of the pamphlet was delayed. While it was in its proof copy it was read by the Russo-German Social Democrat Alexander Helphand, who wrote under the pseudonym of Parvus. Parvus was impressed by Trotsky's analysis and contributed a foreword to the pamphlet in which he amplified the points Trotsky had raised and placed them in the broader context of Russian and European social and economic development.

Parvus

According to Parvus, political radicalism in Western Europe was a characteristic feature of the petty bourgeoisie, the artisans who made a major contribution to the industrial development of their respective countries, before being overwhelmed by the capitalist class. It was artisans like these who created the towns in Western Europe, which for several centuries reflected the culture and the political attitudes of the petty bourgeoisie. In Russia, on the other hand, towns developed more on the Chinese than on the European model. They were administrative centres, bearing a purely bureaucratic character, without the slightest political significance, and as regards economics they were trading bazaars for the gentry and peasant environment that surrounded them. Their development, moreover, was arrested by the growth of capitalism, which began to create large towns in its own image, that is, factory towns and centres of world trade. As a result, in Russia there was a capitalist bourgeoisie, but not the intermediate bourgeoisie, which had given rise to the political democracy of Western Europe (Trotsky 1905: 5).

Like Trotsky, and before him, Plekhanov, Parvus believed that in Russia only the workers could bring about the revolutionary overthrow of tsarism. The revolutionary provisional government in Russia would be a government of workers' democracy. But, Parvus cautioned, it must prepare for the civil war which would follow the overthrow of tsarism. There would be an assault on the workers' government by agrarian and bourgeois liberalism, and treason could be expected from the side of the political radicals and democrats. A Social-Democratic Provisional Government, he believed, could not bring about a socialist revolution in Russia, but it would be able to destroy the autocracy and establish a democratic republic. Such a Provisional Government, Parvus thought, would embark on the lengthy process of transforming Russia politically, but he did not specify how this process might end (Trotsky 1905: 13).

On 9 January 1905 the massacre of a peaceful demonstration in St Petersburg provided the common cause that Trotsky thought was needed to trigger the workers' revolution. A wave of strikes erupted throughout the country in protest, leaving the liberal opposition movement on the political sidelines. The final article in Trotsky's pamphlet was one expressing satisfaction that his prognoses had been proved right. He welcomed the onset of revolution, whose first step, he declared, had lifted the people over scores of steps, which in normal times would have been prolonged and laborious to ascend (Trotsky 1905: 53–64).

Results and Prospects

Trotsky returned to Russia in October 1905, just as the St Petersburg Soviet was being formed, and in this organization Trotsky played a prominent part. For Trotsky, the Soviets, which sprang up all over Russia, were a confirmation that the workers themselves could act as an independent revolutionary force. In December 1905, along with Bogdanov and other members of the Soviet's Executive Committee, he was arrested and imprisoned. It was during this imprisonment that Trotsky wrote *Results and Prospects* (1971b), a work that developed the ideas of *Before 9 January* into his theory of permanent revolution.

Like *Before 9 January*, *Results and Prospects* concentrates on two main points: the character of Russian historical development that would bring the proletariat to power, and the dynamics of the workers government that would lead it in a socialist direction. However, the scope of *Results and Prospects* is much wider than *Before 9 January*. It goes far beyond showing that the workers, rather than the liberals, are capable of establishing a democratic regime in Russia. It seeks to show that the peculiarities of Russia's historical development make it possible for the workers to come to power, and that the logic of their situation would compel them to introduce socialist measures. For the workers' government to survive, it would have to call upon the help of the proletariats of foreign countries, and in this way to make the revolution international.

In speaking of Russia's historical development in *Results and Prospects*, Trotsky repeats what he had said in *Before 9 January* about the relative weakness of the bourgeoisie and the strength of the workers. He makes Parvus's point that Russian towns, unlike those in Western Europe, had no commercial functions, but were mere administrative centres, like those found in Asia (Trotsky 1971b: 179).

In *Before 9 January* Trotsky had mentioned the dominance in Russia of the State apparatus; in *Results and Prospects* this phenomenon was accorded much greater prominence. In this respect, he was following a well-established tradition in Russian historiography, since the conception of a strong, centralized State structure had been put forward by Soloviev, Kliuchevsky and, most recently, by Miliukov. In Trotsky's view, what accounted for the emergence of a powerful State apparatus had been Russia's encounters with its more powerful neighbours, Lithuania, Poland and Sweden.

As a consequence of military pressure from Western Europe, the State swallowed up an inordinately large part of the country's resources, absorbing the incomes of privileged classes, and so hampering their already slow development. It taxed the peasantry to excess, and thus impeded the growth of the population and the development of the productive forces, so the corollary of the burgeoning State was the continued poverty and backwardness of the rest of society.

However, in order to exist and function, and to acquire the resources it required, the State needed a hierarchical organization of estates. This is why it sought to force the development of these structures by Government measures. In order to be able to survive in the midst of better-armed hostile countries, Russia was compelled to set up factories, organize navigation schools, publish textbooks on fortification, and so on. From the end of the seventeenth century the State strove with all its power to accelerate the country's natural economic development, creating new branches of handicraft and machine industry and pursuing a policy of protectionism. According to Trotsky, 'The more a government is centralised and the more independent it is of society, the sooner it becomes an autocratic organisation standing above society' (Trotsky 1971b: 176).

Of course such a State, Trotsky argued, would be a powerful lever for revolution in the hands of the proletariat. Every political party worthy of the name, he declared, strove to capture political power, and thus place the State at the service of the class whose interests it expressed. The Social Democrats would strive for the political domination of the working class.

Having come to power and acquired a powerful State mechanism for transforming society, the Russian workers were unlikely to relinquish it willingly and turn it over to the liberals. Even if the workers' government tried to limit itself to the democratic reforms of the Social-Democratic minimum programme, it would not succeed, but would be forced to implement socialist measures. Trotsky explained how this would come about in the case of the peasantry. On overthrowing the autocracy, the workers' government would stand before the peasants as their liberators. But when the government introduced legislation to protect the agrarian proletarians, this would meet resistance from the peasantry as a whole. The proletariat would then find itself compelled to carry the class struggle into the villages, and in this way to destroy the community of interests existing in peasant society. The logic of events would impel the workers' government towards the introduction of cooperative production under communal control or organized directly by the State. This, Trotsky remarked, was a path leading to socialism (Trotsky 1971b: 212).

A similar situation would arise in industry. Trotsky could imagine a situation in which the workers' government would attempt to introduce an 8-hour working day, a measure included in the minimum programme of the Social-Democratic party. The response of the capitalists might be to close the factories and make the workers unemployed. In that case, the workers' government could expropriate the factories and organize the production in them on a socialized basis. A similar scenario would emerge if the workers' government introduced measures to protect the unemployed, so depriving the capitalist class of its reserve army of labour. In this case too the employers were likely to resort to a lockout, and the workers' government would reply by the expropriation of the factories and the introduction of communal production (Trotsky 1971b: 211–12).

But there were limits to how far the socialist policies of the working class in Russia could go, considering the country's low level of economic development. Sooner or later they would run up against the obstacle of Russia's backwardness. It was therefore Trotsky's conviction that, 'Without the direct State support of the European proletariat the working class of

Russia cannot remain in power and convert its temporary domination into a lasting socialistic dictatorship' (Trotsky 1971b: 237–8).

Russia in the Revolution

In 1909 Trotsky published a collection of articles from the period of the 1905 revolution under the title of *Russia in the Revolution* (*Russland in der Revolution*). The first four chapters: 'Russia's Social Development and Tsarism', 'Russian Capitalism', 'The Peasantry and the Agrarian Question' and 'The Driving Forces of the Revolution' considerably expanded on the historical section of *Results and Prospects*, and in so doing developed the theory of permanent revolution by supporting it with empirical data. The result was to produce an interpretation of Russian history that had permanent revolution at its core.

The first chapter, 'Russia's Social Development and Tsarism' provides an explanation of why the Russian State played such a dominant part in the country's history. Here Trotsky repeats what he had said in *Results and Prospects*: that under military pressure from its Western neighbours, the Russian State had been compelled to develop its industry and technology. In *Russia in the Revolution* he elaborates on how relentless the State was in building up its resources for external defence. It imposed arbitrary taxes on the peasants, which at all times were intolerably heavy and to which the population was unable to adapt itself. In an implicit reference to Chicherin's theory of the origins of the peasant commune, Trotsky adds that to collect the taxes, the State introduced the system of mutual responsibility in the villages (Trotsky 1909: 2).

Surveying modern history, Trotsky gives additional instances of the Russian State responding to military challenges from abroad. He alludes to Peter I's Northern War against Sweden, which obliged him to reorganize the infantry along new lines and to create a fleet. The Crimean War brought Russia into conflict with the economically most powerful European states – England and France – it then became necessary to reorganize the army on the basis of universal conscription. Fiscal and military requirements played a large part in the liberation of the peasants in 1861.

In its need for finance, the Russian State, from the time of Catherine II, relied increasingly on loans from abroad. Thenceforth the European stock exchange became increasingly the source from which tsarism drew its finances. The national debt grew to enormous proportions, so that by Trotsky's time of writing the interest on loans absorbed approximately a third of the treasury's net revenue (Trotsky 1909: 3).

As the Russian State absorbed a disproportionately large part of the surplus product, it inhibited the formation of social estates in the country. European absolutist monarchies reached the height of their power when the feudal aristocracy and the emergent bourgeoisie were equally balanced, and the monarchy could play one off against the other. In Russia, it was not the equilibrium of the economically dominant classes but their weakness that made the Russian bureaucratic autocracy a self-contained organization. In this respect, Trotsky judged, tsarism represented an intermediate form between European absolutism and Asian despotism, being closer to the latter than to the former (Trotsky 1909: 4).

Trotsky's conclusion was that the administrative, military and financial might of absolutism, which enabled it to continue existing after it had outlived its original purpose 'despite and against social development', not only did not exclude the possibility of revolution but also, on the contrary, made revolution the only possible outcome. Moreover, the fact that the growing power of absolutism was constantly widening the gulf between itself and the popular masses guaranteed that the revolution would bear an extremely radical character (Trotsky 1909: 6).

In the chapter on 'Russian Capitalism' Trotsky emphasizes the rapidity with which large-scale industry has been introduced into Russia by foreign investment, encouraged by the State. Whereas only 15 per cent of existing Russian industrial enterprises were created before 1861, 40 per cent had appeared during the last decade. There was no question of this industrial growth being 'natural' or organic. It did not evolve gradually out of small-scale artisan industries because the development of these industries had been prevented by the influx of foreign capital and technology. The industry that was imported into Russia was the most modern, the result of centuries of technological development in Western Europe. This was transported to Russia ready-made, so that Russia had no need to undergo all the social and economic transformations that had gone into its creation in the West.

As foreign enterprises in Russia tended to be large-scale industries, the workforce they employed was correspondingly large. Unlike the peasants, who were scattered over the entire countryside, the young Russian proletariat was concentrated in large masses in the factories and industrial centres. The possibility for concerted action by the proletariat was much greater than for the peasantry (Trotsky 1909: 12–14).

Trotsky's treatment of the 'Peasantry and the Agrarian Question' makes it clear that there can be no suggestion that the countryside might be the source of an indigenous development of capitalism. Because peasant agriculture provided most of the State's budget, which went towards defence and to subsidize foreign firms, the peasants were taxed to such an extent that not only were they left without any surplus but they were also in permanent arrears. They had no means of farming more efficiently, as this would have required financial resources that were unavailable. In these circumstances no social differentiation took place; in the 'black earth zone', Russia's main agricultural area, there was only an equality of poverty.

According to Trotsky, in the Russian countryside there were five million men who could not find employment, as there was insufficient industry to absorb them. On the other hand, the poverty of the villages meant that the domestic expansion of industry was unthinkable without the expansion of the home market and an increase in the purchasing power of the population (Trotsky 1909: 14, 17).

In the fourth chapter, 'The Driving Forces of the Revolution', Trotsky presents what he believes are the implications for the future of the revolution which flow from his survey of the classes and groups in Russian society. He thinks that the bourgeoisie, whether foreign or indigenous, the intelligentsia and the peasantry are all incapable of being an effective opposition to the autocratic regime. Only the proletariat is capable of being the driving force of revolution, and in this sense the Russian revolution is a proletarian revolution. Unlike in *Results and Prospects*, in *Russia in the Revolution* there is no mention of the proletariat requiring international support (Trotsky 1909: 24–37).

One can see that the dynamic behind Trotsky's version of modern Russian history is to show that Russia's indigenous social and economic development is weak, and that this precludes any social class but the proletariat organizing a successful revolution and coming to power. Trotsky wishes to show that any substantive economic development that there has been has come from outside, and that the proletariat is the product of the transfer of foreign capitalism to Russian soil.

This version of Russian economic history is the direct opposite of Lenin's in his *Development of Capitalism in Russia*. Lenin was at pains to emphasize that Russian capitalist development was entirely indigenous, that Russia was a country in which commodity production prevailed, and that capitalist relations in the countryside were causing the stratification of peasant society. Trotsky, on the other hand, takes the view that foreign investment in the Russian economy has made the development of indigenous capitalism impossible. His arguments for this bring him close to the findings of Marx, Danielson and Vorontsov on the obstacles to the circulation of capital in Russia: the purchasing power of the peasantry is too weak to provide a market for Russian industry; peasants are uprooted from the land, but are unable to find work in industry.

For the purposes of his theory, Trotsky is inclined to emphasize external at the expense of internal development. But native capitalism was by no means insignificant, as in fact Trotsky concedes in the remark, 'The textile industry is less dependent on the State. That is why in 1905 Moscow, the textile city *par excellence*, showed a much fiercer, though not perhaps a more energetic, opposition to the autocratic bureaucracy than the Petersburg of the metalworkers' (Trotsky 1909: 26). The dynasties of Moscow merchants, such as the Guchkovs, the Konovalovs, the Krestovnikovs and Tretiakovs, formed an influential group in the economic and political life of the country. They looked with some disdain on the representatives of foreign capital for their supine attitude to the autocracy, and saw themselves as the genuine

Russian business elite. They would also play a prominent part in the 1917 revolution and were well represented in the Provisional Government.

Plekhanov's *History of Russian Social Thought*

Trotsky was not alone in regarding the Russian autocracy as a form of Oriental despotism; the idea appears in the Introduction to Plekhanov's main work of the time, his *History of Russian Social Thought*, which was published in 1914. Because Plekhanov held that all forms of thought were dependent on material conditions, that it was being which determined consciousness, he considered it necessary to place Russian intellectual development within the context of the country's social evolution. He therefore prefaced his work on intellectual history by an essay delineating the historical evolution of Russian society, presenting, in fact, Russian history from what he believed to be a Marxist point of view.

The most striking feature of Plekhanov's interpretation of Russian history is the enormous power and influence he attributes to the State. Indeed he likens the Russian autocracy to the despotisms of the Orient. His materialist method consisted in showing how such an Oriental despotism was produced by Russia's social and economic development. His explanation was that the strong, centralized State organization had emerged as a reaction to the incursions of nomadic and warlike peoples from the East. To account for its continued existence in later times Plekhanov argued that Russia had been a colonizing country, but one which had preserved a system of natural economy. Russia, in other words, had developed extensively but not intensively. Despite its success in colonizing new territories it had retained its ancient forms of social organization, its peasant communes, and these, in the opinion of Friedrich Engels had served as the pillars of despotism everywhere from India to Russia (Plekhanov 1925b: 84, 76–7).

Plekhanov's originality consisted in his characterization of Russia as an Oriental despotism; in other respects his interpretation of Russian history had much in common with those of earlier Russian historians such as Soloviev, Chicherin, and Kliuchevsky, all of whom had emphasized the dominant role of the State in Russian history. What is remarkable in this respect is that historians other than Plekhanov who attempted to provide a Marxist interpretation of Russian history, such as Rozhkov and Pokrovsky, believed that it was mistaken to start from the assumption that the Russian State was all-powerful and then with reference to social and economic factors to explain why this was so. They believed it was incumbent upon Marxist historians to show that the supposed independence of the State was illusory and that what was all-powerful were the economic factors which determined how the State functioned. They, naturally, considered Plekhanov's approach to be mistaken and un-Marxist.

Pokrovsky and merchant capitalism

From his earliest publications, Pokrovsky had contested the idea of a supra-class Russian autocracy, first as a liberal, and then as an adherent of 'economic materialism'. Following the 1905 revolution Pokrovsky had been a member of Bogdanov's *Vpered* (Forward) group, but had left it due to disagreements with Bogdanov over Proletarian Culture. He then allied with Trotsky, collaborating with him on the newspaper *Nashe slovo* (Our Word) during the First World War. Around this time Pokrovsky adopted the theory that the actions of tsarism had been motivated by the interests of merchant capital. Following the October revolution Pokrovsky occupied a leading position in the Soviet regime, being Lunacharsky's deputy at the Commissariat of Education. Pokrovsky had raised no objections to Trotsky's *The Revolution in Russia*, while it remained in its German version, but when it appeared in Russian in 1922 under the title of *1905*, it could not be ignored. Trotsky's scheme of Russian history, like Plekhanov's, was the diametrical opposite of what Pokrovsky had long held. Moreover, Trotsky's version of Russian history contradicted what Pokrovsky taught to his students. The problem, as Pokrovsky saw it, was that:

> Trotsky's book will be *studied*. And we are dealing with an author whose *every* word carries extraordinary weight, whose every pronouncement in the book will be imprinted on thousands of young minds. And due to the lapidary-artistic style in which the book is written, the impression will be so lasting that it will not be erased by the dozens of books that are written with less artistic talent and by authors who carry less authority. (Pokrovsky 1925: 21)

It was incumbent upon Pokrovsky to produce some kind of reply, and this he did in a review article on Trotsky's book, entitled 'Is It True that in Russia Absolutism Existed in Spite of Social Development?'

Pokrovsky opened this review with the declaration that, 'Like every scheme, which is clear and distinct, Trotsky's scheme is easily memorised and assimilated. And this is a great pity. For, first, this scheme is not ours; and second, it is objectively wrong' (Pokrovsky 1933: 133). What, he asks, is this scheme but that which Miliukov put forward without, and Struve with, Marxist terminology, and which has been so recently resurrected by Plekhanov's Introduction to the *History of Russian Social Thought*? According to Pokrovsky, the theory of the supra-class State was in keeping with the liberal policies of Kadets, like Miliukov, or with Mensheviks who sympathized with the Kadets, like Plekhanov. But how was the theory to be reconciled with Bolshevik calls to the proletariat to seize power from the bourgeoisie, when the bourgeoisie did not have power? It seemed to Pokrovsky that: 'We must fight most decisively against this theory, no less energetically than we now fight against religious prejudices. I say further: it is less important to prove that there was no historical Jesus Christ than that a supra-class State never existed in Russia' (Pokrovsky 1933: 135).

It is to Trotsky's merit, Pokrovsky considers, that he has not simply reproduced the argument about the centralized State being formed to protect Russia against the incursions of the Tatars, but he has substituted 'the pressure of Lithuania, Poland and Sweden'. But, Pokrovsky enquires, what could their motives be for attacking Russia? Citing memoirs of visitors to Russia in the sixteenth century, Pokrovsky argues that Russia in the period was a country in which trade was well developed, and in which the tsar and the ruling classes were involved. To Pokrovsky the conflicts with Lithuania, Poland and Sweden that Trotsky had mentioned were ones for Russia to secure trade routes, and it was for this purpose that military modernization was needed.

From the facts adduced, Pokrovsky concludes that to speak of Russia's backwardness missed the point; Russia was 'a new country seized with the development of merchant capitalism, and that it was necessary for it to find a place in the sun along with other, well established competitors. For this Russian merchant capitalism had to rule the country with iron discipline and form a veritable dictatorship. The incarnation of this dictatorship of merchant capital was the Muscovite autocracy' (Pokrovsky 1933: 141–2).

Trotsky's reply to Pokrovsky's review took the form of an article entitled 'Concerning the Peculiarities of Russia's Historical Development'. It appeared in two parts, in *Pravda* for 1 and 2 July 1922. It was an article which Trotsky later reproduced as an appendix to the second edition of *1905* and, later still, to all editions of his *The History of the Russian Revolution*. Trotsky, with reason, obviously considered the question of very great importance, for, in his own words: 'In 1922 Pokrovsky came down upon the historic conception of the author which lies at the basis of the theory of permanent revolution' (Trotsky 1934: 471). Trotsky, no doubt, answered Pokrovsky at such length because it was an opportunity to restate his theory, this time following the successful October revolution, which he took to be a vindication of his ideas. Now he was able to pose the question in terms of how it came about that the proletariat could come to power in a backward country like Russia.

Trotsky conceded that Plekhanov's presentation of Russia's historical development was very close to his own, but thought it false to claim that Plekhanov had used this scheme to justify a bloc with the Kadets. Plekhanov had not drawn the conclusion from it that it was possible for the proletariat to come to power in Russia, but then neither had he drawn any conclusion from another of his unquestionably correct propositions, namely: 'The Russian revolutionary movement will triumph as a working class movement or it will not triumph at all.'

As Trotsky observed: 'Pokrovsky ... flatly denies the primitiveness and backwardness of our economic development, and therewith consigns the

peculiarities of Russian historical development to the realm of legend.'
In Trotsky's view the reason for this oversight was that Pokrovsky was
completely hypnotized by the comparatively extensive development of trade
noticed by him, and also by Rozhkov, in sixteenth-century Russia (Trotsky
1971a: 334).

Perhaps the most telling, and certainly the most vivid, part of Trotsky's
refutation of Pokrovsky was his way of challenging the validity of the
assumption that a high development of trade necessarily denoted economic
progress. This he did, not by reference to history, but to his own experience
of trading during his exile in Siberia, and his acquaintance with a 'dictator
of merchant capitalism'.

> My Siberian employer (in whose office ledger I entered poods and arshins
> for a period of two months), Yakov Andreevich Chernykh ... was in
> practically unlimited control of economic life in the Kirensk district by
> virtue of his trade operations. He bought furs from the Tungus natives,
> he bought church lands from priests in remote districts, and he sold them
> cotton and, especially, vodka ... He was illiterate, but a millionaire (in the
> currency of the time). His dictatorship as a representative of merchant
> capital was unquestioned; he even spoke of the local indigenous
> population as 'my little Tungus folk.' The town of Kirensk . . . was a
> place of residence for police officers of various rank, kulaks in a state of
> hierarchical dependence on one another, a variety of petty government
> officials, and a handful of wretched artisans. I never found any organised
> artisanal trade there as a basis of urban economic life – no corporations,
> no guilds, although Yakov Andreevich was officially listed as a 'merchant
> of the second guild'. (Trotsky 1971a: 336)

By his personal reminiscence Trotsky made the point that his former
employer, who was the living embodiment of the 'dictatorship of merchant
capital' that Pokrovsky spoke of, operated in conditions of extreme
economic backwardness.

Trotsky expressed surprise that Pokrovsky had objected only to the
first chapter of his book, which dealt with tsarism, and not the second,
which was concerned with Russian capitalism, which was also a product
of Russia's economic backwardness. Russian capitalism did not develop
from artisanal trade via the manufacturing workshop to the factory for
the reason that European capital, first in the form of merchant capital and
later in the form of financial and industrial capital, flooded the country at
a time when most Russian artisanal trade had not yet separated itself from
agriculture. Hence the appearance in Russia of modern capitalist industry in
a primitive economic environment, the dominant role of Western European
capital in Russia's economy, and the consequent political weakness of the
Russian bourgeoisie. It was these factors that made the defeat of the Russian
bourgeoisie in 1917 possible (Trotsky 1971a: 339).

Now, in the aftermath of the revolution, Trotsky could add to his theory that Russian economic backwardness had left its mark on the proletariat. It did not have the traditions that Western workers had derived from the guilds; Russian workers had been hurled into the factory boiler straight from the plough. Hence their illiteracy, their lack of technical knowledge, of organization, of culture. These were problems the young Soviet government had to face.

Trotsky concluded by pointing out to Pokrovsky an important aspect of Russian backwardness that had contributed to the downfall of tsarism. This was the inability of the economy to respond adequately to the demands of military operations during the war. With the help of the Allies tsarism was able to deploy the most modern weaponry. But it did not have, and could not have, the means to reproduce these weapons. Nor did it have the means of transporting them with sufficient speed by rail or waterway. In this respect Russia was operating on a more primitive economic base than its enemies or allies (Trotsky 1971a: 344).

Following this exhaustive reply by Trotsky the rest of the polemic became more repetitive and more concerned with clarifying the respective standpoints, particularly on the question of whether tsarist Russia was a colony of the Western powers, a problem of major importance for Soviet historians later in the decade. In 1924 Trotsky published the essay 'Lessons of October', which questioned the right of some of the members of the Soviet leadership to exercise power. In the political struggles which followed Trotsky's dominant position in the regime gradually diminished.

That Pokrovsky's work played a great part in the struggle against 'Trotskyism' is acknowledged by Trotsky himself. In 1937 he recalled: 'The most prominent part in the struggle against "Trotskyism" was accorded to historical questions. These involved both the history of the development of Russia as a whole, as well as the Bolshevik party and the October Revolution in particular. The deceased M. N. Pokrovsky must unquestionably be acknowledged as the most authoritative Soviet historian. For a number of years, he waged, with a vehemence peculiar to him, a struggle against my general views on the history of Russia and especially my conception of the October Revolution. Everything written by the other "communist" critics on this theme was merely parroting the ideas of Pokrovsky' (Trotsky 1962: xxx).

Trotsky's final formulation of his theory of permanent revolution formed the introductory chapter entitled 'Peculiarities of Russia's Development' of his The History of the Russian Revolution published in 1931. This differed substantially from the corresponding chapter in Die Revolution in Russland and 1905. The differences can be accounted for by events that had taken place between 1922 and 1928. Although the dispute with Pokrovsky may have had political overtones, it was nevertheless an exchange of genuine scholarly opinion. One can see from the defence of permanent revolution that Trotsky wrote in response to a denunciatory article by Karl Radek in 1928 that subsequent attacks were entirely politically motivated, and misrepresented Trotsky's views in order to discredit them. The pamphlet in question, entitled *The Permanent Revolution*, reveals less about Trotsky's ideas than the scope and breadth of the campaign waged against them. Issues at stake were not just the application of Trotsky's theory to Russian history and politics but also to the programme and policies of the Communist International, in particular, to its policies in China. Much space in the pamphlet is devoted to the argument that Trotsky's ideas on revolution did not differ greatly from Lenin's, as his opponents argued they did (Trotsky 1971b: 1–157).

A prominent theme that runs through Trotsky's *The History of the Russian Revolution*, is that he, Trotsky, was always in full agreement with Lenin at the key junctures of 1917, and that all of the present-day leadership of the Russian Communist Party, Stalin, Bukharin, Kamenev, Zinoviev, disagreed with Lenin and opposed him. The lesson to be drawn was that, from the time he joined the Bolsheviks, Trotsky was the best Leninist. A telling accusation that Stalin had made in 1927 was that Trotsky did not subscribe to Lenin's dictum that 'Uneven economic and political development is a necessary law of capitalism'. Trotsky's task in the chapter on 'Russia's Historical Peculiarities' was to show that on this theoretical level too, he did not diverge from Lenin.

In the chapter, Trotsky registers his agreement that unevenness is 'the most general law of the historical process'. This declaration brings him into line with Lenin, but the function Trotsky assigns to unevenness is that of a general framework: the assumption that countries develop to different levels at different paces. Trotsky argues that from this universal law of unevenness one can derive another law which he calls the 'law of combined development'. This is a heading under which Trotsky can assemble the ideas which he formerly referred to as 'permanent revolution' (Thatcher 1991: 247–8).

Some of what appears in 'Russia's Historical Peculiarities' is familiar from previous versions of Trotsky's interpretation of Russian history, but there are some significant differences. One is that a much smaller role is assigned to foreign capital in Russia's economic development, and a greater one to indigenous economic development. Here Trotsky does not contend that the rise of commercial towns was forestalled by the influx of foreign capital, but by the fact that at the first sign of crowding, Russian peasants would go deeper into the forest or spread out over the steppe. In this respect Trotsky borrows from Plekhanov the theory of Russia as a country which colonizes at the expense of intensive economic development.

Another difference was in the tone in which Russia's historical peculiarities were treated: now they were presented as a particular instance of a more general law.

Although compelled to follow after the advanced countries, a backward country does not take things in the same order. The privilege of historic backwardness – and such a privilege exists – permits, or rather compels, the adoption of whatever is ready in advance of any specified date, skipping a whole series of intermediate stages. Savages throw away their bows and arrows for rifles all at once, without travelling the road which lay between those two weapons in the past. (Trotsky 1934: 26–7)

This change in focus was understandable, because in recent years Trotsky had been applying his theory to countries other than Russia, to China in particular.

Trotsky repeats that under pressure from the wealthier Europe the Russian State swallowed up a far greater relative part of the people's wealth than in the West, so weakening the position of the possessing classes, and allowing the Russian State to become almost an Asiatic despotism. However, there is no emphasis on the power and independence of the State, and no suggestion that it could be utilized to transform society. This would have contradicted Lenin's contention that in socialist society the State would 'wither away'. Also, in accord with Lenin's thinking, Trotsky attributes a major historic role to the Soviets, which he compares to that played by the Bible in the Puritan Revolution in England and the idea of pure democracy in the French Revolution (Trotsky 1934: 36–7).

It is also noticeable that in his 1931 chapter, Trotsky does not say that it was the weakness of the Russian bourgeoisie that brought the proletariat to power. But he does use the weakness of the bourgeoisie in another connection. This is to explain that in the failed Decembrist uprising of 1825 it was the progressive elements among the nobility that took the place of the bourgeoisie to limit the powers of the autocracy. Similarly, bourgeois liberalism played a very minor part in the liberation of the peasants in 1861. It was the landlords who owned factories who were the first to favour replacing serfdom by wage labour, and the reform was carried out by the bureaucracy aided by liberal landlords. According to Trotsky, the lesson to be drawn from these episodes is that, 'The solution of the problems of one class by another is one of those combined methods natural to backward countries' (Trotsky 1934: 30). This conclusion is not followed by any statement to the effect that in the case of the proletariat, no other class or group can effect its emancipation. Far from opposing 'substitutionism', Trotsky had incorporated it into his theory of permanent revolution.

8

Theories of imperialism

If capitalism had become the universal system, embracing every corner of the globe, as Marx had originally envisaged it would, the question of imperialism, as it emerged on the eve of the First World War, would never have arisen. The world market would have brought homogeneity into the various national economies, and a socialist society would have been created on an international scale. But, as Marx discovered, capitalism did not carry all before it in a village, let alone throughout the world. Given the presuppositions of his system, Marx did not expect to have to explain the phenomenon of imperialism, and this task fell to his successors.

Although works on imperialism by socialist writers of the time have been regarded simply as attempts to explain the phenomenon, to determine why capitalism should evolve in this particular way, this was only one of the aims these writers pursued. Much more pressing was the question of what the implications of this latest phase for the emergence of a socialist society were. The investigation of imperialism or finance capitalism was the form in which prognoses about how socialism would come about were framed.

Rosa Luxemburg

The work on imperialism which is most clearly in keeping with Marx's line of investigation was Rosa Luxemburg's *The Accumulation of Capital*, published in 1913 (Luxemburg 2003). Much of this work is devoted to an analysis of the failure of previous writers to give a satisfactory account of the expanded reproduction of capital. Luxemburg's survey begins with Marx himself, whose mathematical reproduction schemes she analyses in considerable detail (Luxemburg 2003: 79–127). She points out elsewhere, however, that the second volume of *Das Kapital* in which accumulation is discussed is not a finished work, but a manuscript that breaks off half-way through, and so cannot be considered Marx's final word on the subject (Luxemburg 1981: 434). Luxemburg then expounds the solutions proposed by later economic thinkers, such as Tugan-Baranovsky, Struve, Bulgakov and Danielson, and finds them unconvincing (Luxemburg 2003: 145–306).

Luxemburg's own solution to the question of expanded reproduction of capital comes in the section of *The Accumulation of Capital* which begins with the chapter entitled 'The Struggle against the Natural Economy'. Here one encounters Kovalevsky's conception of the two types of factor responsible for the dissolution of primitive communities: slow internal disintegration and the rapid disruption caused by the interference of capitalist powers. Capitalism cannot wait for the primitive communities to dissolve of their own accord; it needs to assimilate them in order to accumulate, but as the natural economy is a barrier to its progress it conducts a war of annihilation against it. According to Luxemburg, the principal methods employed in this struggle are political force (revolution, war), oppressive taxation by the State and cheap goods (Luxemburg 2003: 349).

Luxemburg then proceeds to illustrate these processes with two case studies taken from Kovalevsky's *Communal Landownership*: those of the British in India and the French in Algeria. In both instances the resilience of the traditional communities with their common ownership of land had been overcome by the persistent attacks of the occupying powers. Only with the arrival of the British did the Indian village community, which had survived centuries of war and conquest, finally capitulate when the blight of capitalist civilization succeeded in disrupting the entire social organization of the people. The British artificially created a landed aristocracy at the expense of the ancient property rights of the peasant communities. In Algeria, the French pursued a similar policy in their systematic and deliberate attempts to destroy communal property and establish private property in land, which could then become the object of speculation by the French colonists (Luxemburg 2003: 355–8).

In generalizing from these and other historical examples, Luxemburg concluded that non-capitalist organizations provided fertile soil for capitalism; that capital fed on the ruins of such organizations. She believed that the non-capitalist milieu was indispensable for the accumulation of capital, that the accumulation of capital was a kind of metabolism between the capitalist economy and the pre-capitalist methods of production in which the latter were corroded and assimilated by the former. The implication was that 'capital cannot accumulate without the aid of non-capitalist organisations, nor, on the other hand, can it tolerate their continued existence side by side with itself. Only the continuous and progressive disintegration of non-capitalist organisations makes accumulation of capital possible' (Luxemburg 2003: 397).

The solution to the problem of expanded reproduction of capital that Luxemburg had proposed had earlier been available to Marx. He had been in possession of Kovalevsky's book since 1879 and had studied it thoroughly. Moreover, he was extremely knowledgeable about the evolution of village communities, and especially of the Russian peasant commune, from his extensive reading in the subject. Why did he not use these materials to complete volume two of *Das Kapital* along the lines of Luxemburg's *The Accumulation of Capital*?

Marx's notes on Kovalevsky's book suggest the answer to this question. For Marx the lesson that emerged from Kovalevsky's study was that primitive communities were extremely resilient; they could even withstand contact with capitalism. Where disintegration had taken place, this was through the deliberate actions of occupying powers. In other words, what destroyed pre-capitalist forms of organization were political, rather than economic processes. Moreover, one can see from all of Marx's drafts for volume two of *Das Kapital*, the kind of exposition he envisaged; it would be in terms of an internal dynamic or 'dialectic' of the economic categories. It would have defeated his purpose to resort to an explanation involving wars and revolutions, as Luxemburg had done. And so long as his preferred approach was not available to him, Marx chose to suspend the completion of volume two (White 2016: 117–19).

Hilferding

The work of the Austrian Marxist Rudolf Hilferding, *Das Finanzkapital*, appeared in 1910, and had become extremely influential on socialists at the time of the First World War. Hilferding conceived his book as an extension of Marx's analysis of capitalism to recent economic developments. These developments included the emergence of industrial trusts, cartels and syndicates which limited the play of free-market competition and tended towards monopoly; the erection of high tariff-barriers; the export of capital to undeveloped countries, and increasing rivalry among the capitalist nations to secure spheres of influence in different parts of the world.

Hilferding believed that the factor which explained these phenomena was the emergence of finance capital as a driving force behind recent economic developments. It was industry's need for credit that had given the banks such importance in the economies of capitalist countries, and it was this which had caused industrial and finance capital to coalesce. Any firm that had a guaranteed source of credit had an enormous advantage over the isolated entrepreneur. It was therefore more capable of withstanding crises than its competitors. In the modern world the successful company was one which was linked to finance capital.

Whereas formerly capital had demanded free trade and non-intervention from the State, finance capital sought to dominate markets, and called upon the State to erect tariff barriers to protect its monopolies. When tariff barriers were raised in other countries, finance capital replied by exporting capital in order to set up production behind them. In less developed countries too labour was cheap, and so could be employed to produce values, and thereby counter the tendency of the profit-rate to fall.

The export of capital, in Hilferding's view, was an important factor in equalizing the level of economic development throughout the world. It was one of the positive features in the recent evolution of capital with which he was especially concerned. For him, it appeared that modern capitalism was evolving in a direction that would make the emergence of socialism a distinct possibility. The concentration of the economy had put its central control within easy reach. The fact that industry was dominated by the banks meant that a central bank could exercise control over the whole of social production (Hilferding 1923: 218). In Germany, for example, taking possession of the six large Berlin banks would mean taking possession of the most important branches of larger-scale industry, and would greatly facilitate the initial phases of socialist policy (Hilferding 1923: 473).

It seemed to Hilferding that the contemporary evolution of capitalism was preparing the way for a socialist economy by its tendency towards central regulation. This already existed in what Hilferding called an 'antagonistic form'; it would only remain for a socialist society to render this form benign. In Hilferding's view, if the process of cartelization were taken to its logical conclusion, and only a single cartel remained, then all the characteristic features of the capitalist economy, the fetishism of commodities, the role of money and the reification of relations between people, would cease to exist. As he explained:

> The end result of this process would be the emergence of a general cartel. The whole of capitalist production would be consciously regulated from a single body which would determine the volume of production in all its spheres. Then the determination of prices would be purely nominal and would mean nothing more than the distribution of the total product between the capitalist magnates on the one hand and all the rest of the members of society on the other. Price would then cease to be the result of a reified relationship into which people have entered, but a mere means of accounting and distribution of things by people for people. Money would then play no part. It could disappear altogether, because it is concerned with the distribution of things and not with the distribution of values. The illusion of the objective value of the commodity would disappear along with the anarchy of production, as also would money. (Hilferding 1923: 473)

The extension of the sphere of finance capital also implied that when the socialist revolution came it would be on an international scale. According to Hilferding, 'The proletariat must see that the imperialist policy generates revolution ... and with it the conditions for the victory of socialism' (Hilferding 1923: 471).

In Hilferding's view, finance capital had been singularly successful in winning over the support of most classes in society. This, moreover, applied to the working class, among whom there had emerged a new group, of highly skilled and well-paid salaried workers, whose careers depended on subservience to finance capital. It was the members of this group that most easily became infected with the ideology of imperialism (Hilferding 1923: 444–7).

Thus, from Hilferding's analysis it emerged that finance capital was preparing the ground for the socialist society in two ways: (1) intensively – by the rationalization and centralization of the economy through monopolies to make it amenable to governmental regulation; (2) extensively – by spreading the capitalist economy throughout the world, thus making possible a socialist revolution on an international scale. These were aspects of Hilferding's work which Bukharin, Lenin and other radical socialist thinkers of the time found stimulating and encouraging.

Kautsky

Karl Kautsky published an article entitled 'Imperialism' in *Die neue Zeit* on the eve of the First World War. His first concern in this article was to clarify what the term 'imperialism' meant. Many people used it to designate all the phenomena of modern capitalism – cartels, tariff-barriers, the dominance of finance and the policy of colonialism. This was a usage which linked capitalism necessarily to imperialism. Kautsky, however, pointed out that attempts by nations to extend their territory were as old as written history: that imperialism was the product of highly developed capitalism – the impulse of an industrialized capitalist nation to acquire and annex an increasing amount of agrarian area (Kautsky 1914: 908–9).

This impulse, Kautsky thought, was to be explained by the interchange between agriculture and industry in modern capitalist society. These two sectors of the economy had to work in concert in order to maintain an equilibrium between the means of production and the means of consumption. Whereas this balance had been relatively easy to maintain in the early stages of capitalism, as industry developed, agriculture was increasingly unable to keep pace with its demands, resulting in industrial crises. The solution to the difficulty was to expand the area assigned to agriculture. This was the motive for the acquisition by industrial powers of territories overseas (Kautsky 1914: 916–17).

As there were now several highly industrialized nations competing for overseas agrarian territories, the old era of free trade had come to an end, and each country tried to protect its domain with high tariff barriers. This was the process which had given rise to imperialism. The same process, in Kautsky's view, also spread industrialization to the undeveloped world. For to exploit efficiently its raw materials, the industrialized power had to build railways and other installations, thus raising the economic level of the agrarian territories annexed (Kautsky 1914: 919).

The competition for agrarian territory had given rise to the rivalries among the great powers that had culminated in the present war. But was war an inevitable consequence of imperialism? Kautsky thought not. He could foresee that in the post-war era capitalists would have learnt from experience that war was inimical to their interests and must be avoided at all costs. From a purely economic point of view, Kautsky reasoned, capitalism would come to an end only when all the areas for its agrarian expansion had been exhausted. This was still far from being the case, and the position would not be changed by the war. The possibility remained, therefore, that after the war the great industrial nations would come to an agreement and bring an end to the arms race. This, Kautsky believed, might usher in a new economic era in which the monopolist tendencies in capital would be played out in the sphere of foreign relations. The new 'ultra-imperialism' would be opposed as resolutely as imperialism had been; but in this case the danger of war would have been removed (Kautsky 1914: 920–1).

Like Hilferding, Kautsky believed that the preconditions for socialism were developing within capitalism. But he was aware of a dilemma which this posed: the economic tendency towards annexation of agrarian territories was at variance with the democratic principle, which he held to be essential to the cause of the proletariat. Kautsky was to conclude that although in modern times capitalism had outgrown national boundaries, this need not necessarily lead to the subjection of weak nations by the strong. The interests of capital could be equally, or better, served by close economic ties between economically advanced countries. There should be free unions of equal states. The example for the states of Europe was the United States of America. The peace programme of Social Democracy, Kautsky thought, should be the formation of the United States of Europe (Kautsky 1915: 75).

Kautsky found that his conception of imperialism differed from those of both the left and the right wings in the German Social-Democratic Party. Both groups understood imperialism as the latest form of capitalism. But whereas the Right concluded from this that imperialism should be supported, as a necessary stage on the route to socialism, the Left saw imperialism as the final form of capitalism, and something which should therefore be overthrown forthwith to give way to the socialist system. Kautsky thought both points of view mistaken, because he held that imperialism was neither necessary nor final (Kautsky 1915: 17).

Trotsky

In the years of exile after the 1905 revolution Trotsky had associated with the leading theoreticians of both German and Austrian socialism. These included Kautsky and Hilferding. The intellectual relationship between Kautsky and Trotsky was a close one, but one which the latter chose not to emphasize in later years, since Kautsky had been denounced by Lenin (Trotsky 1974: 24–7). This consideration made Trotsky rather evasive about what his ideas on imperialism had been during the First World War.

Accordingly, the most revealing articles on this subject were never reprinted in his collected works. Nevertheless these supply a valuable insight into what Trotsky's ideas were on the eve of the 1917 revolution.

Hilferding's and Kautsky's conceptions had an obvious attraction for Trotsky because they served to confirm that the coming revolution would necessarily be an international one. This, Trotsky thought, was ensured by the way capitalism had become international in recent times.

> By breaking down the boundaries of nation states to prevent their restricting the development of productive forces, the war destroys them also as a base for social revolution. (Trotsky 1915)

He considered too that within the new monopoly capitalism there were the elements of a regulated socialist economy:

> The direction of this new process is centripetal; it is a process attended by the introduction of rational control and centralised accounting into the blind play of economic forces. This applies not only to the competition between private companies within one nation, but to that between national economies on a world scale. (Trotsky 1915)

Trotsky was especially attracted to Kautsky's conception of a United States of Europe. It was this, he thought, that would be created by the conquest of power by the proletariat.

> The democratic unification of Europe, the creation of a United States of Europe, is the only political form by which the proletariat can resolve the irreconcilable contradiction between modern forces of production and the national exclusiveness of the State organisation. (Trotsky 1915)

Trotsky believed that the creation of a United States of Europe by the socialist revolution would allow the establishment of a dictatorship of the proletariat on an international scale. He envisaged this as being accomplished by a seizure of political power by the proletariat:

> Four and a half decades ago the French proletariat in the aftermath of the Franco-Prussian War anticipated in practice the dictatorship of the proletariat on a national basis. At the present time the problem of social revolution confronts us if not as a world problem in the full sense of the word, then at least as a European one. Every revolutionary movement in its initial stages inevitably strives to break out of its national confines and find the guarantee of its own success in the parallel movements of the proletariat in other countries. The political struggle for social revolution means for the proletariat the struggle for State power. Whereas in 1871, following the experience of the Commune, Marx quite correctly wrote that

the proletariat could not simply and mechanically take over the bourgeois State, but had to transform it according to its own purposes, now we can say that the main direction of this transformation must be the organisation of the dictatorship of the proletariat on an all-European scale, i.e. in the form of the republican United States of Europe. (Trotsky 1915)

What is significant in this passage is that it shows that during the war Trotsky still envisaged the coming revolution as one in which the proletariat would seize control of the State and use its power to bring about socialist transformation of the country. The lesson that he took from the experience of the Paris commune was that the seizure of state power should be on a Europe-wide basis.

Skvortsov-Stepanov

The Russian translation of Hilferding's *Finanzkapital* appeared in 1912. In the following year the translator, Skvortsov-Stepanov, published an article entitled 'Imperialism' in the September and October issues of the Bolshevik journal *Prosveshchenie* (Enlightenment). Skvortsov-Stepanov had collaborated with Bogdanov in translating the three volumes of Marx's *Das Kapital* into Russian and, along with Bogdanov, was engaged in writing a textbook on Marxist political economy (Bogdanov and Skvortsov-Stepanov 1910–25). His study of imperialism was intended to be a chapter of this work (Oreshkin 1968: 95). The article is of some historical significance because it considerably antedates both Bukharin's 'World Economy and Imperialism' (1915) and Lenin's *Imperialism the Highest Stage of Capitalism* (Lenin 1964b). It provides an interesting comparison with these latter two works, and gives an insight into how Bolshevik conceptions of imperialism evolved between 1913 and 1916.

Skvortsov-Stepanov began his article by indicating that he was bringing to the notice of his Russian readership a subject which had been given considerable attention by German socialists. It was one, he said, which explained not only contemporary international affairs, in particular the threat of a European war of unprecedented proportions, but also internal political developments, both in Russia and in Western Europe.

According to Skvortsov-Stepanov one of the most characteristic features of recent economic development was the growth of protectionism. Whereas tariff barriers had originally been designed to protect infant industries, they were now employed by highly developed industrial powers to keep prices high and to overcome competitors. He agreed with Hilferding that protectionism had been transformed from a defensive weapon of the weak into an offensive weapon of the strong (Skvortsov-Stepanov 1930: 261). This had been accompanied by the steady elimination of free competition and the growth of cartels and monopolies. These developments altered traditional relationships between internal and external markets.

The implications for the internal market of industrial cartels depended on the kind of industry in question. An industry such as textiles, which sold its goods to the consumer, was interested in maximizing the number of potential purchasers of its commodities. But for heavy industry, which supplied railways, ships and armaments, the main customer was the government, and it looked on the population of a given territory not as a market for its goods, but as taxpayers who would provide revenue to the State, which would then place orders with the cartels in heavy industry (Skvortsov-Stepanov 1930: 263).

High prices imposed limits on the home market, so that in order to expand its activities capital was forced to 'emigrate'. The emigration of capital could take place in commodity form, but the possibilities for expansion were increased if capital was exported to backward countries as loan capital. The loans would then extend exchange relations in that country, and this in turn would stimulate the demand for fresh loans and increase the capacity of the market for European goods. Emigration of capital was facilitated by the alliance in recent times of industry with the banks, a phenomenon which had been termed by Hilferding 'finance capital' (Skvortsov-Stepanov 1930: 272).

Industrial capital, Skvortsov-Stepanov pointed out, could also emigrate. The example he gave was Belgian capital, which had set up business in Russia. This gave scope for expansion, and meant that Russian tariffs, which had formerly been a barrier, now afforded protection to Belgian industrial concerns inside the country.

Capital was especially attracted to those economically backward countries which were also politically weak. These could be turned into colonies of the economically developed country. Political control of a territory was an effective means of exploiting it while excluding competitors from among other industrially developed nations. There was, however, competition among these nations for the possession of colonial territories. The resulting conflicts led to the European powers' strengthening their armed forces and thus placing fresh orders with the industrial cartels for armaments for their fleets and armies. As a result of the increased militarization more taxes were levied on the population in the home country, and the consumer market was further constricted (Skvortsov-Stepanov 1930: 274–9).

Imperialism also produced its own social basis of support. This was in the mass of functionaries and officials it generated as a result of imperialist activity. It was from among these that the ideologists of imperialism came, people who presented the appetites of finance capital with a quasi-philosophical gloss. Usually this took the form of emphasizing the national identity of the imperialist power and ascribing to it a historical mission of conquest and domination (Skvortsov-Stepanov 1930: 280).

In the long term imperialism undermined its own foundations. The presupposition of the emigration of capital was the difference in economic level between the highly developed metropolitan country and the backward

agrarian territory to which capital was exported. But in emigrating to
a backward country, European capital gave a stimulus to economic
development, and this would eventually even out the difference in economic
level, which had originally prompted capital to emigrate. The receipt of loans
and the introduction of industry encouraged the growth of an indigenous
bourgeoisie in the colonial country. And with this came the beginnings of a
popular movement which strove to achieve national independence from the
imperialist power. The popular movement, according to Skvortsov-Stepanov:

> undergoes a swift evolution, from the reactionary aims of restoring the
> order which has irrevocably passed away, to the aims of agrarian socialism,
> that vague socialism which sees in the peasant-village backwardness of
> its own country especially favourable conditions for realising the ideals
> of Western socialism. And alongside this here and there (e.g. in India and
> Turkey) there even breaks through the modern proletarian struggle, the
> ground for which was prepared by the emigration of European industry.
> (Skvortsov-Stepanov 1930: 283)

Skvortsov-Stepanov considered that whatever the outcome of the
European revolutions, European capitalism had reached the limit of its
expansion. All that remained were the working out of the contradictions
inherent in imperialism: on the international arena the struggle between
rival powers for new annexations and new redivisions of economic territory,
and internally, the struggle between antagonistic social classes; on the one
side the supporters of a capitalist system that had outlived itself, and its
opponents on the other (Skvortsov-Stepanov 1930: 284–5).

Skvortsov-Stepanov's article contained elements and themes that would
be repeated in the works on imperialism by Bukharin and Lenin. These were
(1) that capitalism in modern times had changed from free competition to
monopoly, (2) that there was a new offensive role for tariff barriers, (3) that
modern capitalism was bank or finance capital, (4) that capital was exported,
(5) that the export of capital took place to developed as well as to backward
countries, (6) that there was competition between monopoly capitalist
powers for spheres of investment and colonies, (7) that imperialism created
a social group which supported imperialist activities, (8) that the export of
capital caused economic differences between countries to be reduced, and
(9) that imperialism was the final stage of capitalism and that socialism
would follow.

Bukharin

Bukharin's work 'The World Economy and Imperialism' first appeared in
the Bolshevik journal *Kommunist* in 1915. The political context had altered

considerably since Skvortsov-Stepanov had written his article on imperialism. War had broken out and the socialists of the Second International were divided on what their attitude to it should be. While a minority opposed the war and some took a pacifist position, the vast majority of Russian socialists characterized the war as 'defencist' and gave it their reluctant support. Plekhanov, however, was an ardent supporter of the Allied side and tried to recruit Russian émigrés in France for the war effort. Theories of imperialism in the war years began to reflect the tensions between the various groups and to acquire a polemical edge.

Bukharin does not refer explicitly to Bogdanov, but there is much in Bukharin's approach that is reminiscent of *Tectology*, a work that Bukharin admired. This emerges from Bukharin's remark that the conflicts of imperialism do not hang in the air; that they take place within a particular environment, this environment being the world economy. Bukharin goes on to interpret the disparate effects of finance capital in terms of the interrelation between the world economy and the individual national economies. He treats the relationship of the national economies to the world economy as an organic one, as the relationship of parts to the whole, as subsystems of a total organization. This allowed Bukharin to explain the increasing interdependence of national economies, and at the same time to explain conflict in terms of the divergent interests of the national units of which the world economy was composed.

Bukharin's article was a polemical one, directed against Kautsky and his ideas on 'ultra-imperialism'. In supposing such a development possible, Bukharin considered Kautsky to have overestimated the vitality of the capitalist system. For revolutionary Marxism, Bukharin considered, 'the whole of capitalist development is nothing more than the constant expanded reproduction of the contradictions of capitalism' (Bukharin 1915: 5).

Bukharin was insistent that the world economy and imperialism laid the foundations for a socialist order. Thus:

> The growth of world market connections proceeds apace, tying up various sections of the world economy into one strong knot, bringing ever closer to each other hitherto 'nationally' and economically isolated regions, creating an ever-broader base for the world socialist economy. (Bukharin 1915: 11)

He argued further that the processes of centralization and organization had created a strong tendency towards

> transforming the entire national economy into one gigantic combined enterprise under the tutelage of the financial kings and the capitalist State, an enterprise which monopolises the national market and forms the prerequisite for an organised socialist economy. (Bukharin 1915: 23)

It was also Bukharin's opinion that 'by its very existence an imperialist policy shows that the objective conditions for socialism have ripened' (Bukharin 1915: 44).

In the main, Bukharin's exposition followed Skvortsov-Stepanov's, though at several points Bukharin supplied considerably more factual detail. He noted the increasing internationalization of economic development, as evidenced by the appearance of international cartels and trusts. He also pointed out the dominant role of the banks, and the formation of finance capital by the coalescence of banking and industrial capital.

Like Skvortsov-Stepanov, Bukharin went on to argue that internationalization of capital did not mean the harmonization of interests. It did not put an end to competition for outlets for investment. And despite the tendencies towards cartelization and trustification capitalism retained its anarchic character. This was manifested in the disproportions between the various branches of production of the capitalist economy in general, and in particular between agriculture and industry (Bukharin 1915: 31).

Bukharin followed Hilferding in defining imperialism as the 'policy of finance capital' (Bukharin 1915: 35, 38). Like Hilferding and Skvortsov-Stepanov, he considered the export of capital to be characteristic of finance capital; he repeated Skvortsov-Stepanov's observation that inside another country it enjoyed the protection of the tariff barriers that the country had erected (Bukharin 1915: 32). Since the export of capital might involve the seizure of foreign territories and their subjugation to the monopolies, the imperialist policy of finance capital brought in its train conflicts on an international scale, which had culminated in the present war. The outcome of a finance-capitalist war, Bukharin reasoned, would be a proletarian revolution (Bukharin 1915: 38).

Although Bukharin conceded that there was a tendency towards the formation of a single world trust, as Hilferding had suggested, he believed that such a smooth route to a socialist society was unlikely. Bukharin's reasoning for this drew upon the methodology of Bogdanov's *Tectology*. His argument was that such an accord would require that the parties to the agreement hold equal or approximately equal positions in the world market. If this were not the case, then it would always be more beneficial for the stronger contestant to continue the competition. The chances of 'national' capitalist groupings ever achieving the necessary degree of economic and political parity Bukharin considered to be negligible (Bukharin 1915: 44–5). The arguments Bukharin had advanced against Hilferding's world trust also applied to the kind of 'ultra-imperialism' which Kautsky had in mind.

Bukharin expanded his article into a pamphlet, and in December 1915 Lenin supplied it with a preface. Besides expressing general approval for Bukharin's work, Lenin indicated which aspect of Bukharin's pamphlet he found most useful. This was the rebuttal of Kautsky's conception of imperialism, and what Lenin said on that subject contained the embryo of what he would write some months later in *Imperialism, the Highest Stage of Capitalism*. This was that:

> There is no doubt that the trend of development is towards a single world trust absorbing all enterprises without exception and all states without exception. But this development proceeds in such circumstances, at such a pace, through such contradictions, conflicts and upheavals … that inevitably imperialism will burst and capitalism will be transformed into its opposite long before one world trust materialises, before the 'ultra-imperialist', world-wide amalgamation of national finance capitals takes place. (Lenin 1969: 98)

Here Lenin accepts Bukharin's argument that finance capital is developing in the direction of an all-embracing world trust, but that this is unlikely to come about because the component elements are so diverse. Lenin, however, does not adopt Bukharin's tectological approach and terminology, but restates Bukharin's argument in more general terms.

In an article entitled 'The Imperialist Robber State' published in December 1916 in the journal *Die Jugend-Internationale* (The Youth International) Bukharin developed his ideas on finance capital in times of war. He began by pointing out that the slogan 'defence of the fatherland' was a misleading one, because in fact what was being defended was not the country or the population, but the State organization. Moreover, the State was a historical entity, an institution which had arisen as an organization of the ruling class for holding down and exploiting the oppressed class. It was, correspondingly, destined to disappear with the socialist revolution and the end of class rule. Here Bukharin recalled Engels's words in *Anti-Dühring* that the State would 'wither away' (Lenin 1972: 103).

In the era of finance capital, and especially during the war, the syndicates and economic monopolies had merged with the State apparatus and other organizations of bourgeois society to compose a modern Leviathan predatory State. State regulation of production was being introduced, so that the national economy was increasingly becoming a State economy. In these circumstances the proletariat would have to adjust its tactics to combat this formidable adversary, and it was the task of social-democrats, Bukharin maintained, to stress their hostility to the State in principle. 'He is a traitor to socialism', Bukharin declared, 'who, like the social-patriots of today, incites the workers to mutual extermination under the pretext of the defence of the fatherland, that in reality is an offensive action by the State, the mortal enemy of the socialist proletariat.' In order to dissociate himself from charges of anarchism Bukharin claimed that what distinguished socialists from anarchists was not that the former were in favour of the State while the latter were not, but that socialists advocated a centralized economy whereas anarchists called for a decentralized one (Lenin 1972: 103).

In a comment on Bukharin's article in the journal *Sbornik Sotsial-Demokrata* (The Social-Democrat's Miscellany) for December 1916, Lenin disputed Bukharin's distinction between socialists and anarchists. The appropriate distinction to be drawn in the question of the State, he maintained, was that socialists were in favour of utilizing the existing State and its institutions to effect the transition from capitalism to socialism. This transitional form was the dictatorship of the proletariat, which was also a State. The anarchists, on the other hand, wanted to abolish the State, to 'blow it up'. For socialists, the State would gradually wither away after the bourgeoisie had been expropriated. Lenin said that he intended to return to this important subject in a further article (Lenin 1964c: 165–6).

Lenin

According to Pokrovsky, who himself was involved in the project, Lenin's work on imperialism was conceived as the introductory volume to a series of booklets on the belligerent countries in the Great War. The series, which was sponsored by Gorky's journal *Letopis* (Chronicle) was aimed at a mass readership. These circumstances had an influence on the precise form Lenin's work was to take. Although intended as a critique of Kautsky, it could not be a purely polemical work. Its educational function demanded that it should have a systematic character, and because the editorial board of *Letopis* was favourably disposed towards Kautsky, adverse comment on the latter could not be a salient feature of the work. Accordingly, in the original version overt criticism of Kautsky was confined to the notes. Difficulties created by the war prevented this version being published, and Lenin's *Imperialism* only appeared in 1917. Although the published work could be rather more polemical than the original variant, the structure of the work remained unchanged (Pokrovsky 1969: 368–72).

The systematic form of *Imperialism* is apt to give the impression that Lenin, drawing upon the work of earlier writers such as Hobson, Bukharin and Hilferding, had formulated an independent theory of imperialism, which he then found to conflict with ideas espoused by Kautsky. In actuality the critique of Kautsky is what constitutes the central core of Lenin's theory of imperialism, and it is this which determines the way the work is structured.

Lenin began his exposition by restating ideas that had become generally accepted by socialists in recent years, namely that free competition had given way to monopoly, and that this had brought with it 'socialization of production', that is, a step in the transition towards socialism (Lenin 1964b: 205). This statement, however, was immediately followed by the observation that monopoly had by no means eliminated competition, and that between the two types of capitalism considerable friction was still bound to arise. From the start Lenin was concerned to demonstrate that the monopoly stage of capitalism did not bring with it the end of conflict in the economic sphere.

The next important point that Lenin wished to make was that in the latest stage of capitalism the banks had acquired a new role. Whereas formerly they had functioned as modest middlemen, now they had become powerful monopolies and had come increasingly to 'coalesce' (here Lenin used Bukharin's term) with industry. Industry in the monopoly stage of capitalism was dominated by the banks and by the financial oligarchies which controlled them (Lenin 1964b: 223).

A characteristic feature of monopoly capitalism, Lenin stated, was the export of capital. Whereas free-enterprise capitalism had exported commodities, monopoly capitalism exported capital. The motive was to acquire higher profits than could be earned at home. In more economically backward countries profits were high because labour, land and raw materials were cheap. The world had already been divided up into spheres of interest which were the special preserve of the various international cartels. Lenin was at pains to emphasize, however, that this division was by no means stable, and that as the relative strength of the capitalist groupings altered there would be competition for more advantageous shares (Lenin 1964b: 241–5).

And, like the international cartels, the various capitalist nations had already divided all the territories of the world up among themselves, so that no area remained unclaimed. What would follow could only be the struggle to redivide the world, once the balance of economic power changed. This it was bound to do, since Lenin believed that 'finance capital and trusts do not diminish, but increase the differences in the rates of growth between the various parts of the world economy' (Lenin 1964b: 274). Future prospects in this regard gave no hope of any lasting stability.

Lenin disagreed with Kautsky's definition of imperialism as 'the striving of every industrial capitalist nation to bring under its control or to annex all large areas of agrarian territory', since he considered that the characteristic of imperialism was its striving to gain control not only of agrarian territories, but even of the most highly industrialized regions. Kautsky's mistake had been to think of imperialism as driven by industrial, and not, as was the case, by finance capital (Lenin 1964b: 268).

This same characteristic of imperialism Lenin was to use to counter any prospect of the ultra-imperialism Kautsky had envisaged. He did this by arguing that monopoly capitalism was capitalism in decay. The financial oligarchy was a parasitic class or stratum of society which 'took no part in any enterprise whatsoever'. It made its living by exporting capital and by living on dividends. It had no interest in developing industry and, indeed, was quite capable of impeding technical innovation in order to safeguard its position. Finance capital was not a capital which showed prospects for future development. It was capitalism in decline, the final stage of capitalism before it was transformed into socialism (Lenin 1964b: 276–85).

Lenin concluded his argument by using his characterization of imperialism as finance capital to explain the failure of the international labour movement to oppose the current war. He stated that the receipt of high monopoly profits by the capitalists enabled them to pay relatively generous wages to a minority of the workforce, and so gain the support of this 'labour aristocracy'. It was this group which fostered 'opportunism' within the working-class movement, an 'opportunism' which found its most characteristic incarnation in the leadership of the Second International. This was an argument which adapted slightly Skvortsov-Stepanov's idea of a social stratum whose economic interests coincided to some extent with those of finance capital (Lenin 1964b: 283–5).

The theory of the 'labour aristocracy' and the conception of finance capitalism as capitalism in decay were ideas which had not been present in Bukharin's article. These reinforced the main idea common to both Bukharin and Lenin: that economic development proceeded unevenly and that, therefore, the world capitalist system would never reach a stage of perpetual stability, of 'ultra-imperialism'.

Although *Imperialism, the Highest Stage of Capitalism* was not published until 1917, as early as the summer of 1915 Lenin had made his views known on the uneven nature of capitalist development and the implications of this for the proletarian revolution. On that occasion his arguments were directed against the idea of a United States of Europe as envisaged by Kautsky and Trotsky. He pointed out that:

Uneven economic and political development is a necessary law of capitalism. It follows that the victory of socialism is, at the beginning, possible in a few capitalist countries, even in one, taken separately. The victorious proletariat of that country, having expropriated the capitalists and organised socialist production at home, would rise against the rest of the capitalist world. (Lenin 1964a: 342)

Clearly, it was assumed by both Lenin and Trotsky that the extent of the revolution would be determined by the limits of the capitalist, national or international, entity in which it took place. At that time, the point at issue between Lenin and Trotsky was on how far unification of these entities was possible. Lenin did not dispute Trotsky's idea that the aim of the proletariat should be the capture of State power, and that the latter should be achieved on a European scale. In the summer of 1915 Lenin himself still conceived of the 'dictatorship of the proletariat' in terms of centralized political control. The continuation of the passage quoted above, for example, is as follows:

The political form of a society in which the proletariat is victorious, in which it has overthrown the bourgeoisie, will be a democratic republic, centralizing ever more the forces of the proletariat of a given nation or nations in the struggle against the states that have not yet gone over to socialism. It is impossible to abolish classes without a dictatorship of the oppressed class, of the proletariat ... . (Lenin 1964a: 342)

At the end of 1915, therefore, there was still a great deal of consensus among Russian socialists about what a proletarian revolution would be. It would involve the seizure of power in one or more countries where finance-capitalist monopolies had laid the foundations of a planned economy. Even Lenin, who emphasized the uneven nature of capitalist development, accepted that there was a world market, and that although the transition to socialism would not take place in all countries simultaneously, but be a staged process, it was one which would eventually embrace all countries in the world.

Bogdanov

Skvortsov-Stepanov's article on 'Imperialism' had originally been intended as a chapter in the textbook on economics that he was writing in conjunction with Bogdanov. Bogdanov, however, had objected strongly to the chapter and refused to include it in the book. In the light of how Bogdanov viewed the economic causes of the war and how he viewed the collapse of the Second International one can deduce what he found reprehensible in Skvortsov-Stepanov's chapter. There were two main issues at stake. One was the theory that imperialism found support among the relatively highly paid stratum of workers who benefited from it. This was the stratum referred to as the 'workers' aristocracy', whose support for the war had led to the collapse of the Second International. In Bogdanov's opinion, what caused working-class support for the war was the weakness of a distinctly proletarian culture, which had led the working class to accept the values of the bourgeoisie.

The other point of contention was Hilferding's basic thesis: this was that finance capital, by subordinating the branches of industry to itself, was preparing the way for a future centrally directed socialist economy. In Bogdanov's view, the control exercised by the central banks over industry was by no means as decisive as Hilferding maintained. The banks in practice seldom intervened in the running of the economic units under their control, and that intervention was mostly indirect, through concealed economic pressure. 'However great', Bogdanov concluded, 'the economic power of finance capital, and however broad its field of operation, its real organizing function is less profound, the bond of its systems less close and firm than even in the lowest forms of cartels and syndicates. This bond is reminiscent of the vassal-suzerain relationship of loosely-connected feudal groupings' (Bogdanov and Skvortsov-Stepanov 1918: 142).

In an article entitled 'World Crises Peaceful and Military' serialized in the journal *Letopis* during the summer of 1916 Bogdanov set out what he considered to be the causes of the war and the reasons for the failure of socialist internationalism to prevent it. There were, he considered, three different forces involved. The first was that of the economic bonds, the mutual relations between buyers and customers. These bonds increased as international trade broadened and deepened. This growth necessarily slowed down as the world market was saturated and its extension to non-capitalist countries was completed, and the stage of constant distribution between states was reached.

The second of the purely economic forces was that of 'pressure', one that arose from the competition between different capitalist nation states for an increased share of the world market. The growth of the forces of pressure would necessarily accelerate as the world market approached saturation point. If the growth of the force of bonds slowed down and the growth of the force of pressure accelerated, then the difference between them would rapidly lessen. However, the catastrophe would not come when the two forces were exactly equal, but earlier, due to the operation of the third force, that of the military (Bogdanov 1916a: 115–17).

The military force also grew parallel with the increase in world competition between states. When the other two forces approached equilibrium, the build-up of military force would upset the balance and precipitate a military crisis. This sequence of events, according to Bogdanov, explained why the driving force of the crisis was the military element and why the war was unexpected by the capitalists of all countries, since the predominance of the economic forces was that of bonds.

For Bogdanov the war was a spontaneous phenomenon, comparable to the kind of crises of overproduction that occurred during peacetime. Whereas in peacetime crises had their origin in the overproduction of commodities, the war was a crisis of overproduction of organized human forces, in their manner characteristic of the capitalist state: in the form of militarism. The war would not end until this kind of overproduction, which had accumulated in the nation states of the world system, had been eliminated (Bogdanov 1916b: 153).

Bogdanov devoted considerable attention in 'World Crises, Peaceful and Military' to the question of proletarian culture. It was paradoxical, he said, that although one associated the bourgeoisie with individualism and anarchy, and the proletariat with organization and discipline, in fact the bourgeoisie had a much higher level of organization than the proletariat. This was shown by the fact that the bourgeoisie maintained a dominant position in society, and in particular their superior level of organization had been decisively demonstrated in the summer of 1914, when the Socialist International had collapsed and the workers had followed the bourgeoisie in supporting the war. According to Bogdanov, this was because the bourgeois culture was well established, while that of the proletariat was only in its infancy (Bogdanov 1916b: 135).

Bogdanov held that the organized nature of human collectives was determined by all the things that give them unity in the practical direction of thoughts and attitudes. This, moreover, was not done only by formal organizations. The organizing form was much wider and more general, and without it those organizations would not even be possible. This was the whole intellectual culture of the collectives: the combination of its customs, morals, laws, science and art. All this was combined in the world-outlook specific to the given collective.

When the great crisis broke out, the weakness of the new shoots of culture was immediately revealed, in their inability to play an independent role. The old bourgeois State culture, almost without opposition, carried the day, uniting its forces with nationalist-patriotic slogans. The internationalism of the working classes at once disintegrated, because it existed only as a feeling or an attitude of the masses; it could only be a real force to be reckoned with if it were the incarnation of a particular and integral mass culture (Bogdanov 1916b: 136). The implication of this analysis was that the working class needed its own culture to withstand that of the bourgeoisie, and that the creation of a specifically proletarian culture was a matter of urgency.

9

Marxism and revolution

The events of 1917 were a crucial episode in the development of Marxism in Russia. It was the occasion on which the various theories of socialism were tested against the actuality of revolution. In a country enervated by the strains of three years of war the tsarist autocracy had collapsed in February 1917. Its place was taken by a Provisional Government which consisted largely of former members of the State Duma. Simultaneously with the Provisional Government there had been formed the Petrograd Soviet by those members of the socialist parties who remained at liberty in the city. Both organizations faced the problems of how to deal with an economy in crisis and how to prosecute the war. On the latter issue the policy of the Provisional Government was to continue the war to a victorious conclusion; the Mensheviks and Socialist Revolutionaries who formed the majority on the Soviet were of the opinion that the war should be continued, but only as a defensive one, with no territorial annexations.

Marxism on the State

Stimulated by Bukharin's article on the 'Imperialist Robber State', during January and February 1917 Lenin intensively researched the question of the attitude of Marx and Engels to the State, noting down excerpts from their various published works and private correspondence. He also made notes from the polemic that Kautsky and Pannekoek had conducted on the subject of the State. The materials were contained in a notebook to which Lenin had given the title 'Marxism on the State'. This was, presumably, the title that he would have given to the finished article.

Lenin had got as far as drawing up the outline for his intended publication when the February revolution erupted in Russia. As a result, the work was written not in exile in Geneva but in Lenin's Finnish retreat of Razliv when he was forced to quit Petrograd after the 'July Days'. It was thus able to take account of the first six months of the revolution in Russia. The finished work, now extended into a pamphlet, bore the title of *The State and Revolution*, and was first published in 1918.

As it was published after the Bolsheviks came to power, it might appear that *State and Revolution* had no effect on the events of 1917. This is true insofar as the finished work could not reach an audience until the following year. But the ideas contained in it were ones that influenced Lenin's actions in 1917, and in particular the policies outlined in the 'April Theses' (Lenin 1964e). A comparison of 'Marxism on the State' with *The State and Revolution* shows that at the time of the February Revolution Lenin's ideas on the State were already well formulated. This can be seen from the note that Lenin wrote to Kamenev in July 1917 in which he says: '*Entre nous*: if they do me in, I ask you to publish my notebook: "Marxism on the State" (it got left behind in Stockholm). It's bound in a blue cover. It contains a collection of all the quotations from Marx and Engels, likewise from Kautsky against Pannekoek. There are a number of remarks and notes, and formulations. I think it could be published after a week's work' (Lenin 1967: 434).

Following Bukharin, Lenin began his exposition of the Marxist approach to the State by referring to what Engels had said on the subject. The most general pronouncements were in *The Origin of the Family, Private Property and the State* (Marx and Engels 1970), where Engels had characterized the State as an institution that had arisen at a certain stage of economic development, when society had been divided into classes. With the end of class society the State too would cease to exist, and the machinery of the State would be relegated to the Museum of Antiquities, where it would take its place along with the spinning wheel and the bronze axe. The same position had been repeated in *Anti-Dühring*, where Engels had made the memorable declaration that in classless society, 'the State is not abolished. It withers away'. This statement, Lenin hastened to emphasize, did not signify that revolution was superfluous, as some commentators believed; the 'withering away' referred to the proletarian State after the proletariat had come to power (Lenin 1964d: 395–7).

The dictatorship of the proletariat

A concept that Lenin was anxious to document was 'the dictatorship of the proletariat'. The phrase occurs repeatedly in 'Marxism on the State', but chiefly in Lenin's comments, only twice in actual quotations. One of these is from Engels in his 'Critique of the Draft Programme of the German Social-Democratic Party' in 1891, and one from Marx's 'Critique of the Gotha Programme' of 1875. In this latter document Marx wrote:

Between capitalist and communist society lies the period of the revolutionary transformation of the one into the other. Corresponding to this is also a political transition period in which the State can be nothing but the revolutionary dictatorship of the proletariat. (Lenin 1972: 28)

For the second edition of *The State and Revolution* published in 1918 Lenin had found another reference to the dictatorship of the proletariat in a letter from Marx to Weydemeyer written in March 1852. Here Marx stated that 'the class struggle necessarily leads to the dictatorship of the proletariat and that this dictatorship itself only constitutes the transition to the abolition of all classes and to a classless society' (Lenin 1972: 411). The discovery prompted Lenin to add another section to the text of his pamphlet in order to include it.

The concept of the dictatorship of the proletariat was to be extremely useful to Lenin because he employed it to justify the repressive measures that he took against opposition to Bolshevik rule in the early years of the Soviet regime. It was important for him, therefore, to show that the concept had a genuine Marxian pedigree. Although the concept may have been derived from Marx, its use was not. When Marx spoke of the dictatorship of the proletariat, he meant literally 'the proletariat', and not a group of radicals who professed to act on its behalf.

An important dimension in 'Marxism on the State' was the investigation of the lessons on the State that Marx had drawn from the experience of the Paris Commune of 1871. In *The Civil War in France* Marx had observed: 'One thing especially was proved by the Commune, viz., that "the working class cannot simply lay hold of the ready-made State machine and wield it for its own purposes"'. On this statement Lenin remarked: 'This passage, taken by itself, is unclear, it leaves a kind of loophole for opportunism' (Lenin 1972: 8). Of course the fact that Marx had not stated clearly what he meant by 'not simply lay hold of the ready-made State machine' opened the way for different interpretations. Trotsky's had been one of these, when he advocated organizing the dictatorship of the proletariat on an all-European scale, in the form of the republican United States of Europe.

Lenin, as the editor of a collection of Marx's letters to Kugelmann, had the explanation of what Marx meant to hand. In a letter written in April 1871, Marx had told Kugelmann that whereas previous French revolutions had involved the transfer of the bureaucratic-military machine from one hand to another, the next revolution in France would smash it. This, he said, was what the Communards were attempting to do, and was the preliminary condition for every real people's revolution on the Continent. Marx directed Kugelmann to the last chapter in his *Eighteenth Brumaire of Louis Bonaparte* in which he had declared that all revolutions had perfected the State machine instead of smashing it (Lenin 1972: 9–11).

A people's revolution

In *The State and Revolution* Lenin drew attention to the words that Marx had used: 'a real people's revolution on the Continent'. In Europe in 1871, Lenin commented, there was not a single country in which the proletariat constituted a majority of the people. A 'people's revolution', consequently, could only be such if it embraced both the proletariat and the peasantry. These were the two classes that constituted 'the people'. Lenin did not say so explicitly, but here was the justification for implementing the dictatorship in Russia, a country in which the proletariat constituted only a minority of the population (Lenin 1972: 421–2).

But what did Marx intend to put in place of the smashed State machine? Lenin believed that it would be a socialist republic modelled on the Paris Commune. He listed the policies of the Commune that met with Marx's approval. These included:

1 The abolition of the standing army and the substitution for it of the armed people.

2 Municipal councillors elected by universal suffrage to be revocable at any time.

3 The police stripped of political attributes and turned into revocable executives.

4 Public service to be performed at workmen's wages.

5 The Commune was to be a working body, not a parliamentary one, executive and legislative at the same time.

6 It would not simply decide once in three or six years which member of the ruling class was to represent the people in Parliament.

In Lenin's view the Commune had replaced the smashed State machine by increased democracy. But the increase had given rise to a new kind of structure, a case of 'quantity becoming transformed into quality' (Lenin 1972: 43–4).

As to the practicality of the measures, Lenin argued that there could be no thought of abolishing the bureaucracy at once, everywhere and completely; that was utopia. But to smash the old bureaucratic machine at once and to begin immediately to construct a new one that would permit the gradual abolition of all bureaucracy – that was not utopian. It was the actual experience of the Commune, and was the immediate task of the revolutionary proletariat.

Like Bukharin, when talking about the abolition of the State, Lenin felt the need to distinguish his ideas from those of the anarchists, who also advocated the destruction of the State. He pointed out that although Marx had fought against the anarchists, he did not deny that the State would disappear with the disappearance of social classes. But he maintained that the workers should not renounce the use of arms, of organized violence, that is, of the State, to crush the resistance of the bourgeoisie.

There is an essential element of *The State and Revolution* that is not reflected in the collection of quotations that constitutes 'Marxism on the State'. That is the economic aspect of smashing the State structure, and in this Lenin draws upon the works of Hilferding and Bukharin rather than of Marx and Engels. Lenin observed that capitalist culture had created large-scale production, such things as factories, railways, the postal service, and the like. On this basis the great majority of the functions of the old State power had become simplified and could be reduced to the exceedingly simple operations of registration, filing and checking, so that they could be performed by every literate person and performed for ordinary workmen's wages (Lenin 1964d: 426). Lenin was particularly impressed by the way the modern postal service worked. For him, it showed that 'the mechanism of social management is here at hand'. The immediate aim of the proletarian revolution would be 'to organise the whole national economy on the lines of the postal service, so that the technicians, foremen, book-keepers as well as all officials receive salaries no higher than "a workman's wages"' (Lenin 1964d: 432).

In 'Marxism on the State' there are a few tentative mentions of the Soviets, which suggests that Lenin envisaged that this could be the form that the 'commune state' would take. This is confirmed by the 'April Theses' and other pronouncements following his return to Petrograd in 1917 (Lenin 1972: 19). The situation on the ground, however, thwarted the implementation of this idea.

The workers' movement in Petrograd in February 1917 had been led by the Vyborg District Committee of the Bolshevik fraction of the RSDLP, which included a group of veteran worker participants in the 1905 revolution in Sormovo, the industrial suburb of Nizhnii Novgorod. The movement had begun as demonstrations against the war, and the shortages and deprivation that the war had brought with it. Street battles were fought against the police, causing many casualties, but by 27 February the workers had brought the Petrograd garrison on to their side. When it was clear that the revolution had triumphed, it was joined by many of the radical intelligentsia who had hitherto held aloof. These were overwhelmingly 'defencist' members of the Menshevik and Socialist Revolutionary parties. It was they who established the Petrograd Soviet, which from its very inception had a 'defencist' character. In an attempt to forestall this development, the Vyborg District Committee issued a manifesto, emphasizing the anti-war character of the workers' movement and calling for the creation of a Provisional Revolutionary Government at the Finland Station. But the momentum for the creation of a Soviet in the Duma building proved to be overwhelming. The Petrograd Soviet not only supported the war effort but also gave its, albeit conditional, support to the Provisional Government, which had been formed at the beginning of March, largely from former members of the State Duma (White 1979).

In the middle of March, Stalin, Kamenev and Muranov returned from exile in Siberia, and took over the leadership of the Bolshevik fraction and the editorship of *Pravda*. In face of resistance from the existing Bolshevik leaders, the returnees favoured the policies of giving conditional support to the Provisional Government and pursuing a defencist policy with regard to the war. This was the situation in Petrograd when Lenin returned on 14 April. It is worth recounting these events because one gains the impression from Trotsky's chapter, 'The Re-Arming of the Party', in his *The History of the Russian Revolution* that before Lenin's return all of the Bolshevik leadership had shared the opinions of Stalin and Kamenev, and that what came as a surprise to them in Lenin's 'April Theses' was their anti-war stance and their opposition to lending support to the Provisional Government. In fact the element that was novel in the 'April Theses' was their ideas on the 'commune state'.

The 'April Theses'

The most immediate issues taken up by the first three 'Theses' were the war and the Provisional Government (Lenin 1964e: 21–4). As the war still enjoyed widespread support, there was no mention of turning the imperialist war into a civil war. The 'Theses' began by defining the circumstances in which a genuine defensive war would be possible. Under the existing government, a government of capitalists, the war could only be an imperialist war. A truly defencist war could only be fought when the government was in the hands of the workers and the poorest sections of the peasantry.

The second 'Thesis' stated that the revolution was at a transitional stage. Owing to lack of class-consciousness and organization, the proletariat had allowed political power to be acquired by the bourgeoisie. In the second stage, however, power would pass into the hands of the proletariat and the poorest sections of the peasantry. In the third 'Thesis' Lenin was adamant that there should be no support for the Provisional Government. The falsity of its promises should be exposed, so that everyone would understand the futility of 'demanding' that this capitalist government should not act in the interest of the capitalists. Here Lenin had in mind those people, including his fellow-Bolsheviks Stalin and Kamenev, who supported the Provisional Government 'in so far as' it acted in the interests of the proletariat.

In the fourth 'Thesis' Lenin introduced the idea that the only form of government for Russia should be the Soviets, and that all power ought now to pass to the Soviets throughout the country. The immediate obstacle to this happening at the present time was that the Petrograd Soviet was dominated by Mensheviks and Socialist Revolutionaries who believed that the Provisional Government should be maintained in power, and that the function of the Soviet was merely to monitor its activities. Accordingly, the course of action Lenin advocated was patient persuasion to win a majority to the side of the Bolsheviks.

The fifth 'Thesis' reads like a summary of 'Marxism on the State'. It stated:

> Not a parliamentary republic – to return to a parliamentary republic from the Soviets of Workers' Deputies would be a retrograde step – but a republic of Soviets of Workers', Agricultural Labourers' and Peasants' Deputies throughout the country, from top to bottom.
>
> Abolition of the police, the army and the bureaucracy, i.e., the standing army to be replaced by the arming of the whole people.
>
> The salaries of all officials, all of whom are elective and revocable at any time, not to exceed the average wage of a competent worker. (Lenin 1964e: 24)

In agrarian policy Lenin considered that more emphasis should be put on the Soviets of Agricultural Labourers' Deputies. All landed estates should be confiscated and placed at the disposal of these agrarian Soviets. As far as economic policy was concerned, the 'Theses' demanded the immediate amalgamation of all banks in the country into a single bank, the activities of which were to be monitored by the Soviet of Workers' Deputies (Lenin 1964e: 23). This demand shows the influence of Hilferding and his conception of finance capital. Hilferding had believed that control of the chief banks in the country would make it possible to regulate the entire economy. It was at this point that Lenin made his only reference to socialism in the entire 'Theses'. It was not, he insisted, 'the immediate aim to "introduce" socialism, but only to bring social production and the distribution of products at once under the control of the Soviets of Workers' Deputies' (Lenin 1964e: 24).

The 'Theses' concluded with a list of party tasks including: the immediate convocation of a party congress; alteration of the party programme on the questions of imperialism, the State and the minimum programme; the change of the party's name from Social-Democratic to Communist. A more long-term objective was the creation of a new International.

Lenin's 'Theses' were discussed at the Petrograd Conference of the Bolshevik Party on 14 April. On the whole they were received favourably, and one speaker at least, Kalinin, thought that their contents were not particularly novel. He drew attention to the fact that the Manifesto the Bolsheviks had issued during the February revolution did not differ substantially in its content from the points Lenin had made in his 'Theses'. In Kalinin's opinion, the only thing that was new in Lenin's 'Theses' was the proposition that the Soviet of Workers' Deputies was the only form of government (Institut marksizma-leninizma pri TSK KPSS 1958: 18). Some days later Lenin's 'Theses' met with opposition at the Seventh Congress of the RSDLP, a fact noted by Bogdanov in an article occasioned by Lenin's return to Petrograd.

Bogdanov on Lenin's 'April Theses'

In an article entitled 'What Is It That We Have Overthrown?' published in the newspaper *Novaia zhizn* (New Life) on 17 May 1917, Bogdanov deplored the way Lenin had exerted his authority on the Bolsheviks by insisting that they accept the policies set out in the 'April Theses'. To him it implied that the Bolsheviks had succumbed to authoritarian attitudes, that they showed deference to Lenin simply because he was a leader. To Bogdanov this boded ill for the future: an authoritarian political party could not but create an authoritarian society. In his view:

> Every organisation, on achieving a position of decisive influence in the life and ordering of society, quite inevitably, irrespective of the formal tenets of its programme, attempts to impose on society its own type of structure, the one with which it is most familiar and to which it is most accustomed. Every collective re-creates, as far as it can, the whole social environment after its own image and in its own likeness. And if this structure is of the authoritarian type, based on the domination-submission model, albeit only in the intellectual sphere, it will inevitably give rise to authoritarian tendencies in the ordering of society itself, however democratic, communist etc. the programme of the organisation might be. (Bogdanov, 17 May 1917)

In Bogdanov's opinion, the fact that the autocracy had been overthrown meant very little, when authoritarian attitudes pervaded society, not only on the right, but also on the left of the political spectrum. Bogdanov was aware that there was opposition to Lenin among the Bolsheviks, and that it was possible that many of them, perhaps the majority, would not follow the line he had laid down. But, he claimed, even Lenin's critics shared the authoritarian attitudes of their leader. If a rank-and-file party member had arrived back in Russia the way Lenin had done, and rejected the existing party programme, insisting that it be replaced, he would not have been taken seriously. But since it was the *leader* who had arrived, he and his opinions were treated with deference. The basic feature of the authoritarian way of thinking, Bogdanov contended, was in the acceptance of a qualitative difference between the ruler and the ruled.

The conclusion that Bogdanov drew from this was that although the fall of the tsarist regime had overthrown authoritarianism politically, authoritarian attitudes continued to survive culturally. And they did so among the most progressive elements of the population, let alone among the unenlightened masses. What it would take to eliminate them, Bogdanov stated, was a 'cultural revolution', a term which he introduced for the first time (Bogdanov, 17 May 1917).

Bogdanov went on to argue, as he had done in his 1914 and 1916 writings, that the war had taught socialists a great lesson. Why, he asked, had it been able to destroy the international brotherhood of the workers so easily; why did most of the proletariat and its ideologists in the belligerent countries submit so blindly to the leadership of the bourgeoisie? This was, he said, because the socialist way of thinking existed only in an embryonic form, and was powerless to cope with the new challenges confronting it on a global scale. The socialist as a cultural type was and remained essentially bourgeois. The proletariat was still a long way from having elaborated its own particular modes of thought. In Russia, Bogdanov believed, even the democratic cultural type was a stage that still had to be reached. For that reason, he urged: 'We must have a cultural revolution' (Bogdanov, 17 May 1917).

The policy that Lenin urged on the Bolsheviks on his return to Russia prompted Bogdanov to publish a critique of the 'April Theses' in the *Bulletin of the Moscow Soviet of Workers' Deputies*, entitled 'The Commune State'. On Lenin's call for a republic of Soviets, Bogdanov remarked that the Soviets were organs of revolutionary struggle, a means of furthering the revolution, but were unsuitable as permanent organs of government. Soviets were not elected on a uniform basis, and the proportion of delegates to electors varied widely throughout the country. Some towns had one delegate for every fifty inhabitants, others had one for every hundred, others again for every two hundred, and so on. This did not matter in the revolution, but as a permanent State organization this was obviously less suitable than a parliamentary democratic republic (Bogdanov 1990: 345).

Another impracticality of Lenin's programme, to Bogdanov's mind, was in his idea that 'the salaries of all officials, all of whom are elective and subject to recall at any time, not to exceed the average wage of a competent worker'. To Bogdanov this went against elementary economic sense. Work, such as that of an organizer, which was prolonged, intensive and complex, demanded a great expenditure of energy from the human organism. It would therefore need a corresponding assimilation of energy, that is, more plentiful and more complex consumption. If a commissar or a minister exhausted his mental and nervous energy in his post, so as to be incapacitated for several years, and received the same 200–300 roubles as a competent turner, what turner would want to be a minister? If everyone were to be paid the same, the end result would be that the most demanding and responsible posts would be held either by the children of the bourgeoisie, who had an alternative income, or by intriguers who did not scruple to supplement their incomes by corruption (Bogdanov 1990: 348). To Bogdanov, Lenin's programme was an extreme example of maximalist thinking. It lacked any organizational analysis, but was inspired by the faith that the revolution would somehow deliver up the desired results.

Trotsky joins Lenin

In his *The History of the Russian Revolution* Trotsky is at pains to show that he and Lenin were at one in their evaluation of the February revolution, and that his analysis of it coincided with Lenin's in the 'April Theses'. A perusal of the articles that Trotsky wrote in March 1917 in New York does not bear this out. In fact at that time Trotsky viewed events within the framework of his theory of permanent revolution. In an article written in April he argues that it is wrong to class the Russian revolution as a bourgeois revolution on the pattern of the French revolution. The reason Trotsky gives is a concise statement of permanent revolution:

> In the Great French Revolution of the eighteenth century the driving force was the petty bourgeoisie, holding under its influence the peasant masses. Where do we have in Russia a petty bourgeoisie? Its economic role is insignificant. Russian capitalism from its very beginning began to develop in its highest centralised forms. The Russian proletariat confronted the Russian bourgeoisie as a class to a class, as far back as the eve of the first Russian revolution of 1905. In this way there is a profound difference between the Russian revolution and the French revolution at the end of the eighteenth century. (Trotsky 1924–25: 24)

Trotsky also believed that, as the Russian bourgeoisie was dependent on the London stock exchange, the Allies had played an important part in the formation of the Provisional Government (Trotsky 1924–25: 27).

That in 1917 Trotsky still adhered to his theory of permanent revolution is clear from the pamphlet written between the July Days and the October revolution entitled *What Further? (Results and Prospects)*. Trotsky's answer to the question of 'what came next' was that all power should go to the Soviets, and this power would be used in the interests of the workers. For the establishment of control over the economy the proletariat had very valuable examples in the West, in particular, the German 'war socialism'. Even if the Soviets had full power and the workers had control over production and distribution, this still would not be socialism, because the bourgeoisie would resist any such development. However, as Trotsky explained:

> Having thrown off the shackles of capitalist power, the revolution would become *permanent*, that is, uninterrupted. It would apply State power not to entrench the regime of capitalist exploitation, but, on the contrary, to overcome it. Its final success on this path would depend on the success of the proletarian revolution in Europe. (Trotsky 1917: 6)

In July of 1917 Trotsky, along with his group of Social Democrats, the 'Mezhraiontsy', which included Lunacharsky and Pokrovsky, joined the Bolsheviks. It was a recognition on Trotsky's part that the future lay with Lenin, though at that particular juncture the Bolsheviks were being hunted down as German agents and instigators of an abortive coup against the Provisional Government. Trotsky was captured and imprisoned; Lenin had to go into hiding in Finland. However, the tide turned in September, with the defeat of the attempted overthrow of the Provisional Government by General Kornilov. Trotsky went on to be one of the leaders of the October revolution, the architect of the Red victory in the Civil War, an influential figure in every sphere of Soviet policy, and a leading light in the Communist International.

For Trotsky the alliance with Lenin brought enormous benefits. But the price he had to pay was the subordination of his intellectual and literary talents to the cause of furthering the cult of Lenin. He did this with every appearance of sincerity, so that one has no grounds for doubting that he did it willingly. But Trotsky's desire to show that he was always a Leninist, when in fact he was not, necessarily introduces an element of distortion into his writings. This is not obvious because Trotsky is a consummate master of the written word; among his Russian Marxist contemporaries he has no rival. One is naturally inclined to believe that someone who writes so artistically and persuasively must write truthfully. But the evidence does not point in that direction.

Trotsky's espousal of Leninism meant that he repudiated the criticism of Lenin's concept of the party that Trotsky himself had given in his 1904 pamphlet *Our Political Tasks*, with its critique of 'substitutionism'. He now accepted Lenin's concept and did not repeat his prediction that its substitution methods would necessarily lead to dictatorship. When that dictatorship did in fact come about in the person of Stalin, he did not explain it as he had done in 1904, but advanced a new – and less convincing – hypothesis in his book, *The Revolution Betrayed*. This was that in conditions of shortages of goods, a queue formed, and someone was needed to control the queue (Trotsky 1970: 112).

As the title suggests, Trotsky was of the opinion that in the Stalin era the socialist aims of the Russian revolution had not been attained and that the revolution had degenerated. As a Leninist, Trotsky did not believe that this degeneration could have occurred during Lenin's lifetime, but had come about with Stalin's rise to power and his espousal of the policy of 'socialism in one country'. This deprived the Soviet State of the support that an international revolution would have provided. Trotsky did not accept that the suppression of opposition movements within Soviet Russia, in which he took an active part, might have contributed to the rise of the Stalin phenomenon. For ideological reasons, Trotsky's works do not reveal the element of continuity, which undoubtedly existed, between the Lenin and the Stalin eras.

Lenin and the banks

Why was Lenin so sure that the accession of the Bolsheviks to power would be the beginning of a socialist revolution? The answer is that he had absorbed completely Hilferding's analysis of finance capital. Following Hilferding, Lenin believed that the banks dominated industry, and that once nationalized the banking system could be used by an incoming socialist government to establish centralized control over the entire economy. Although Hilferding is not mentioned by name, his ideas pervade Lenin's writings during 1917, in particular, his two main pamphlets on economics: *The Impending Catastrophe and How to Deal with It* and *Can the Bolsheviks Retain State Power?*

In *The Impending Catastrophe*, Lenin, in an implied reference to Hilferding's contention that control of the whole German economy could be established by taking hold of the six major Berlin banks, remarks that in Germany there were only four very large private banks of national importance; in America there were only two. In other words, the process of centralization had gone even further since Hilferding wrote. Lenin agreed that in this way the banks 'regulated the economic life' of their respective countries, but that this regulation consisted in 'squeezing' the workers to the point of starvation, while guaranteeing the capitalists profits higher than before the war (Lenin 1964d: 333–4). Here Lenin was endorsing Hilferding's idea that prior to the introduction of socialism economic regulation existed in an 'antagonistic' form.

In the pamphlet *Can the Bolsheviks Retain State Power?* Lenin takes up the question of adapting the legacy of capitalism to socialist purposes. Whereas he advocates that the institutions of the State should be smashed, this must not happen to the economic structures which capitalism has created: the banks and the cartels, because through them it will be possible to regulate the economy. He argues as follows:

> In addition to the chiefly 'oppressive' apparatus – the standing army, the police and the bureaucracy – the modern State possesses an apparatus which has extremely close connections with the banks and syndicates, an apparatus which performs an enormous amount of accounting and registration work, if it may be expressed this way. This apparatus must not, and should not, be smashed. It must be wrested from the control of the capitalists; the capitalists and the wires they pull must be cut off, lopped off, chopped away from this apparatus; it must be subordinated to the proletarian Soviets; it must be expanded, made more comprehensive, and nation-wide. And this can be done by utilising the achievements already made by large-scale capitalism. (Lenin 1964f: 106)

He then goes on to say that:

Capitalism has created an accounting apparatus in the shape of the banks, syndicates, postal service, consumers' societies, and office employees' unions. *Without big banks socialism would be impossible.*

The big banks are the 'State apparatus' which we need to bring about socialism, and which we take ready-made from capitalism; our task here is merely to lop off what capitalistically mutilates this excellent apparatus, to make it even bigger, even more democratic, even more comprehensive. (Lenin 1964f: 106)

By his declaration that '*without big banks socialism would be impossible*' (emphasis in the original JW) Lenin indicates that he has accepted Hilferding's argumentation completely. Because in Russia the process of cartelization and the centralization of banking had not gone as far as it had in Germany, Lenin envisaged completing this process through compulsion once the Bolsheviks had taken power. Accordingly, the measures he advocated were: amalgamation of all banks into a single bank, and State control over its operations, nationalization of the syndicates and compulsory syndication of industrialists, merchants and employers generally.

Questions of socialism

In November 1917 Bogdanov published a collection of his recent writings which included an article entitled 'War Communism and State Capitalism' where he contested the idea, put forward by his friend Bazarov, that the measures of State regulation necessitated by the war could be regarded as a transition stage to a socialist society. According to Bogdanov, the army in general, in peace and in wartime, was an enormous consumer commune with an authoritarian structure. A mass of people live at the expense of the State, distributing among themselves goods from the producing apparatus, which they consume uniformly. In peacetime the commune was a small part of society as a whole, and had no great influence upon it. In wartime, however, the commune grows in extent and in importance for the country. Its influence on society in terms of structure and culture increases enormously. The character of this influence is determined by two distinctive features of the military apparatus: its authoritarian structure and its consumer communism.

As it was obvious that in time of war countries experienced an expansion of authoritarianism, Bogdanov did not consider it necessary to dwell on this topic. His main interest in the article was to examine the dynamics of the military consumer commune in wartime conditions, its gradual extension from the army to the rest of society.

The first stage in the process was the maintenance of soldiers' families by the State so that millions of people were either wholly or partly supported at State expense. This was quite irrespective of any function they might perform in production. And it was not as if they were State employees; they were supported simply because they had the right to have their needs supplied. This was an extension of the soldiers' commune in the country.

The destructive course of the war extended the consumer commune even further. The shortage of goods was exacerbated by the uneven way they were distributed, hence a rationing system was introduced. This gave the purchaser the right to buy a given quantity of goods, but that did not guarantee that the goods in question would be available, and at a price that could be afforded. The solution was to control prices and the supply of goods, leading to a further extension of consumer communism and restrictions on the private ownership of goods.

With continuing economic decline the regulation of the supply of goods turned out to be futile without regulation of their production, because capitalists had no incentive to produce rationed goods, from which they could not gain any profit. The State was forced to exercise control over branches of production and to determine the extent of that production. Subsequently this control was extended to the distribution of raw materials, implements and the labour force. While the State control of supplies could lead to the merger of whole sectors into syndicates, the regulation of production could necessitate the compulsory formation of trusts, the merger of whole sectors into corporate organizations with the complete loss of independence for individual enterprises.

This, Bogdanov explained, was how 'state capitalism' came about. Its point of departure was military consumer communism, and its driving force was the progressive decline of the economy. Its organizing method was rationing and restrictions enforced by authoritarian-compulsory means. To understand this system it was essential to bear in mind that it arose out of consumption, and through distribution had entered the sphere of production. This sequence of events was the exact opposite of the normal course of development. There it was the development of production which determined changes in the forms of distribution and consumption. In tectological terms, normal growth was one of progressive changes in the social organism. In 'state capitalism' the processes were of decline, destruction, simplification, that is, these were regressive phenomena.

Bazarov had argued that state capitalism was a transitional form between capitalism and socialism, an idea that Bogdanov disagreed with strongly. He pointed out that there was an enormous difference between socialism, which was primarily a new form of cooperation, and 'war communism', which was a special form of social consumption. If state capitalism really was the first stage of a socialist revolution, then it would be the outcome of the progressive driving forces of capitalism, of the culmination of the class struggle of the proletariat. In fact state capitalism embodied class cooperation of nations for the purpose of destruction, and was a regressive phenomenon.

Bogdanov conceded that 'maximalism' such as that of Bazarov was a comparatively broad and influential current, but that it was a mirage generated by the conditions of war communism. It was dangerous, Bogdanov warned, because it could encourage adventures that would result in cruel defeat (Bogdanov 1990: 343–4). Bogdanov remarked ruefully that Lenin had come to head a government which proclaimed a 'socialist' revolution, but in practice was trying to carry out a war-communist one. This of course made the position immeasurably more utopian (Bogdanov 1990: 348).

Bogdanov devoted considerable attention in his article to considering what features of war communism were likely to remain after the end of the war. As it happened, in Russia the World War shaded into the Civil War, which lasted until 1921, so that war communism had a greater longevity than Bogdanov might have expected. And in fact the features of the economic system which was in force in Soviet Russia between 1918 and 1921 are remarkably accurately described in Bogdanov's article. The essence of that system was precisely that it was an attempt to manage scarce resources in a spiral of economic decline. Bogdanov himself took pride in his analysis of war communism, giving it a special mention in the autobiographical sketch which he wrote in 1925 (Bogdanov 1995: 19).

The nationalization of the banks

On coming to power in October 1917, the Bolsheviks had attempted to take over the banking system with which to control the whole national economy, but had found it much more difficult than anticipated. Before the State Bank could be occupied by the Red Guards, the private banks had succeeded in getting many millions of roubles into their possession. These were then placed at the disposal of anti-Bolshevik organizations, and were disbursed as a month's advance wages to all State employees who would agree to go on strike and boycott the Bolshevik regime. The new Soviet government had great difficulty in withdrawing money from the State Bank to pay for running expenses.

As a measure to counter the sabotage of the private banks the Soviet government issued a decree on 14 December nationalizing the banks and making banking a State monopoly (Akhapkin 1970: 62). The following day the Petrograd and Moscow branches of the private banks were occupied by Red Guards and a Commissar put in charge to ensure that no funds were withdrawn and hidden. This measure only partially broke the sabotage, since the Bank Clerks' Union called its members out on strike. As it was not possible to find the requisite number of trained accountants to keep the banks open, for the latter part of December and the first two weeks of January the banks were closed (Price 1921: 165–6, 209–11). When the private banks opened again, it was observed that 'not a trace remained of the intention to centralize the operations of the banks' (Kowalski 1990: 48).

When Bukharin reviewed *The State and Revolution* in the spring of 1918, he made no mention of those passages in it where Lenin advocated using the banks as a means of controlling the economy, or those which argued that the administration of the economy had become simplified under capitalism. These sections of Lenin's work had already become obsolete. Nevertheless, Bukharin thought that there was enough of value in *The State and Revolution* to make it an essential work of reference for every communist. In Bukharin's view, Lenin's reconstruction of Marx's thinking on the role of the State under capitalism, in the future communist order, and in the transition period, was much to be commended. These were ideas that had been obscured and distorted by the Social Democrats, and Lenin's revival of them served to draw a clear distinction between the attitudes of Social Democrats and Communists to the State (Kowalski 1990: 51).

The organization tasked with dealing with bank saboteurs was the All-Russian Extraordinary Commission for the Struggle against Counter-Revolution and Sabotage (Vcheka), chaired by Feliks Dzierżyński, that had been set up on 7 December 1917. The Vcheka in its various guises was to survive well after the problem with the banks had been resolved.

This initial period of Bolshevik rule is instructive because its dynamic is the adaptation of theory to the realities of the situation. Because the banks do not fulfil the function that theory has allotted to them, as being the means of controlling the whole national economy, but, on the contrary, act as an obstacle to the smooth transition to socialism, the solution is the use of force in an attempt to compel them to behave as theory dictates. The violence that characterized the Bolshevik regime from its earliest days arose from the misplaced optimism about the ease with which the transition could be made from the existing structures to the new.

The fate of the workers' party

In an article entitled 'The Fate of the Workers' Party in the Present Revolution' published in January 1918 Bogdanov analysed the significance of the Bolshevik seizure of power. His starting point was a comparison between the revolutions of 1905 and 1917. Although both involved the proletariat and the peasantry, the revolution of 1917 differed from 1905 in that it took place in the unprecedented conditions of the World War, thus ensuring a major role in it for the soldiers, the peasants in uniform. The widespread desire for peace in 1917 had brought a mass influx of both workers and soldiers into the Bolshevik party, the party which promised peace. The change in the membership meant that the Bolsheviks were no longer the party of the workers, but of the workers and soldiers (Bogdanov 26–27 January 1918b).

Because Bogdanov considered that the continuation of the war would have meant the irreversible economic and cultural decline of Russia, he viewed the seizure of power by the Bolsheviks and their conclusion of peace as historically inevitable. He saw the seizure not as a conspiracy, but as the eruption of spontaneous forces brought about by the ruinous continuation of the war. It was this that had brought the Bolsheviks to power.

The fact that the Bolsheviks were a workers' and soldiers' party had determined how the party had behaved on coming to power. Since the party was made up of two class cohorts with different levels of culture, the tectological 'law of the leasts' ensured that the political standpoint of the whole party, its programme, tactics and methods, would be dictated by the group with the lower cultural level. Consequently, for all practical purposes, the workers'-soldiers' party was simply a soldiers' party.

Whereas the working class viewed political activities in terms of labour and skill, the soldiery saw them in terms of physical force, as an offensive. This was evidenced by the way the Bolsheviks attempted to take over the banking system. This system, as Bogdanov explained, was an enormously complex mechanism, beyond the comprehension of even most economists. The crude methods employed in nationalizing the banks destroyed the networks of deposits and withdrawals on which they were based and made the banking system unworkable (Bogdanov 26–27 January 1918b).

Shortly after the October revolution Bogdanov was invited by Lunacharsky to join the Commissariat of Education of the new Soviet Government. He refused on the grounds that the atmosphere of the barracks which prevailed in the new Soviet government was not one in which he believed he would be able to live and work. For him comradely relations were the principle on which the new culture ought to function (Bogdanov 1990: 352–5).

In the immediate post-revolutionary period Bogdanov occupied himself with organizing the Proletarian Culture (Proletkult) Movement, which would inculcate into the working class an autonomous proletarian culture that would enable it to escape from the baneful influence of the bourgeoisie that had dragged it into the carnage of the recent war. Bogdanov explained that: 'To give a class an all-round education, unequivocally directing the collective will and thinking, can only be done by elaborating an autonomous intellectual culture. The bourgeois classes had it – therein lay their strength; the proletariat lacked it – therein lay its weakness' (Bogdanov 1918a: 1).

10

Towards the 'Short Course'

Bukharin

The Bolshevik revolution was a turning point in the history of Marxism, not only in Russia but also throughout the world. From then on Russia was regarded as the country in which Marxism had triumphed. Marxists everywhere looked on the Russian Communist party as the organization which knew how to make a socialist revolution, and saw it as the organization to emulate. This attitude was encouraged by the Bolsheviks and was a central theme of the Communist International, which was founded in 1919. A consequence of the Bolsheviks' coming to power was that in the Soviet period Marxist theory took on an apologetic role, that of defending and justifying Soviet practice. Lenin's *The State and Revolution* was the first work to fulfil this function. When it was published in 1918 its significance was no longer that of directing how the revolution was to be carried out, but of providing the rationale for the dictatorship of the proletariat and the Bolsheviks' refusal to institute a representative democracy.

The first substantial theoretical work published in the Soviet era was *The ABC of Communism* by Bukharin and E. A. Preobrazhensky, which appeared in 1919. The idea that mastery of the banks will provide control of the economic system no longer appears, and the description of how a socialist system will function draws upon Bogdanov's ideas. The portrayal of the distribution system of communist society is reminiscent of Bogdanov's in *Red Star*.

> Products are ... neither bought nor sold. They are simply stored in communal warehouses, and are subsequently delivered to those who need them. In such conditions, money will no longer be required ... The main direction will be entrusted to various kinds of book-keeping offices or statistical bureau. There, from day to day, account will be kept of production and all its needs; there also it will be decided whither workers

must be sent, whence they must be taken, and how much work there is to be done. (Bukharin and Preobrazhensky 1969: 116–18)

The similarity between *Red Star* and *The ABC of Communism* is not fortuitous, since Bukharin was an admirer of Bogdanov's book. It is remarkable, however, to reflect that the best vision of a socialist economy that was available to the Bolsheviks in the revolutionary era was one that was taken from Bogdanov's novel.

After 1917 Bukharin emerged as the principal Marxist theoretician of the Soviet regime. His *Economics of the Transition Period* was published in 1920 as the Civil War drew to a close. This book re-assessed Marxist thinking about socialism in the light of the experience of the young Soviet regime. Its main emphasis was that the transition to socialism could not be smooth, and involved a great deal of hardship and privation. The idea that capitalism had created the institutions that could be taken over as they stood by a socialist government would have to be abandoned. Socialist revolution involved the disruption of the existing economic system, and with it a severe loss of production in all sectors.

One example of an idea that had to be abandoned was Hilferding's contention that the seizure of possession of six large Berlin banks by the proletariat would give it control over the whole of industry. Bukharin pointed out that it had been empirically proved that nothing of the kind took place; in reality the seizure of the banks merely undermined the commanding power of capital. In explaining why this was the case, Bukharin reproduced Bogdanov's argument that the control of the banks over industry was much looser and more indirect than Hilferding had imagined. The banks could not control industry

> for the reason that the banks 'rule' industry on the basis of specific relations of money credit. The mode of connection is here the mode of credit connection, and it is just this which collapses when the proletariat seizes possession of the banks. (Bukharin 1979: 89)

In other words, the rationale that Lenin had given for a smooth takeover of the institutions of capitalism had been mistaken.

How did Bukharin explain the revolution in Russia? He did this with the help of *Tectology* and Bogdanov's concept of the 'the law of the leasts'. According to Bukharin, the individual capitalist states were linked together in a chain-like connection as component elements of an integrated world system. A crisis causing disturbance of equilibrium in one part of the system would inevitably spread to the others. The world war created just such a crisis, so that the system of world economy began to disintegrate.

'With which links of the chain', Bukharin asked, 'was this collapse bound to begin?'. His answer was that: 'It stands to reason that it was bound to begin with those links that were the weakest in terms of capitalist organisation' (Bukharin 1979: 168). When Lenin read this passage in Bukharin's book he commented in a marginal note:

> Untrue: with the moderately weak link. Without a certain level of capitalism nothing would have happened here in Russia. (Bukharin 1971: 221)

Given Lenin's hostility to Bogdanov, which is well reflected in other marginal notes, it is not surprising that he was not impressed by Bukharin's application of Bogdanov's 'law of the leasts'. Lenin was emphatically not an adherent of the 'weakest link' theory.

What Lenin did admire in Bukharin's book was the chapter on 'extra-economic compulsion in the transition period', which justified the use of force not only against landowners and capitalists, the enemies of the proletariat, but against the proletariat itself. Bukharin agreed that under communism there would be absolute freedom, and that there would be no kind of external regulation of relationships between people. In the transition period, however, compulsion was necessary, because the proletariat was not a homogeneous group; while some parts of it, the vanguard, were advanced, relatively broad circles bore the stamp of the capitalist commodity world. To make the majority of workers conform to the standards of the vanguard, compulsory discipline was needed. Because this discipline was imposed by the working class on the working class for its own interests, it differed fundamentally from the discipline and compulsion formerly imposed on it externally by the bourgeoisie.

For Bukharin the use of force against the peasantry was absolutely necessary because it resisted the system of compulsory labour and the attempts to restrain the free market in grain. There was, moreover, no alternative to compulsion since the exhausted cities could offer no equivalent for the grain that they requisitioned (Bukharin 1979: 157–66).

In the long run, Bukharin argued, proletarian compulsion in all its forms, 'from shootings to labour service', would serve the purpose of creating a classless society (Bukharin 1979: 165). Following the period of intense class struggle, when society had fragmented, a new equilibrium would be established in which class divisions became blurred and finally disappeared altogether. When this came about, compulsion, in every form, would disappear once and for all.

A question that Bukharin raised in *Economics of the Transition Period* was: Were those methods and categories of thinking that Marx applied to capitalist society valid for the time in which capitalism had broken down and the foundations were being laid for a socialist society? The answer to this question had already been prefigured in the opening sentence of his book. This was that theoretical political economy was the science of a social economy that was based on commodity production, that is, the science of an unorganized social economy (Bukharin 1979: 57). In other words, Marx's analysis of capitalism was not applicable to the planned economy that Russia was in the process of creating. With reference to the economic phenomena of the time, Bukharin argued that there were no commodities, no value, no wages, no profit or surplus value and no commodity fetishism (Bukharin 1979: 146–56). A question that Bukharin did not ask himself was: to what extent had these categories of a capitalist economy been developed in Russia prior to the 1917 revolution? It could just as well have been argued that the Russian economy had not sufficiently advanced to be characterized by these categories than to argue that it had somehow surpassed them

Oppositions

The Red victory in the Civil War had been at enormous cost in human life. Economically, the country was devastated, both its agriculture and its industry in ruins. In 1920 the system of compulsory grain requisitions was still in force causing deprivation to the peasantry without being able to feed adequately the diminishing urban population. The militarization of the Soviet State had encouraged centralization of power and the suppression of popular initiative. The restrictions on press freedom and other civil rights that had been introduced by the Bolsheviks on their accession to power as temporary measures had become permanent. Sympathetic socialist visitors to Soviet Russia in 1920 such as Alexander Berkman, Emma Goldman and Bertrand Russell, who had expected to find there the makings of a socialist society, were quickly disillusioned by the reality that confronted them, and which they documented in contemporary accounts.

While the Red Army was still quelling peasant revolts up and down the country, a number of opposition movements emerged during the course of 1920. One of these was the Workers' Opposition which called for greater rights for the trade unions in the running of the economy. The theoretical case of the Workers' Opposition was made by Alexandra Kollontai, who called for a return to the elective principle, freedom of expression and the elimination of bureaucracy by making all officials answerable to the public at large. She pointed out that the aspirations of the Workers' Opposition were in keeping with the dictum of Marx and Engels that the creation of socialism must be the affair of the workers themselves (Kollontai 1977: 199). In the context of 1920–21 this dictum had become subversive and associated with opposition movements.

Another opposition movement, the Democratic Centralists, argued that since coming to power the Bolshevik party had betrayed its own ideals. They opposed the bureaucratic centralism of Lenin's Central Committee and insisted that every important question should be discussed by the party rank-and-file before decisions were taken.

The most serious opposition movement, however, was that by the sailors at the Kronstadt naval base on the Gulf of Finland at the beginning of 1921. It was a dangerous rebellion since the sailors were an armed force and located near Petrograd, where they were likely to attract wide support among the workers. The demands of the sailors included ones that could be classed as basic human rights: democratically elected Soviets, freedom of speech and the press for workers, peasants and left socialist parties, the release of political prisoners from socialist parties. The response of the Soviet government was to storm the Kronstadt fortress, imprison the sailors on the mainland, and shoot them in batches over the next few months (Serge 1963: 115–31).

The feature that the opposition movements had in common was that the demands they put forward were for the democratic forms that the Bolshevik party itself professed to subscribe to. But in the situation following the Civil War the call for democracy was a threat to the very existence of the Bolshevik regime.

At the Tenth Party Congress in March 1921 Bukharin justified the rejection of the demands by the Workers' Opposition and the Democratic Centralists in the same terms as he had justified the use of force in *Economics of the Transition Period*. His argument was that it was impossible to have formal democracy because in that case the working class would be swallowed up in the petty-bourgeois peasant masses. Even working-class democracy would be extremely dangerous because the advanced group of workers was a small minority among the vast majority who were subject to petty-bourgeois influences through its ties with the villages.

Bogdanov himself took no part in any opposition movement, but the anti-authoritarian spirit which suffused his writings, which were still being published, was a standing reproach to Lenin's government. There was an echo of this in Kollontai's pamphlet *The Workers' Opposition*, and the very concept of 'democratic centralism' owed its existence to Bogdanov. Also important politically was what Bogdanov's writings did not say. Nowhere did Bogdanov endorse Lenin's use of the term 'the dictatorship of the proletariat', the formula by which the Bolsheviks justified their resort to force against the people. Its absence in Bogdanov's writings implied his refusal to accept the Bolshevik regime's legitimacy. In the circumstances, it is understandable that Bogdanov's ideas would have the potential to inspire democratic opposition to the Soviet regime.

In September 1920 Lenin had launched his campaign against Bogdanov with the publication of a new edition of *Materialism and Empiriocriticism*. For this Lenin commissioned V. I. Nevsky to write a foreword, whose basic message was that Lenin's work was still valid because, despite its appearance of novelty, *Tectology* embodied the same idealist principles as *Empiriomonism* and other of Bogdanov's writings that Lenin had criticized in the first edition of his book. The reissue of Lenin's *Materialism and*

Empiriocriticism with Nevsky's foreword had the effect of encouraging a vigorous anti-Bogdanov campaign in the press.

The adoption of Plekhanov as the approved interpreter of Marxist theory was encouraged by Lenin as a means of countering Bogdanov's influence. During the debate on the trade unions in January 1921 Lenin had remarked: 'Let me add in parenthesis for the benefit of young party members that it is impossible to become a conscious, genuine communist without studying – and I mean studying – everything that Plekhanov has written on philosophy, because nothing better exists in the international literature on Marxism' (Lenin 1973a: 100). He urged that the Soviet State should demand that professors of philosophy should have a knowledge of Plekhanov's exposition of Marxist philosophy and the ability to impart it to their students. Apparently, such professors were not in abundance in 1921, so that the followers of Plekhanov, A. Deborin and L. Ortodoks were invited to lecture at the Sverdlov University, despite the fact that both of them had been Mensheviks.

The official endorsement of Plekhanov as the approved interpreter of Marxism lasted until Lenin's death in 1924, from which time Leninism became the official Soviet doctrine. From 1920 Bogdanov's name disappeared from the historical record. He was not mentioned in histories of the Bolshevik party, and his works were not referred to. This situation persisted right up to the fall of the Soviet Union. Had it not been for his negative mention in Lenin's *Materialism and Empiriocriticism*, a major figure in Russian intellectual history would have passed completely into oblivion.

Stalin's *Fundamentals of Leninism*

Following Lenin's death, Stalin delivered a series of lectures entitled 'On the Foundations of Leninism' which were published in *Pravda* in April and May 1924. The lectures are most renowned for being the occasion on which Stalin announced his theory of 'socialism in one country', a theory which he attributed to Lenin.

The other thing that Stalin attributed to Lenin in the lectures was the revolutionary theory that, 'The front of capital will be pierced where the chain of imperialism is weakest, for the proletarian revolution is the result of the breaking of the chain of the world imperialist front at its weakest link.' In 1917 the chain of the imperialist world front proved to be weaker in Russia than in the other countries. It was there that the chain broke and provided an outlet for the proletarian revolution (Stalin 1953: 100).

This was a remarkable assertion because, as we know, Lenin did not subscribe to the theory that 'the chain of imperialism broke at its weakest link'. In fact, he would have nothing to do with a theory that was couched in terms of chains and links because it quite obviously had its source in Bogdanov's *Tectology*.

Yet, one can understand why Stalin made the attribution. If, as Lenin maintained, the revolution in Russia was a socialist one, it was incumbent upon him to explain how it was that in an economically backward country like Russia, where the proletariat was in a minority, a socialist revolution was possible. The historically accurate answer to this question was that in 1917 Lenin had believed, following Hilferding, that the creation of trusts and syndicates by finance capital had prepared the ground for a socialist society, and that by gaining control of the banks one could establish a centrally controlled economic system. Unfortunately, this idea had turned out to be illusory, and one simply took a pragmatic approach to problems as they arose.

Historical accuracy, however, was not among Stalin's priorities and, most probably at Bukharin's suggestion, he attributed Bogdanov's idea to Lenin, who of course was unable to protest. The ruse was successful because not only was the false attribution not noticed and exposed but the statement that the chain of imperialism broke at its weakest link was held up as Lenin's most characteristic theoretical postulate.

Stalin's *Fundamentals of Leninism* contained a less obvious, but no less important theoretical doctrine. This was that 'Leninism is Marxism of the era of imperialism and the proletarian revolution'. On the face of it, this was a fairly innocuous formulation. But the corollary, which Stalin did not spell out, was rather more significant. It was that Marx's writings applied only to the era of capitalism. In this idea Stalin was adopting the doctrine that Bukharin had introduced in his *Economics of the Transition Period*, that the categories of capitalism did not exist in the time of the transition to socialism. Bukharin took up the doctrine in his 1924 essay on 'Lenin as a Marxist', arguing that there were developments in capitalism that Marx was not familiar with, because they did not exist in his times, such as the formation of trusts and syndicates (Bukharin 1988: 58–9). This division into the Marxism of Marx and the Marxism of Lenin, propounded by Stalin and Bukharin, was a very convenient one for the Soviet regime. It could publish the most complete editions of Marx and Engels's works, but these would have only an academic or an antiquarian significance. They would have no bearing on any actions the regime took. These would be justified by the more flexible 'Leninism'.

A further step in the direction of separating the Soviet reality from Marxist theory came in 1925 with the 'Debate on Political Economy' held in the Communist Academy in Moscow. The target here were books like the *Course of Political Economy* written by Bogdanov and Skvortsov-Stepanov which treated the subject historically. The implication of this was that the categories of political economy were valid for more than just the capitalist period, but were found in different historical epochs. In defence, Skvortsov-Stepanov presented a well-researched paper with numerous quotations from Marx's works, showing that Marx's method had not only been abstract but also historical. Bukharin, for his part, inquired of Skvortsov-Stepanov whether Bogdanov in his novel *Red Star* used the categories of bourgeois political economy (Bukharin 1925: 301).

The problem for Bukharin, Preobrazhensky and all those who opposed the historical approach to political economy was that when Lenin had reviewed Bogdanov's *Short Course of Political Economy*, which treated the subject historically, he had been much in favour of Bogdanov's approach, declaring it to be 'exactly how one ought to expound political economy'. Various ingenious pretexts were advanced to explain why Lenin could not have meant what he said.

The arguments advanced by Bogdanov and Skvortsov-Stepanov were to no avail. The issue had been decided in advance, and henceforth it was a matter of Soviet doctrine that Marx's analysis in *Das Kapital* applied to a capitalist society only, and that the categories of political economy were valid only in bourgeois society.

Economic planning

If the prospect that Hilferding had held out of the seizure of six banks being sufficient to gain control of the national economy, then the Bolsheviks would have fallen heir to a ready-made planning system nurtured within the capitalist order. Even when this turned out not to be the case, it was still believed that a planned economy was the hallmark of a socialist system. However, now it would be necessary to create the socialist planned economy from scratch.

In March 1920 Trotsky expressed his approval of the notion that workers now had to 'shift in accordance with a single economic plan, on orders from central economic organisations', and he justified the militarization of labour by claiming that such a plan was already in operation. L. N. Kritsman also advocated the need for a single economic plan in a pamphlet written at the end of 1920. How he envisaged the planning process was:

> The preparation of a single economic plan consists in establishing, firstly how much of what there is and how much can be obtained, and secondly, how much of what is needed – and the economic plan itself consists in deciding how much of what should be received (produced, prepared within the country or brought in from abroad), and in the provision of each organ of the national economy with everything it needs to fulfil the tasks it has been set. (King 1999: 73–4)

In January 1921 Bogdanov gave a lecture entitled 'The Organizational Principles of a Unified Economic Plan' to the first Congress of the Scientific Organization of Labour. It was a significant lecture because in it he formulated the principles of Soviet economic planning. Bogdanov's definition of a planned economy was one in which all its parts are systematically coordinated on the basis of a unified and methodically elaborated economic plan. In this way the economy as a whole would be treated as a system in the tectological sense. The essence of this approach was expressed in the two propositions:

1   Every organized whole is a system of activities, unfolding in a particular environment and in constant interaction with it. Thus, society is a system of human activities in the natural environment and in a process of struggle against its resistances.

2   Every part of an organized system exists in a particular functional relationship to the whole. Thus, in society every branch of the economy, every enterprise, every worker fulfils its own particular function.

These propositions were the points of departure for establishing the equilibrium of the system and its further development. Bogdanov stressed that equilibrium came first and development second.

The equilibrium of the economic system depended on there being a balance between production and distribution. Since production provided all the products for distribution, and distribution in its turn served to support production, it was possible to define the conditions for equilibrium, namely: the equilibrium of the social economy is possible where each one of its elements by means of distribution receives all the necessary means to fulfil its social-productive functions.

As a result of the interdependence of the sectors of the economy, the expansion of the economic system as a whole is subject to the 'law of the leasts', making the expansion depend on the rate of development of its most backward parts. If, say, for a new cycle of production, some of the necessary elements can be obtained in a quantity that is increased by only 2 per cent over the previous one, but other elements can grow by 4, 6, 9 per cent, in such a case even the expansion of the other branches can only take place successfully within the limits of 2 per cent. If they exceed this rate, it will be to no purpose, and will probably cause a bottleneck (Bogdanov 1996: 300–7). One finds these arguments repeated by Bukharin in the debates about Soviet industrialization.

Industrialization debates

V. G. Groman and Bazarov were among the Soviet economists who were influenced by Bogdanov's argument that the economy should be seen as a unified system tending towards equilibrium, and as a system of chains which could be no stronger than the weakest link. It followed that planning should be concerned above all to ensure proportionality between the different sectors of the economy (King 1999: 75).

One of the earliest ideas was that a single economic plan should take the form of a 'balance sheet' of the entire economy. This would constitute, in Bazarov's words, 'a stable system of dynamic equilibrium'. In April 1922 the work on compiling such a balance sheet, which was to serve as a basis for the single economic plan, was begun. The task, however, turned out to be much more complex than anticipated, so that when the preliminary figures were published in 1925, they were not complete enough to take the form of the projected balance sheet.

In Bazarov's view, there were two distinct approaches to planning: there was the one which extrapolated from existing resources and projected these into the future, which he termed 'genetic'; and there was the approach which set goals and targets to be attained, which he called 'teleological'. He believed that both of these approaches were valid, though the genetic approach should predominate. Originally these terms had no political connotations, but by the end of the 1920s, they had become part of the factional struggle between the Left and the Right. 'Teleology' was regarded as a term of approval for those who wished to go beyond the market framework, whereas 'genetic' was an abusive term for those, like Bukharin, who wanted to preserve the market relations of the New Economic Policy (NEP), which had been introduced in 1921.

By 1925–26 Russian industrial output had regained its pre-war levels, as existing productive capacity was restored. The question then arose: how to transform the country in a socialist direction by an expansion of the industrial sector. Preobrazhensky based his approach on the way that Marx had described the means by which the resources for capitalism had been amassed in Britain, by 'primitive accumulation'. This had involved the expropriation of the peasantry, enclosures of agricultural land and the exploitation of the colonies. These methods, Preobrazhensky stressed, were not open to Soviet Russia. Nevertheless, in 'primitive socialist accumulation' something of the kind must take place, since the peasantry were the main source of accumulation for Soviet industrialization.

Preobrazhensky argued that after the revolution the peasantry had more resources than before, because they were now less burdened by taxation and other compulsory payments to the State and the landowners. As a result, they had more effective demand for industrial goods that industry in its present state was powerless to supply. In Preobrazhensky's view, the Soviet State should use its position as the supplier of most industrial goods and, as the monopolist of foreign trade, to pump resources out of the private sector and so finance the State's investments in the expanding socialist industrial sector. To achieve this the relationship between industry and agriculture would not be based on equal exchange. The peasants would have to pay relatively more for industrial goods than what they received in return for their grain. This would provide the resources to build up industry, and at a comparatively rapid pace. Peasants would benefit from rapid industrialization, because this would increase the quantity of goods for them to buy. At the same time, it would mechanize agriculture and make them more productive.

For Preobrazhensky there was a difference in principle between the nationalized industrial sector controlled by the Soviet State on the one hand, and the private sector of peasants and capitalists on the other. Whereas in the private sector the law of value operated, in the State sector it was the law of 'primitive socialist accumulation' (Nove 1992: 121–4).

Bukharin thought that Preobrazhensky's programme would alienate the peasantry and endanger the regime's survival. A regime which was at war with the peasantry could not be strong. The peasants would not produce or deliver their surplus grain without an incentive, and Preobrazhensky's 'non-equivalent exchange' would eliminate market incentives that NEP gave them. It would mean a return to requisitioning. Bukharin recognized that the growth of industry would be slow, since it would depend on the peasants' willingness to save and supply the State with food surpluses. The road to socialism would be 'at a snail's pace', but, on the positive side, it would maintain the worker–peasant alliance (Nove 1992: 119–21).

Despite their differences on the pace of industrialization, both Bukharin and Preobrazhensky shared the assumption that the equilibrium of the Soviet economy must be maintained. However, by the end of the 1920s this assumption was beginning to be questioned by Stalin. The article that Bukharin published in *Pravda* on 30 September 1928, entitled 'Notes of an Economist', under the pretext of criticizing Trotsky, in reality is directed against Stalin, and puts the case for equilibrium in the strongest terms. This article is the most 'tectological' of Bukharin's writings of the period and, significantly, echoes arguments that Bogdanov had used against Preobrazhensky.

Although, Bukharin conceded, he had regarded the science of economics as applying only to the capitalist world, and the science of the planned economy applying only to socialist society, he believed nevertheless that lessons could be drawn from the capitalist experience. An important lesson to be learnt was that successful industrialization depended on a thriving agriculture, that industry was dependent on the prosperity of the peasants. Conversely, agriculture depended on the growth of industry for its mechanization. If, for the sake of 'pumping over' of resources from agriculture to industry, a pricing policy were introduced in favour of industry and against agriculture, the peasants would reduce their production of grain. And, Bukharin warned:

> If any branch of production regularly fails to recover its production costs plus a certain increment, that corresponds to a certain proportion of surplus labour and can serve as the source of expanded reproduction, then that branch of production either stands still or *regresses*. (Bukharin 1982: 316)

At the time Bukharin was writing, the Soviet regime was beset with the problem of grain collection, and Stalin was invoking the Soviet criminal code to discourage hoarding. Stalin did not readjust the State price for grain, which might have alleviated the situation, but instead embarked upon the policy of forced collectivization of agriculture. The policy was accompanied by a political campaign against the 'Rightists', among whom Stalin numbered Bukharin.

The end of equilibrium

In a speech made to the Conference of Marxist-Agrarians in 1929 Stalin denounced the theory of equilibrium that had hitherto been the assumption of Soviet economists. He declared:

> You know, of course, that the so-called theory of 'equilibrium' between the sectors of our national economy is still current among Communists. This theory, of course, has nothing in common with Marxism. Nevertheless, it is a theory that is being spread by a number of people in the camp of the Rightists. (Stalin 1949: 149)

Stalin maintained that objectively the purpose of the theory was to defend the position of individual peasant farming, to act as a theoretical weapon in the struggle against the collective farms.

In place of the theory of equilibrium, Stalin invoked the Marxist concept of 'expanded reproduction'. He pointed out that whereas Soviet industry expanded year upon year, the economy of small peasant farms did not. It not only failed to show expanded reproduction, but in the majority of cases was unable to achieve even simple reproduction. In order to make agriculture capable of expanded reproduction it was necessary to combine the small peasant farms into large collective farms, employing machinery and scientific methods of farming. Such farms would be capable of further development and would be able to achieve expanded reproduction.

Soon after this speech Groman and Bazarov were arrested on the charge of belonging to the so-called counter-revolutionary organization of Mensheviks, and of wrecking activities. The end of equilibrium in Soviet economic theory meant the adoption in practice of the conception of unbalanced growth, leading to severe bottlenecks and shortages in the years that followed (Belykh 1990: 579–80).

Leninskii sbornik

Bukharin's dictum that Marx and Engels's writings only applied to the era of capitalism ensured that the Soviet regime would not feel threatened by the publication of any works penned by the founders of Marxism. One of the most important offshoots of the Socialist Academy (later the Communist

Academy) was the Institute of Marx and Engels, presided over by the Marxist scholar David Ryazanov. The Institute's journal *Arkhiv K. Marksa i F. Engel'sa* (Marx–Engels Archive) published manuscript writings of Marx and Engels, as well as scholarly articles on the history of socialism. The drafts of Marx's letter to Vera Zasulich appeared in the *Arkhiv* in 1924, and Engels's 'Dialectics of Nature' in 1925. The Lenin Institute was established on Lenin's death in 1924. It was headed by Lev Kamenev, who edited the journal *Leninskii sbornik* (Lenin Miscellany), which published those of Lenin's writings that had not appeared elsewhere.

As part of the campaign against Bukharin and the 'Rightists', Stalin published Lenin's comments on Bukharin's *Economics of the Transition Period* in *Leninskii sbornik* in November 1929. This was intended to show that Lenin had been critical of Bukharin's ideas and, even more damning, that Bukharin had been influenced by Bogdanov. The downside of this manoeuvre was that it revealed that Lenin had not agreed with the 'weakest link' interpretation of the October revolution attributed to him by Stalin and Bukharin. Sure enough, the discrepancy was noticed and was the subject of an article in *Pravda* on 16 December 1929. Stalin, however, replied immediately, claiming that Bukharin's 'weakest link' theory was entirely different from Lenin's (Stalin 1949: 143).

In the September 1929 and December 1930 issues of *Leninskii sbornik* there appeared the collection of manuscripts known as the 'Philosophical Notebooks'. Nothing was published in this journal that Stalin had not approved and, as the publication of Lenin's comments on Bukharin's book illustrates, Stalin used the journal for political purposes. The question thus arises: What did Stalin want to accomplish by publishing Lenin's notes on philosophy?

The obvious answer to this is that it contributed to the Lenin cult that Stalin had fostered by showing Lenin as an adept of Marxist theory. This was something not generally accepted since, as Bukharin pointed out in his article 'Lenin as a Marxist', Lenin was widely thought of, both inside and outside the party, as a man of action but not as a Marxist theoretician (Bukharin 1988: 50). In this context, the notes on philosophy could be held up as proof that Lenin was a master of Hegelian dialectics.

But beyond this, Stalin wanted to show that in the development of Marxism there was a distinct Leninist stage. This was in line with the Soviet orthodoxy that Leninism was Marxism of the era of imperialism and proletarian revolution. The idea, however, was resisted by David Ryazanov, the Director of the Marx and Engels Institute. Ryazanov and his Institute consequently came under attack for their failure to give Lenin his due. To these criticisms Ryazanov replied:

> that it was only after he became acquainted with the correspondence of Marx and Engels did Lenin apply himself to a more profound study of materialist dialectics ... and that therefore there could be no talk of

Leninism as a new, higher, method of scientific investigation as compared with the method of Marxism, that one could only speak of the dialectical method of Marx, Engels and Lenin. (Rokitianskii and Miuller 1996: 312)

Ryazanov's principled stand had dire consequences. Ryazanov was replaced as Director of the Marx and Engels Institute by V. V. Adoratsky, and his Institute was merged with the Lenin Institute to form the Marx, Engels and Lenin Institute attached to the Central Committee of the Communist Party, thus placing it firmly under Stalin's control.

It emerges from what Ryazanov said that the impulse for Lenin to commence the study of Hegelian philosophy at the outbreak of the First World War was the reading of the Marx–Engels correspondence. Moreover, this correspondence established the continuity between Marx and Engels on the one hand and Lenin on the other. Lenin copied out Marx's and Engels's words and absorbed their opinions. As Ryazanov argued, in this situation there could be no suggestion of a distinct Leninist stage of Marxism. Consequently, although Lenin's notes on the Marx–Engels correspondence form an integral whole with the 'Philosophical Notebooks', only the 'Philosophical Notebooks' were published in *Leninskii sbornik* and later in Lenin's *Collected Works*. Lenin's notes on the Marx–Engels correspondence were published only much later, under Khrushchev, in 1956.

But if reading the Marx–Engels correspondence could not be given as the reason for Lenin's philosophical studies in 1914, what other explanation could there be? This explanation was provided by Adoratsky in the Preface to the second instalment of the 'Philosophical Notebooks' in December 1930. It was that:

Lenin's enormous contribution consists in the fact that he rescued dialectics from the simplification, the vulgarisation, the transformation into sophism, as was the case with the renegades of the II International Kautsky, Vandervelde, Otto Bauer and others, and reconstructing it in the form that it had with Marx. (Adoratskii 1930: 19)

This explanation of Adoratsky's is the origin of the interpretation of the 'Philosophical Notebooks' as the regeneration of dialectical Marxism, which had been vulgarized by the theoreticians of the Second International. This interpretation is still current today, though it is not history, but a piece of Soviet ideology approved, and perhaps even invented, by Stalin.

Istpart

How history was written, especially the history of the Bolshevik party and how it came to power, was important to the Soviet regime from the very start of its existence. There were two main stages in the early interpretations of the October revolution. The first stage was from 1918 to 1920, and coincided with the period of the Civil War, when the Bolshevik government was hard-pressed by internal and external adversaries, and needed to project a sympathetic image to potential friends. It wanted to refute the charge that it had come to power by a *coup d'état*. The work which embodies the required interpretation of the October revolution is Trotsky's pamphlet *From October to Brest-Litovsk*, which was written while Trotsky was attending the peace negotiations with the Germans and Austrians at Brest-Litovsk.

In *From October to Brest-Litovsk* Trotsky is adamant that the process that brought the Bolsheviks to power was not a *coup d'état*. On the contrary, taking power was a measure that was forced upon the Bolsheviks by the circumstances and by the insistence of the workers. One finds the same interpretation in John Reed's famous book *Ten Days that Shook the World*, in which the Bolshevik leadership is harangued by a 'rough worker' to take power into their hands. Trotsky's pamphlet was the prototype for later programmatic works which set out an official interpretation of events that all other works were expected to follow.

The second stage was from 1920 onwards, by which time the tide of the Civil War had turned in the Reds' favour, and when the Second Congress of the Communist International met in Moscow in the summer of 1920. Hopes were high that the Russian revolution might be exported to Western Europe. In these circumstances the 'defensive' interpretation of the October revolution was abandoned in favour of one that emphasized the role of the Bolshevik party in organizing and leading the seizure of power in October 1917. The new doctrine was voiced by Lenin in his pamphlet *Left Wing Communism an Infantile Disorder*. This was that the October revolution had been successful due to the organization and iron discipline of the Bolshevik party (Lenin 1966: 24). It was a formula that Lenin recommended to the international communist movement.

In 1920 there was formed Istpart, the Commission for the study and publication of materials on the history of the Bolshevik party and the October revolution. Its chairman was M. S. Olminsky, a veteran revolutionary, who had published a historical work on the origins of the Russian absolutist State, and had edited a collection of memoirs of pioneers of Social Democracy in Russia. Party history was a field too sensitive to be left to historians, and tended to be dominated by party functionaries like Nevsky, Ya. A. Yakovlev and E. M. Yaroslavsky. From its inception Istpart set about establishing a monopoly on all sources relating to its field of interest, so that its version of events could not be challenged by alternative interpretations. Istpart's journal, *Proletarskaia revoliutsiia* (Proletarian Revolution) became one of the main sources for materials on the Russian revolutionary movement, and on the October revolution of 1917 in particular.

Of course the new interpretation called for the publication of a new programmatic history of the October revolution. The task of editing this work was entrusted by Olminsky to Trotsky. The actual writing was done by Yakovlev, the resulting work being a short pamphlet entitled *On the Historical Significance of October*, published in 1922 (Iakovlev 1922). This was the first work to deal with the February as well as the October revolution. Yakovlev contrasted these two revolutions, showing that in February the workers had been unable to seize power because of their lack of organization, whereas October had been a successful proletarian revolution because of the leadership of the Bolshevik party. The lesson for Proletkult, the Workers' Opposition and any other group which believed in workers' autonomy was clear: to be successful the labour movement needed party leadership.

A key function of the history of the October revolution was in emphasizing the importance of members of the party leadership. Prominent figures such as Lenin, Trotsky, Zinoviev and Kamenev were attributed important roles in bringing the Bolsheviks to power. Thus, the question was not 'Who played important parts in the October revolution?' It was 'What important roles in the October revolution did so-and-so play?' Trotsky was a major beneficiary of such honorific attributions until 1924, when he turned the convention on its head and, by denying that Zinoviev and Kamenev had played significant roles in the October revolution, undermined their positions in the party leadership.

The publication of Lenin's writings was indispensable if events were to be interpreted from a Leninist point of view. K. N. Ostroukhova, for example, in recalling her work for Istpart revealed the method employed when she had written a series of articles for *Proletarskaia revoliutsiia* on Lenin's campaign against the boycott of the Second and Third Dumas. This was an important subject because it formed part of the argument in Lenin's *Left-Wing Communism an Infantile Disorder*. According to Ostroukhova:

> I was worried about my ability to expound these complex themes correctly. M. S. Olminsky gave me advice: first of all study Lenin's works, his pronouncements on the question of intra-party struggle in these years ... I remember that in writing the article 'Social Democracy and the Elections to the Third State Duma' I took my guidance chiefly from Lenin's article 'Against the Boycott'. (Ostroukhova 1967: 94–5)

By structuring historical events around Lenin's writings in the way Ostroukhova describes there was inevitably produced a version of history proving that events had confirmed the correctness of Lenin's views. The logic of the situation eventually led to the history of the Bolshevik party and the October revolution becoming a kind of exegesis on Lenin's writings. The culmination of the process came in 1928 when Istpart was incorporated into the Lenin Institute. As Olminsky explained: 'The question of a merger arose inevitably: it was impossible to conceive of the history of the party without Lenin or the history of Lenin without the party' (White 1985: 344).

Pokrovsky

The establishment of Istpart had the effect of designating an area of special ideological significance and removing it from the province of academic historical study. The people on the staff of Istpart, therefore, were not chosen for their historical scholarship, but for their political reliability, a fact noted with some annoyance in 1923 by N. A. Rozhkov who, though a former Menshevik, was a historian of some standing and one with an interest in the history of the Russian revolutionary movement (Rozhkov 1923: 71–4). By the same token, however, the remainder of Russian history was left for scholarly study, including the social and economic conditions which led up to the 1917 revolution. Political control over this area was only established in 1931 following Stalin's letter to *Proletarskaia revoliutsiia*.

Pokrovsky was fortunate in his polemic with Trotsky because in the following year Trotsky fell out of favour with the party leadership. Pokrovsky's articles against Trotsky's conception of Russian historical development merged into the general anti-Trotsky campaign. Because Pokrovsky had argued in favour of Russia's having an autonomous economic development, one not dominated by foreign capital, his articles against Trotsky were held to lend weight to the case for the building of socialism in one country. This impression was reinforced in 1927, when two students of the Institute of Red Professors, Alypov and Tsvetkov, asked Stalin to clarify what his position was on the origins of the Russian autocracy. They had noticed that in his speech at the Tenth Party Congress Stalin had said that the centralized State in Russia had not been formed by the economic development of the country, but as a means of defence against the Mongols and other eastern peoples. Did this mean that Trotsky was right when he asserted that in its development the Russian State had overtaken economics? Stalin replied: 'As for the theory of the "autocratic structure", I must say that basically I do not share comrade Trotsky's theory, whereas I consider comrade Pokrovsky's theory correct in the main, although it is not without its overstatements in simplifying the economic explanation of the rise of the autocracy' (Nechkina 1990: 243). This passage was omitted from Stalin's *Works*, but it was referred to in a report of Pokrovsky's address to the First Congress of Marxist Historians published in the journal *Istorik-Marksist*. In his address Pokrovsky confessed that in the explanation of historical events he tended to overstate the economic factor and that: 'This was noticed by comrade Stalin during the discussion between Pokrovsky and Trotsky. Recognising Trotsky's scheme as completely un-Marxist, comrade Stalin noted the correctness of Pokrovsky's scheme, only pointing out that it suffered from some simplification, consisting in the exaggeration of the role of the economic factor' (Pokrovsky 1929: 234–5).

In 1925 N. N. Vanag, one of Pokrovsky's students, published the monograph *Finance Capital in Russia before the World War*. Vanag took

as his starting point Lenin's conception of imperialism as being the merger
of finance or bank capital with industrial capital. This merger had taken
place in Russia, but whereas the industry had been Russian, the finance
capital had been foreign. Russian monopoly capitalism, therefore, was
not an independent system but more a link in a chain of a more powerful
system: that of Anglo-French-Belgian finance capital. According to Vanag,
foreign capital controlled three quarters of the whole banking system, and
of this the largest share was in the hands of the French banking consortium
(53.2%). The Germans controlled 36.4 per cent and the British 10.4 per
cent. That is, the Entente powers controlled 63.6 per cent and the Germans
36.4 per cent of all foreign investment in Russian industry. Vanag's study
was followed by others which confirmed his findings, the only differences
between them being the precise extent of Russia's dependence on foreign
capital.

Pokrovsky accepted fully Vanag's findings, and adjusted his conception
of modern Russian history accordingly. But if Pokrovsky saw Vanag's work
chiefly as a means of perfecting his own historical conceptions, others were
more sensitive to its political implications. In 1928 at the First Conference of
Marxist Historians, P. O. Gorin expressed what must have been in the minds
of many delegates. He pointed out: 'The views of Vanag on the role of foreign
capital in Russia are close to those of Trotsky. The latter, in the preface of his
book *1905*, also ignores the role of indigenous capital in Russia. The ideas of
Vanag and Trotsky are exactly alike' (Gorin 1929: 234). Other participants
in the conference recommended that Vanag should take the approach Lenin
had in his *The Development of Capitalism in Russia*, focusing on indigenous
rather than foreign investment in the Russian economy.

Eventually the Trotskyist label began to be applied to Pokrovsky himself.
It occurred in 1931 in a chapter of the *History of the Communist Party*
edited by Yaroslavsky (Iaroslavskii 1930–33). It was asserted that: 'In
denying the independent character of Russian imperialism, Pokrovsky,
Vanag and Kritsman have regarded Russia as a colony of French and English
imperialism.' There then followed accusations of a 'revision of Leninism',
'Trotskyist prose' and other political abuse which Pokrovsky rejected as
having no justification.

Vanag himself in 1932 had published a letter in *Istorik-Marksist* in which
he said that he considered it necessary 'to condemn most decisively the point
of view which presents tsarist Russia as a colony of Western-European
imperialist countries. This theory serves as a basis for the Trotskyist
thesis that the building of socialism is impossible in our country' (White
2005: 181).

Stalin made his presence felt by Soviet historians in a dramatic and
forceful manner in October 1931when *Proletarskaia revoliutsiia* published
his letter to the editorial board of the journal. The letter entitled 'Some
Questions Concerning the History of Bolshevism' complained that the
journal had published an article by a certain Slutsky, which suggested that

Lenin might have underestimated the danger of centrism in the German Social-Democratic Party. There were some historical matters, Stalin asserted, which were axiomatic truths and were not subject to discussion. Any attempt to do so was, in his opinion, the smuggling of 'Trotskyist contraband' into historical literature. Stalin's letter singled out for special criticism Yaroslavsky's party history in which Pokrovsky had been criticized. It was Pokrovsky's opponents who now found themselves under a cloud.

In May 1934 the Soviet government recommended that school textbooks should be produced which presented their factual material in a chronological order and avoided 'abstract sociological schemes'. A number of groups were established to draw up outlines for the proposed textbooks, Vanag being put in charge of the group concerned with the history of the USSR. In August of 1934 the outlines were read and commented upon by a panel consisting of Stalin, A. Zhdanov and S. Kirov. The panel found that Vanag's outline was unsatisfactory in a number of ways, including the rather surprising one that '… the dependent role both of Russian tsarism and Russian capitalism on that of Western Europe … remains unexplained.' Vanag was to pay dearly for this oversight and was shot as an 'enemy of the people' (White 2005: 182–3).

Russia's colonial status

The report of the jury for the history textbook competition was published in *Pravda* on 22 August 1937. It was stated that the authors had in the main complied with the guidelines and avoided abstract sociological schemes; but among the shortcomings which remained, a prominent defect was that: 'The Stalin thesis that Russia was beaten "because of its military backwardness, because of its cultural backwardness, because of its governmental backwardness, because of its industrial backwardness, because of its agricultural backwardness", which provides one of the most important keys to Russian history in the last centuries, has not been understood by several authors of textbooks.' The report went on to say that if Russia's backwardness was not understood, the part played by Soviet power in transforming Russia from a poor and weak country into a rich and powerful one would not be appreciated. Now, apparently, the theme of Russian backwardness, which had been associated with Trotsky until 1930, was to be attributed to Stalin (White 2005: 185).

In the same year as the jury reported, Stalin drew up an outline for the projected textbook on the history of the Russian Communist Party. Symptomatically, he was especially anxious that the authors of the textbook should mention the 'petty-bourgeois' nature of the country in order to explain the great variety of currents and fractions within the party, and in the working class as a whole, against which it was necessary to wage an unrelenting struggle (Stalin 1937: 34). The published version of the *History*

of the Russian Communist Party (Bolsheviks): A Short Course, which
appeared in 1938, duly stressed Russia's backwardness with the assertion:

> That Russia entered the imperialist war on the side of Entente ... was
> not accidental. It should be borne in mind that before 1914 the most
> important branches of Russian industry were in the hands of foreign
> capitalists, chiefly those of France, Great Britain and Belgium, that is,
> of the Entente countries ... All these circumstances, in addition to the
> thousands of millions borrowed by the tsar from France and Britain in
> loans, chained tsardom to British and French imperialism and converted
> Russia into a tributary, a semi-colony of those countries'. (*History of the
> CPSU (B)*, 1939: 162)

This idea was of course consistent with the theory of the 'weakest link',
which also was reproduced in the *Short Course*. This stated that:

> Lenin showed that it is just this unevenness of development of capitalism
> that gives rise to imperialist wars, which undermine the strength of
> imperialism and make it possible to break the front of imperialism at its
> weakest point. (*History of the CPSU (B)*, 1939: 168)

The *Short Course*

The context in which the *Short Course* appeared was the aftermath of the
forced collectivization of agriculture, the industrialization of the country
with enormous human and material cost and, most recently, the purges,
which had destroyed a great part of the old intelligentsia. A climate of fear
and suspicion pervaded all walks of life, encouraged by calls for vigilance in
the face of all-pervasive internal wreckers and saboteurs. The *Short Course*
was designed to provide Soviet propagandists with an 'encyclopedia of
Marxism-Leninism', to instruct them in what their attitudes to the history
of the recent past should be: lack of this kind of political tempering had led
to members of the intelligentsia falling into the clutches of foreign spies and
their Trotskyist-Bukharinist and bourgeois nationalist agents.

An article in *Pravda* on 15 November 1938 set out the objectives that
the *Short Course* was meant to achieve. The first of these was that it was
meant to replace all previous textbooks on the subject, and put an end to
the existence of different interpretations of the history of the Communist
party. The *Short Course* would be the version approved by the party Central
Committee, and thus be the official version of events.

The *Pravda* article explained that an important feature of the *Short
Course* was that in propaganda it would put an end to the artificial division
into Marxism and Leninism that had come about over the past few years.
Henceforth the doctrine would be referred to as Marxism–Leninism. In

other words, Stalin was eradicating the distinction that he and Bukharin had created in 1924 to allow the emergence of a specifically Soviet approach to economics. In the circumstances of 1938, the change could only have symbolic significance. It signalled a new stage in Marxism which called for a new definition of Leninism. This was: 'Leninism is the further development of Marxism in the new conditions of the class struggle of the proletariat, the Marxism of the epoch of imperialism and proletarian revolution, the Marxism of the epoch of the victory of socialism in one sixth of the world.' The Leninism of the new stage was 'active Leninism', and an example of this kind of Leninism was the collectivization of agriculture.

A feature of Marxism–Leninism was that, in addition to the *Short Course*, propagandists were encouraged to refer to the first-hand sources of Marxism. There were the works of Marx, Engels, Lenin and Stalin. The doctrine of Marxism–Leninism placed Stalin on a par with Marx, Engels and Lenin. This did not mean, however, any radical break with the existing practice of Soviet Marxism to base itself on Lenin's interpretation of Marx's doctrines (Marcuse 1971: 38–9).

The encouragement to read works of the four great theoreticians of Marxism – from, of course, the perspective of 'Marxism-Leninism' – meant that there should be suitable editions of these works readily available. That there were not, prompted criticism of the Institute of Marx, Engels and Lenin. Adoratsky was contrite in the face of the shortcomings of his Institute. He explained that the followers of the wrecker Ryazanov had been expelled, but that the Institute had still been unable to fulfil its functions satisfactorily. The institute was brought under the direct control of the party Central Committee.

The *Pravda* article stated that the approach of the *Short Course* to historical events would be impersonal; it would eschew the biographical approach common in other works, and avoid reference to individuals. In fact the *Short Course* did not adhere consistently to this principle, and singled out people for special praise or, more frequently, for condemnation. But of course it was convenient not to refer to those individuals who had fallen victim to the reign of terror, which was still being conducted as the book was being published.

According to the *Pravda* article, an aim of the *Short Course* was to avoid simplification or vulgarization in its exposition. It intended to avoid the schematism characteristic of the Pokrovsky school, which recounted events in a distorted way, viewing them from the perspective of the present day, rather than in the context of contemporary conditions. This was a laudable aim, but the approach adopted by the *Short Course* was the exact opposite: it was in fact simplification, vulgarization and the evaluation of events from the perspective of the late 1930s. This was unavoidable because the book was intended for a wide audience, primarily the new Soviet intelligentsia which was emerging to replace the one that had been destroyed in the purges. The book was distributed in tens of millions of copies (Wetter 1964: 212).

This was a manual which told that cohort how to think; it was written in unambiguous terms, so that there could be no doubt about whom one should be for, and whom one should be against.

Content

The *Short Course* has for its central figures Lenin and Stalin and, for the later sections, Stalin alone. Only Lenin and Stalin have right on their side; other protagonists and currents of opinion are regarded as enemies or wreckers. Trotsky, Bukharin and their supporters are never acknowledged to have made any positive contribution to the success of the Bolsheviks, and are presented as inveterate saboteurs or traitors.

This implacable attitude is projected backwards even to the opening sections of the *Short Course*, to the way the *narodniki* are treated. They are presented as a major ideological force, though no actual *narodnik* or work of *narodism* is mentioned. The first fact revealed about the *narodniki* is that they were 'opponents of Marxism'. Consequently, 'Narodism had to be completely *smashed* ideologically if the further spread of Marxism and the creation of a Social-Democratic party were to be assured'. This schematic presentation of events has very little relation to reality; '*narodism*' in the sense used by the *Short Course* never existed.

As the Introduction to the *Short Course* explains, the history of the Communist party is a succession of struggles against *narodniki*, Mensheviks, Anarchists, and within the party itself, against Trotskyists, Bukharinists and other anti-Leninist groups (*History of the CPSU (B)* 1939: 1). Characteristic of the *Short Course*'s treatment of these groupings and individuals was the attribution to them of exaggerated views which they did not hold, thus making the Leninist view seem reasonable by comparison.

This was the case in dealing with Bogdanov, Lunacharsky and Bazarov. 'These people', the *Short Course* asserted:

> claimed that in the main they were Marxists, but that they wanted to 'improve' Marxism by ridding it of certain of its fundamental principles. In reality, they were hostile to Marxism, for they tried to undermine its theoretical foundations, although they hypocritically denied their hostility to Marxism and two-facedly continued to style themselves Marxists. The danger of this hypocritical criticism lay in the fact that it was calculated to deceive rank-and-file members of the Party and might lead them astray. The more hypocritical grew this criticism, which aimed at undermining the theoretical foundations of Marxism, the more dangerous it was to the Party, for the more it merged with the general campaign of the reactionaries against the Party, against the revolution. Some of the intellectuals who had deserted Marxism went so far as to

advocate the founding of a new religion (these were known as 'god-seekers' and 'god-builders'). (*History of the CPSU (B)* 1939: 102–3)

The readers of the *Short Course* were unlikely to have read Bogdanov's *Tectology* or Lunacharsky's *Religion and Socialism*, and so would not be in a position to question this tendentious and garbled version of events.

What added some credibility to the *Short Course*'s characterization of Bogdanov and his associates was the quasi-sociological explanation of the intellectual currents of the post-1905 period. This was:

> The defeat of the revolution of 1905 started a process of disintegration and degeneration in the ranks of the fellow-travellers of the revolution. Degenerate and decadent tendencies grew particularly marked among the intelligentsia. The fellow-travellers who came from the bourgeois camp to join the movement during the upsurge of the revolution deserted the Party in the days of reaction. (*History of the CPSU (B)*, 1939: 101–2)

According to the *Short Course* it was this decadent movement which gave rise to the ideas of Bogdanov, Lunacharsky, Bazarov and others. The grain of truth in this explanation is that quite often the intellectuals who joined the revolutionary movement in 1905 left it when the movement was defeated. What is not true is that Bogdanov and his friends were part of this phenomenon. On the contrary, the party schools they ran on Capri and in Bologna were designed to make good the loss of the intellectuals who had deserted the workers' movement. A mark of how influential the *Short Course* became is that one can still come across the 'decadent' explanation of Bogdanov's and Lunacharsky's ideas in Western works to the present day.

Dialectical and Historical Materialism

The passage on Bogdanov is an important one in the *Short Course* because it is a preliminary to the section in chapter four entitled 'Dialectical and Historical Materialism', written by Stalin. Here, over thirty pages, Stalin sets out the theoretical side of Marxism as he believes it ought to be understood. His approach is practical since he repeats several times that a correct understanding of the subject is essential if one is not to make mistakes in policy. His approach is also didactic in that he systematically defines the terms he uses and provides examples mainly from the Soviet experience.

Stalin begins by stating that dialectical materialism is the world outlook of the Marxist–Leninist party. It is called dialectical materialism because its approach to the phenomena of nature, its method of studying and apprehending them is *dialectical*, while its interpretation of the phenomena of nature, its conception of these phenomena, its theory, is *materialistic*

(*History of the CPSU (B)* 1939: 105). Stalin then goes on to define 'dialectics' and 'materialism' separately.

According to Stalin, dialectics regards the phenomena of nature, not in isolation, as metaphysics does, but in relation to other phenomena. Also, in contrast to metaphysics, dialectics holds that nature is not in a state of rest and immobility but in a state of continuous movement and change. Here Stalin cites in support of this latter contention the opinion of Engels in 'The Dialectics of Nature'. A further contrast between metaphysics and dialectics is that whereas the former saw change as a continuous process, the latter envisaged rapid transformations from quantity to quality. Lastly, contrary to metaphysics, dialectics holds that contradictions are inherent in all things, an idea which Stalin supported by a quotation from Lenin's 'Philosophical Notebooks' (*History of the CPSU (B)* 1939: 109).

Stalin's three characteristics of dialectics had no inner connection; they were offered to the reader of the *Short Course* as individual aphorisms. Nor did they have any particular philosophical connotations, being more in the character of homespun wisdom than socialist theory. The practical implications of the laws of dialectics, moreover, were somewhat predictable.

According to Stalin, a lesson that could be drawn from the dialectical point of view on change, 'if one were not to err in policy', is that 'one must be a revolutionary, not a reformist'. The implication of contradictions' being in the nature of things was that one should not conceal the contradictions of the capitalist system, but disclose and unravel them (*History of the CPSU (B)* 1939: 111).

Having given his definition of dialectics, Stalin then proceeded to explain what materialism was. Defining 'materialism' and 'matter' was something that had caused Plekhanov great difficulty, but caused Stalin no problems. His method was to contrast materialism with idealism, and to define idealism in such a way that it appeared absurd to hold such a view. Thus, according to Stalin, contrary to idealism, which denies the possibility of knowing the world and its laws, which does not recognize objective truth, which holds that the world is full of 'things-in-themselves' that can never be known, Marxist philosophical materialism holds that the world and its laws are fully knowable. In support, here Stalin quoted the passage from Engels's *Ludwig Feuerbach*, which argued that the most telling refutation of idealism was practice, experiment and industry, the fact that people were able to replicate natural processes and to make accurate predictions from scientific data (*History of the CPSU (B)* 1939: 113). Stalin, however, did not cite in this connection, as Engels had done, Marx's 'Theses on Feuerbach'.

In terms of 'historical materialism', Stalin held that the factor that determined the life of society was its mode of production. It followed that, 'if it were not to err in policy', the party of the proletariat must, both in the drafting of its programme and in its practical activities, proceed primarily from the laws of development of production, from the laws of the economic development of society. There then followed a disquisition on the relationship of the productive forces of society to its relations of production, and how these corresponded exactly in the Soviet Union. The section on 'historical materialism' concluded by reproducing the famous passage from Marx's Preface to the *Contribution to the Critique of Political Economy* in which Marx outlined his conception of the base and superstructure of society, and of how people's consciousness was determined by their social being.

In the fraught atmosphere of 1938 people's critical faculties were suspended. The Soviet philosopher M. B. Mitin said of the *Short Course* that 'the treasury of Marxism-Leninism has been enriched by a work, which, no doubt, stands on the first rank beside such classical theoretical works as the *Communist Manifesto, Das Kapital* and *Imperialism the Highest Stage of Capitalism*' (Maslov 1990: 100–1). Quite clearly it was nothing of the kind: it was a plodding scholastic work of semi-fiction, but judgement upon it was stamped with the fear and menace of the times. The *Short Course* may not have been on a par with the works that Mitin mentioned, but for a time its influence was greater than that of any of them. It was essential reading for generations of Soviet citizens, and was the obligatory template for all works of history and philosophy produced during Stalin's lifetime, and indeed beyond.

Very little remains in the *Short Course* of the conceptions that are incorporated in Marx's *Das Kapital*. In their journey through the Russian revolutionary movement and the creation of the Soviet State, Marx's ideas were emptied of their original content in such a way that only the outer shell remained. If one's knowledge of Marx's writings came only from the *Short Course*, it would be impossible to reconstruct what Marx's original intention could have been. In particular, it would be impossible on the evidence of the *Short Course* to deduce why it was that Marx should have taken up the study of Russia.

After Stalin's death in 1953 measures were taken by Khrushchev, and later by Gorbachev, to undo the damage that had been done to Soviet scholarship by the practices of the Stalin era. One should not underestimate the achievements of the post-Stalin period in this regard. In fact, some of the sources used in the present work were published at this time. However, the problem for Soviet leaders was that they dared not tamper too far with the precepts of 'Marxism-Leninism' for fear of undermining the legitimacy of the Soviet regime.

Moreover, there was the difficulty that historical perceptions have their own momentum. Once a version of history has gained currency, however erroneous it may be, it is difficult to correct. The omission from it of particular events or personalities, or the inclusion in it of spurious phenomena, is not appreciated. Allied to this is the problem of collective memory. The generation of Soviet theorists who first moulded party history to suit political conjunctures has long since left the scene. How can later generations correct these distortions of fact, when they do not recognize that they are in fact distortions? For these reasons, Stalin's *Short Course* continued to exercise an influence right up to the demise of the Soviet regime. To the present time one can still encounter conceptions of Russian and Soviet history that are derived from that source.

Concluding remarks

In her day, Mrs Thatcher was fond of referring to the Soviet Union as a 'Marxist State', the implication being that Marx was responsible for all the infamies perpetrated in the Soviet era. But was she right? Does Marx carry the blame for the crimes of Stalinism? For what we have seen from the history of Marxism in Russia, there is very little continuity between Marx and Stalin. But that is not to say there is none. Terminology such as 'class struggle' and 'dictatorship of the proletariat' provided justification for the use of force throughout the Soviet period. Otherwise, the evolution of Marxist thought in Russia is a progressive distancing from the Marxist ideas that had first entered Russia in the 1870s.

As we have seen, this evolution was initiated by Marx himself. His interest in Russia, and Russians' interest in his ideas, came at a time when Marx was revising his original plans for his 'Critique of Political Economy'. He was eliminating the Hegelian framework and revising fundamentally his initial conceptions of how capital circulated and reproduced itself on an expanded scale. Marx never succeeded in completing his project, and when he died in 1883 he left an ambiguous intellectual legacy to his followers that was subject to a variety of interpretations.

A more conscientious literary executor than Engels might have left the second and third volumes of *Das Kapital* in their unfinished state, and not implied that the problems Marx had encountered and worked on for over a decade did not exist. He might have published selections from the Russian material with Marx's annotations, as Kovalevsky and Chuprov had suggested. That would at least have pointed Marx's successors in the right direction, and showed that Marxism was a work in progress and not a finished system.

Since after 1868 Marx had been intent on eliminating the Hegelian element from his economic writings, it was misleading of Engels to imply that his own preoccupation with updating Hegel's *Philosophy of Nature* was one shared by Marx, and was the basis for Marx's theoretical works. The theory of knowledge which Engels attributed to Marx in his pamphlet *Ludwig Feuerbach* was not the one which underlay Marx's economic writings, and was not one from which the concept of 'commodity fetishism' could be derived.

It was not Engels, but Bogdanov, who, like Marx in his *Economic and Political Manuscripts of 1844*, held that the distorted view of reality which gave rise to 'commodity fetishism' arose from the fragmentation of the individual in civil society that the division of labour had brought about. Like Marx too, Bogdanov saw the solution in a society in which people would not be trapped in a single role, but could engage in a variety of activities according to their inclinations.

Sieber was quite correct in seeing in Engels's *Anti-Dühring* nothing beyond contemporary scientific thinking. But his opinion was used by Plekhanov to argue that Sieber did not understand 'dialectics', and so to discredit him. Plekhanov's rise to prominence and Sieber's early death were causes that prevented a commentator on Marx, who by rights should occupy a unique place in the history of Marxist thought, from being better known. An important insight of Sieber's was the ability to distinguish in Marx's writings what was central to his thought and what was the embellishment of Hegelian terminology. His judgement on this was given Marx's full endorsement. Had Sieber's commentary on Marx been given the weight it deserved, the acceptance of Plekhanov's conception of Marxist philosophy as 'dialectical materialism' would have been impossible. It is for this reason that the rise of Plekhanov necessarily involved the eclipse of Sieber.

Lenin's *What Is To Be Done?* represented a major breach with a basic principle of both Marx and Engels, which was that 'the emancipation of the working class is the affair of the working class itself'. It is significant that the two men took the principle so seriously that they declared that they could not cooperate with people who openly stated that the workers were too uneducated to emancipate themselves and must be freed from above, by representatives of other classes (Marx and Engels 1970: 94). The entire history of the Bolshevik party is an illustration of the wisdom of this proposition. The pretension of a group of intellectuals to know what the real objective interests of the working class might be, in face of the expression of the concrete demands of actual workers, is the definition of tyranny. Trotsky perceived this in 1904, when he warned of the dangers of 'substitutionism', a warning which was fully vindicated by later events. By that time, however, Trotsky himself was an active participant in, and apologist for, that same 'substitutionism'.

An important break in any continuity there might be between Marx and Stalin was made by Bukharin when he denied the existence of the categories of capitalist political economy in the Soviet state, arguing that Marx's economic ideas did not apply to the emerging socialist system. This idea was reinforced by Stalin's pronouncement in 1924 that Leninism was the Marxism of the era of imperialism and proletarian revolution. The ideology of the Soviet State was thereby held to be Leninism rather than Marxism. Following Stalin's 'revolution from above' in 1929 what determined Soviet policy was the personal will of the dictator.

A characteristic phenomenon in the evolution of Marxist ideas in Russia is the generation of a historical mythology. This begins with Engels's *Ludwig Feuerbach*, whose account of the emergence of Marx's ideas is at variance with contemporary evidence, including Engels's own early writings. Plekhanov is the arch-spinner of historical mythology with his creation of the '*narodnik*' current of agrarian socialism, whose intellectual ancestors were Herzen and Chernyshevsky and, prior to them, the Slavophiles. This myth was first debunked by Mikhailovsky, who had been classed as a '*narodnik*' by Plekhanov, but rejected the label and denied that any such current existed.

What was Lenin's revolutionary theory? What was the insight that Lenin had that led him to believe that socialism in Russia was possible? We know from Lenin's writings what this was: it was the Hilferdingian idea that, because the banks controlled industry, it was sufficient to take over the banks in order to have the basis for a centralized socialist economic system. Because this idea did not work, Hilferding and his ideas disappeared from Soviet discourse, and Stalin declared Lenin's revolutionary theory to be that 'the chain of imperialism broke at its weakest link'. There was also a change of emphasis when dealing with Lenin's leadership in the Bolshevik revolution. It became less on Lenin's theoretical pronouncements and more on the actual process of taking power in October 1917. What had been a relatively uneventful and peaceful accession to power in Petrograd was portrayed a decade later in an Eisenstein film as a major military operation. It is symptomatic, however, that there were more casualties in the making of the film than there had been in the actual event.

Trotsky's most famous works, his *The History of the Russian Revolution* and his autobiography *My Life*, were both written in exile, and with the acceptance of the Lenin cult. The materials in the volumes of his *Collected Works*, published in Moscow in the 1920s, are also selected to give a pro-Lenin gloss on Trotsky's literary output. But Trotsky's earlier versions of the theory of permanent revolution, particularly in his book *1905*, show him as a thinker who bases his ideas on a much better grasp of Russian economic history than Lenin did in his *Development of Capitalism in Russia*. For Trotsky, the role of foreign capital in the Russian economy is decisive, and it is the dominance of this capital which determines the weakness of the Russian bourgeoisie and its liberal aspirations. This was true in 1905, and applied just as well in 1917. Only political considerations made it necessary for Trotsky to modify the introduction to *The History of the Russian Revolution* in deference to Lenin.

The culmination of myth-making is Stalin's *Short Course*. It is not history, but politics in a historical guise. It is a work in which every sentence has been hammered out to achieve the desired effect. Its purpose is to give legitimacy to Stalin's rule, and every alleged historical event is held to be a step leading towards the regime that had emerged by 1938. Moreover, the *Short Course* did not exist in isolation. Every textbook, every monograph,

every collection of documents published for the next thirty years or so had
to conform to its interpretations, so that the *Short Course* could not be
challenged by independent research. Even more pernicious was Stalin's
doctrine, enunciated in his letter to the journal *Proletarskaia revoliutsiia*
in 1931, that there existed in history certain axioms that could not be
questioned. This is a doctrine that effectively destroys history as a discipline,
and no doubt this was Stalin's intention.

There are no axioms in history; there is no historical 'fact' that cannot
be questioned. This is especially true in Russian and Soviet history, where
the influence of ideology on historiography has been so great. In these
circumstances there is particular need to approach accepted versions of
events critically. To do this it is necessary to have an understanding of what
the political and ideological considerations were that determined a given
historical version. It is to be hoped that the present work will go some way
towards raising awareness of the ideological element in Russian and Soviet
historiography, and by doing this, assist in overcoming its influence.

BIBLIOGRAPHY

Adoratskii, V. (1930), 'Predislovie', in N. I. Bukharin, V. M. Molotov and
  M. A. Savel'ev (eds), *Leninskii sbornik: Volume 12*: 3–23, Moscow
  and Leningrad: Gosizdat.
Akhapkin, I. (1970), *First Decrees of Soviet Power*, London: Lawrence & Wishart.
Aleksandrov, V. A. (1976), *Sel'skaia obshchina v Rossii (XVII- nachalo XIX v.)*,
  Moscow: Nauka.
Antonov, V. (1962), *Russkii drug Marksa: German Aleksandrovich Lopatin*,
  Moscow: Sotsekgiz.
Avenarius, R. (1905), *Kritika chistogo opyta v populiarnim izlozhenii
  A. Lunacharskogo*, Moscow: S. Dorovatskii i A. Charushnikov.
Belykh, A. A. (1990), 'A. A. Bogdanov's Theory of Equilibrium and the Economic
  Discussions of the 1920s', *Soviet Studies*, 42 (3): 571–82.
Berdyaev, N. (1901), 'Bor'ba za idealizm', *Mir Bozhii*, 10 (6): 1–26.
Bogdanov, A. A. (1899), *Osnovnye elementy istoricheskogo vzgliada na prirodu.
  Priroda. Zhizn'. Psikhika. Obshchestvo*, St Petersburg: S. Dorovatskii i
  A. Charushnikov.
Bogdanov, A. A. (1906a), *Iz psikhologii obshchestva*, St Petersburg: Delo.
Bogdanov, A. A. (1906b), *Kratkii kurs ekonomicheskoi nauki*, Moscow:
  S. Dorovatskii i A. Charushnikov.
Bogdanov, A. A. (1908), *Prikliucheniia odnoi filosofskoi shkoly*, St Petersburg:
  Znanie.
Bogdanov, A. A. (1910a), *Otchet pervoi vysshei sotsial-demokraticheskoi
  propagandistsko-agitatorskoi shkoloi dlia rabochikh (avgust-dekabr; 1909
  goda)*, Paris: Izdanie Soveta Shkoly.
Bogdanov, A. A. (1910b), *Padenie velikogo fetishizma. (Sovremennyi krizis
  ideologii). Vera i nauka. (O knige V. Il'ina 'Materializm i empiriokrititsizm')*,
  Moscow: S. Dorovatskii i A. Charushnikov.
Bogdanov, A. A. (1911), *Kul'turnye zadachi nashogo vremeni*, Moscow:
  S. Dorovatskii i A. Charushnikov.
Bogdanov, A. A. (1916a), 'Mirovye krizisy, mirnye i voennye', *Letopis'*, 5: 113–24.
Bogdanov, A. A. (1916b), 'Mirovye krizisy, mirnye i voennye', *Letopis'*, 4: 133–53.
Bogdanov, A. A. (1917), 'Chto zhe my svergli?', *Novaia zhizn'*, 17 May.
Bogdanov, A. A. (1918a), 'Tovarishchi!', *Proletarskaia kul'tura*, 1.
Bogdanov, A. A. (1918b), 'Sud'by rabochei partii v nyneshnei revoliutsii',
  Novaia zhizn', 26 January.
Bogdanov, A. A. (1925), 'Roza Liuksemburg protiv Karla Marksa', in A. S.
  Shutskever (ed.), *Kak rozhdalas' partiia bol'shevikov: Literaturnaia polemika
  1903–04 gg.*; Sbornik: 167–75: Priboi.

Bogdanov, A. A. (1984), *Red Star: The First Bolshevik Utopia*, Bloomington: Indiana University Press.

Bogdanov, A. A. (1989), *Tektologiia: Vseobshchaia organizatsionnaia nauka*, Volume 1, Moscow: Ekonomika.

Bogdanov, A. A. (1990), *Voprosy sotsializma: Raboty raznyh let*, Moscow: Politizdat.

Bogdanov, A. A. (1995), *Neizvestnyi Bogdanov: V 3-kh knigakh*, Volume 1, Moscow: ITS 'AIRO-XX'.

Bogdanov, A. A. (1996), *Bogdanov's tektology*, Centre for Systems Studies, University of Hull, UK.

Bogdanov, A. A. (2003), *Empiriomonizm: Stat'i po filosofii*, Moscow: Respublika.

Bogdanov, A. A. and I. I. Skvortsov-Stepanov (1918), *Kurs politicheskoi ekonomii*, 2nd edn, Moscow: Tsentral'nyi Knizhnyi Sklad M. S. R. i K. Deputatov.

Bogdanov, A. A. and I. I. Skvortsov-Stepanov (1910–25), *Kurs politicheskoi ekonomii*, St Petersburg: Izd. t-vo 'Znanie'.

Bogucharskii, V. I. (1912), *Aktivnoe narodnichestvo semidesiatykh godov*, Moscow: Izd-vo M. i. S. Sabashnikovykh.

Bogucharskii, V. I. (1970), *Revoliutsionnaia zhurnalistika semidesiatykh godov: Vtoroe prilozhenie k sbornikam 'Gosudarstvennyia prestupleniia v Rossii'*, Rostov-na-Donu, Düsseldorf: Donskaia rech'; Brücken-Verlag.

Brusnev, M. I. (1923), 'Vozniknovenie pervykh sotsial- demokraticheskikh organizatsii: (Vospominaniia)', *Proletarskaia revoliutsiia*, 2 (14): 17–32.

Bukharin, N. I. (1915), 'Mirovaia ekonomika i imperializm', *Kommunist*, (1–2).

Bukharin, N. I. (1925), 'Chto takoe politicheskaia ekonomiia?', *Vestnik Kommunisticheskoi Akademii*, 11.

Bukharin, N. I. (1971), *Economics of the Transformation Period, with Critical Remarks by Lenin*, New York: Bergman.

Bukharin, N. I. (1979), *The Politics and Economics of the Transition Period*, Edited with an introduction by Kenneth J. Tarbuck. Translated by Oliver Field, London: Routledge.

Bukharin, N. I. (1982), *Selected Writings on the State and the Transition to Socialism*, Translated, edited, and introduced by Richard B. Day. With forewords by Stephen F. Cohen and Ken Coates, Nottingham: Spokesman.

Bukharin, N. I. (1988), *Izbrannye proizvedeniia*, Moscow: Izdatel'stvo politichrskoi literatury.

Bukharin, N. I. and E. Preobrazhensky (1969), *The ABC of Communism: Introduced by E. H. Carr*, Harmondsworth: Penguin Books.

Carr, E. H. (1933), *The Romantic Exiles: A Nineteenth-Century Portrait Gallery*, London: V. Gollancz.

Carver, T. (1980), 'Marx, Engels and Dialectics', *Political Studies*, 28 (3): 353–63.

Chernyshevskii, N. G. (1937), *Izbrannye sochineniia: Volume 2*, Moscow-Leningrad: Gosudarstvennoe sotsial'no-ekonomicheskoe izdatel'stvo.

Chernyshevskii, N. G. (1949), *Polnoe sobranie sochinenii v piatnadtsati tomakh: Volume 9*, Moscow: 'Khudozhestvennaia. Literatura'.

Chernyshevskii, N. G. (1950), *Polnoe sobranie sochinenii v piatnadtsati tomakh: Volume 5*, Moscow: 'Khudozhestvennaia. Literatura'.

Chicherin, B. N. (1998), *Liberty, Equality and the Market: Essays by B. N. Chicherin*. Edited and Translated by G. M. Hamburg, New Haven and London: Yale University Press.

Comte, Auguste (1875–77), *System of Positive Polity*, 4 vols. London: Longmans Green.

Danielson, N. F. (1880), 'Ocherki nashego poreformennogo obshchestvennogo khoziaistva', *Slovo*, 10: 77–143.

Donald, M. (1993), *Marxism and Revolution: Karl Kautsky and the Russian Marxists, 1900–1924*, New Haven, CT: Yale University Press.

Engels, F. (1886), 'Ludwig Feuerbach und der Ausgang der klassischen deutschen Philosophie', *Die neue Zeit*, 4 (4): 145–57.

Engels, F. (1888), *Ludwig Feuerbah und der Ausgang der klassischen deutschen Philosophie: Revidirter Sonder-Ausdruck aus der 'Neuen Zeit'*, Mit Anhang: Karl Marx über Feuerbach vom Jahre 1845, Stuttgart: Dietz.

Falkowski, M. and T. Kowalik (1957), *Początki marksistowskiej myśli w Polsce: Wybór publicystiki z lat 1880–1885*, Warsaw: Panstwowe wydawnictwo naukowe.

Flerovskii, N. (1869), *Polozenie rabochego klassa v Rossii: Nabliudeniia i issledovaniia N. Flerovskogo*, St Petersburg: Izd. N. P. Poliakova.

Frankel, J. (1963), 'Economism: A Heresy Exploited', *Slavic Review*, 22 (2): 263–84.

Gorin, P. O. (1929), 'Discussion on Vanag's Paper', *Istorik marksist*, 11: 234.

Grin, T. I. (1985), *Perevodchik i izdatel' 'Kapitala': Ocherk zhizni i deiatel'nosti Nikolaia Frantsevicha Daniel'sona*, Moscow: 'Kniga'.

Harding, N. (1981), *Lenin's Political Thought*, London: MacMillan.

Harstick, H.-P. (1977), *Karl Marx über Formen vorkapitalistischer Produktion: Vergleichende Studien zur Geschichte d. Grundeigentums 1879–80*, 1st edn, Frankfurt/Main, New York: Campus-Verlag.

Haxthausen, A. v. (1866), *Die ländliche Verfassung Russlands. Ihre Entwickelungen und ihre Feststellung in der Gesetzgebung von 1861*, Leipzig: F. A. Brockhaus.

Haxthausen, A. v. (1972), *Studies on the Interior of Russia*, Edited with an introduction by S. Frederick Starr, Chicago & London: University of Chicago Press.

Hegel, G. W. F. (1969), *Science of Logic*. Translated by A. V. Miller, London: Allen & Unwin.

Herzen, A. (1956), *Selected Philosophical Works*, Moscow: Foreign Languages Publishing House.

Hilferding, R. (1923), *Das Finanzkapital: Eine Studie über die jüngste Entwicklung des Kapitalismus*, Wien: Verlag der Wiener Volksbuchhandlung.

History of the CPSU (B): Short Course (1939), Moscow: Foreign Languages Publishing House.

Iakovlev, I. A. (1922), *Ob istoricheskom smysle Oktiabria*, Moscow: Gosizdat.

Iaroslavskii, E. M. ed. (1930–33) *Istoriia VKP(b)*, Moscow: Partizdat.

Institut marksizma-leninizma pri TSK KPSS (1958), *Sed'maia (aprel'skaia vserossiiskaia konferentsiia RSDRP (Bol'shevikov): Protokoly*, Moscow: Gospolitizdat.

Kant, I. (1950), *Immanuel Kant's Critique of Pure Reason*. Translated by Norman Kemp Smith, London: MacMillan.

Karataev, N. K. (1958), *Narodnicheskaia ekonomicheskaia literatura: Izbrannye proizvedeniia*, Moscow: Sotsekgiz.

Kautsky, K. (1914), 'Der Imperialismus', *Die neue Zeit*, 32 (21): 908–22.

Kautsky, K. (1915), *Nationalstaat, imperialistischer Staat und Staatenbund*, Nürnberg: Fränkische Verlagsanstalt.

Kazakov, A. P. (1969), *Teoriia progressa v russkoi sotsiologii kontsa XIX veka (P.L. Lavrov, N.K. Mikhailovskii, M.M. Kovalevskii)*, Leningrad: Izd-vo Leningradskogo universiteta.

King, F. (1999), 'The Russian Revolution and the Idea of a Single Economic Plan 1917–28', *Revolutionary Russia*, 12 (1): 69–83.

Kleinbort, L. M. (1923), *Nikolai Ivanovich Ziber*, Petrograd: 'Kolos'.

Kolakowski, L. (1992), *Main Currents of Marxism: Its Origins, Growth and Dissolution*, Oxford: Oxford University Press.

Kollontai, A. (1977), *Selected Writings of Alexandra Kollontai*, London: Allison and Busby.

Koniushaia, R. P. (1948), *Arkhiv K. Marksa i F. Engel'sa: Volume 11*, Moscow: Gospolitizdat.

Koniushaia, R. P. (1952), *Arkhiv K. Marksa i F. Engel'sa: Volume 12*, Moscow: Gospolitizdat.

Koniushaia, R. P. (1985), *Karl Marks i revoliutsionnaia Rossiia*, Moscow: Politizdat.

Kovalevskii, M. M. (1876), *Ocherk istorii raspadeniia obshchinnago zemlevladeniia v kantone Vaadt*.

Kovalevskii, M. M. (1879), *Obshchinnoe zemlevladenie, prichiny, khod i posledstviia ego razlozheniia*, Moscow: F. B. Miller.

Kowalski, R. I. (1990), *Kommunist: A Weekly Journl of Economic, Political and Social Opinion.: The Organ of the Moscow Regional Bureau of the Russian Communist Party (Bolshevik)*, Edited with introduction, notes, appendices and index by Ronald I. Kowalski, Millwood, New York: Kraus International Publications.

Krupskaya, N. (1970), *Memories of Lenin*, London: Panther.

Lafargue, P. (1905), 'Persönliche Errinerungen an Friedrich Engels', *Die neue Zeit*, 23 (44): 556–61.

Lenin, V. I. (1930), 'Philosophical Notebooks', *Leninskii sbornik*, 12.

Lenin, V. I. (1960a), *Collected Works: Volume 1*, Moscow: Progress Publishers.

Lenin, V. I. (1960b), *Collected Works: Volume 3*, Moscow: Progress Publishers

Lenin, V. I. (1960c), *Collected Works: Volume 4*, Moscow: Progress Publishers.

Lenin, V. I. (1961), *Collected Works: Volume 38*, Moscow: Progress Publishers.

Lenin, V. I. (1962), *Collected Works: Volume 14*, Moscow: Progress Publishers.

Lenin, V. I. (1963), *Collected Works: Volume 19*, Moscow: Progress Publishers.

Lenin, V. I. (1964a), *Collected Works: Volume 21*, Moscow: Progress Publishers.

Lenin, V. I. (1964b), *Collected Works: Volume 22*, Moscow: Progress Publishers.

Lenin, V. I. (1964c), *Collected Works: Volume 23*, Moscow: Progress Publishers.

Lenin, V. I. (1964d), *Collected Works: Volume 25*, Moscow: Progress Publishers.

Lenin, V. I. (1964e), *Colleted Works: Volume 24*, Moscow: Progress Publishers.

Lenin, V. I. (1964f), *Colleted Works: Volume 26*, Moscow: Progress Publishers.

Lenin, V. I. (1966), *Collected Works: Volume 31*, Moscow: Progress Publishers.

Lenin, V. I. (1967), *Collected Works: Volume 37*, Moscow: Progress Publishers.

Lenin, V. I. (1968), *Konspekt 'Perepiski K. Marksa i F. Engel'sa 1844–1883 g. g.'*, Izdanie vtoroe, Moscow: Politizdat.

Lenin, V. I. (1969), *Polnoe sobranie sochinenii: Volume 27*, Moscow: Politizdat.

Lenin, V. I. (1970), *Podgotovitel'nye materialy k knige 'Razvitie kapitalizma v Rosii'*, Moscow: Politizdat.

Lenin, V. I. (1972), *Marxism on the State: Preparatory Material for the Book 'The State and Revolution'*, Moscow: Progress Publishers.

Lenin, V. I. (1973a), *Collected Works: Volume 32*, Moscow: Progress Publishers.

Lenin, V. I. (1973b), *Collected Works: Volume 5, May 1901–February 1902*, Moscow: Progress Publishers.

Lih, L. T. (2005), *Lenin Rediscovered: What Is To Be Done? in Context*, Boston: Brill.

Listovki bol'shevistskikh organizatsii v pervoi russkoi revoliutsii 1905–1907 gg.: sbornik v trekh chastiakh., Volume 1 (1965), Moscow: Gospolitizdat.

Lunacharskii, A. V. (1908), *Religiia i sotsialzm: Volume 1*, St Petersburg: Shipovnik.

Lunacharskii, A. V. (1911), *Religiia i sotsializm: Volume 2*, S. Peterburg: Shipovnik.

Lunacharskii, A. V., K. Radek and L. Trotsky (1991), *Siluety: Politicheskie portrety*, Moscow: Politizdat.

Luxemburg, R. (1981), *Gesammelte Werke: Volume 5, Ökonomische Schriften*, 2nd edn, Berlin: Dietz.

Luxemburg, R. (2003), *The Accumulation of Capital*, London [u.a.]: Routledge.

Maksim Kovalevskii 1851–1916. Sbornik statei (1918), Petrograd.

Marcuse, H. (1971), *Soviet Marxism: A Critical Analysis*, Harmondsworth: Penguin.

Martov, L. (2004), *Zapiski sotsial-demokrata*, Moscow: ROSSPA.

Marx, K. (1867), *Das Kapital: Kritik der politischen Oekonomie*, Erster Band. Buch I: Der Produktionsprocess des Kapitals, Hamburg: Verlag von Otto Meissner.

Marx, K. (1872), *Le Capital: Traduction de M. J. Roy, entièrement revisée par l'auteur*, Paris: Lachatre.

Marx, K. (1885), 'Der franzözische Materialismus des 18 Jahrhunderts', *Die neue Zeit*, 3 (9).

Marx, K. (1886), 'Letter to *Otechestvennye zapiski*', *Vestnik Narodnoi Voli*, 5.

Marx, K. (1927), 'Iz chernovoi tetradi K. Marks', *Letopisi marksizma*, 4: 56–62.

Marx, K. (1970), *A Contribution to the Critique of Political Economy*, Moscow: Progress Publishers. First published 1859.

Marx, K. (1973), *Grundrisse: Foundations of the Critique of Political Economy (rough draft)*, London: Allen Lane.

Marx, K. (1976), *Capital: A Critique of Political Economy / Karl Marx*, Introduced by Ernest Mandel. Vol.1 / translated [from the German] by Ben Fowkes, Harmondsworth: Penguin; London: New Left Review.

Marx, K. (1978), *Capital: A Critique of Political Economy*, Volume 2, Harmondsworth: Penguin Books.

Marx, K. and F. Engels (1908), *Pis'ma Karla Marksa i Fridrikha Engel'sa k Nikolaiu-onu s prilozheniem mest iz ikh pisem k drugim litsam*, St Petersburg: [s.n.].

Marx, K. and F. Engels (1913), *Der Briefwechsel zwischen Friedrich Engels und Karl Marx, 1844 bis 1883, herausgegeben von A. Bebel und Ed. Bernstein*, Stuttgart: J. H. W. Dietz Nachf.

Marx, K. and F. Engels (1967), *K. Marks, F. Engel's i revoliutsionnaia Rossiia*, Moscow: Politizdat.

Marx, K. and F. Engels (1969a), *Selected Works in three volumes: Volume 1*, Moscow: Progress Publishers.
Marx, K. and F. Engels (1969b), *Selected Works in three volumes: Volume 2*, Moscow: Progress Publishers.
Marx, K. and F. Engels (1970), *Selected Works in three volumes: Volume 3*, Moscow: Progress Publishers.
Marx, K. and F. Engels (1975), *Collected Works: Volume 3*, London: Lawrence & Wishart.
Marx, K. and F. Engels (1983), *Collected Works: Volume 40*, London: Lawrence & Wishart.
Marx, K. and F. Engels (1987a), *Collected Works: Volume 42*, London: Lawrence & Wishart.
Marx, K. and F. Engels (1987b), *Collected Works: Volume 25*, London: Lawrence & Wishart.
Marx , K. and F. Engels (1988), *Collected Works: Volume 43*, London: Lawrence & Wishart.
Marx, K. and F. Engels (1989a), *Collected Works: Volume 24*, London: Lawrence & Wishart.
Marx, K. and F. Engels (1989b), *Collected Works: Volume 44*, London: Lawrence & Wishart.
Marx, K. and F. Engels (1991), *Collected Works: Volume 45*. London: Lawrence & Wishart.
Marx, K. and F. Engels (1992), *Collected Works: Volume 46*. London: Lawrence & Wishart.
Marx, K. and F. Engels (1995), *Collected Works: Volume 47*, London: Lawrence & Wishart.
Marx, K. and F. Engels (2001), *Collected Works: Volume 49*, London: Lawrence & Wishart.
Maslov, N. N. (1990), 'Iz istorii rasprostraneniia stalinizma', *Voprosy istorii KPSS*, 7.
Mehring, F. (1902), *Aus dem literarischen Nachlass von Karl Marx, Friedrich Engels und Ferdinand Lassalle*, Stuttgart: Dietz.
Mikhailovskii, N. K. (1897), *Sochineniia: Volume 4*, St Petersburg: B. M. Vol'f.
Mikhailovskii, N. K. (1909), *Polnoe sobranie sochinenii: Volume 7*, St Petersburg: M. M. Stasiulevich.
Nechkina, M. V. (1990), 'Vopros o M. N. Pokrovskom v postanovleniiakh partii i pravitel'stva 1934–1938 gg. o prepodavanii istorii i istoricheskoi nauki: (K istochnikovedcheskoi storone temy)', *Istoricheskie zapiski*, 118: 232–46.
Nezhdanov, P. (1898), *Nravstvennost'*, Moscow: Tipografiia I. A. Balandina, Volkhova, D. Mikhailova.
Nikolaevskii, B. (1929), 'Russkie knigi v bibliotekakh K. Marksa i F. Engel'sa', *Arkhiv K. Marksa i F. Engel'sa*, 4: 355–423.
Nove, A. (1992), *An Economic History of the USSR 1917–1991*, 3rd edn, London: Penguin Books.
Ocherki po filosofii marksizma. Filosofskii sbornik (1908), St Petersburg: Zerno.
Ocherki po istorii 'Kapitala' K. Marksa (1983), Moscow: Politizdat.
Ocherki realisticheskogo mirovozzreniia. Sbornik statei po filosofii, obshchestvennoi nauke i zhizni (1904), St Petersburg: S. Dorovatskii i A. Charushnikov.

Oreshkin, V. V. (1968), *Voprosy imperializma v rabotakh bol'shevikov-lenintsev: Dooktiabr'skii period*, Moscow: Nauka.

Ostroukhova, K. A. (1967), 'O rabote v Istparte', *Voprosy istorii KPSS*, 6: 92–9.

Partiia narodnoi voli (1905), *Literatura sotsial'no-revoliutsionnoi partii 'Narodnoi voli.'*, n.p.: Tip. Partii sotsialistov-revoliutsionerov'.

Pipes, R. (1964), 'Narodnichestvo: A Semantic Inquiry', *Slavic Review*, 23 (3): 441–58.

Plekhanov, G. V. (1896), *Beiträge zur Geschichte des Materialismus*, Stuttgart: Dietz.

Plekhanov, G. V. (1909), *Anarchism and Socialism*, Translated with the permission of the author by Eleanor Marx Aveling. With an introduction by Robert Rives LaMonte, Chicago: Charles H. Kerr.

Plekhanov, G. V. (1924), *Sochineniia: Volume 1*, Moscow: Gosizdat.

Plekhanov, G. V., (1925a), *Sochineniia: Volume 3*, Moscow: Gosizdat.

Plekhanov, G. V. (1925b), *Sochineniia: Volume 20*: Moscow: Gosizdat.

Plekhanov, G. V. (1961), *Selected Philosophical Works*, Moscow: Foreign Languages Publishing House.

Pokrovskii, M. N. (1925), *Marksizm i osobennosti istoricheskogo razvitiia Rossii*, Leningrad: Priboi.

Pokrovskii, M. N. (1929), 'Leninizm i russkaia istoriia', *Istorik Marksist*, 11: 235–6.

Pokrovskii, M. N. (1933), *Istoricheskaia nauka i bor'ba klassov: Volume 1*, Moscow-Leningrad: Gosudarstvennoe sotsial'no-ekonomicheskoe izdatel'stvo.

Pokrovskii, M. N. (1969), 'Kak rozhdalsia "Imperializm"', in A. P. Smirnova and V. A. Chanova (eds), *Vospominaniia o Vladimire Il'iche Lenine: Volume 2*: 368–72, Moscow: Politizdat.

Problems of Idealism. Essays in Russian Social Philosophy, Translated, edited and introduced by Randall A. Poole (2003), New Haven and London: Yale University Press.

Price, M. P. (1921), *My Reminiscences of the Russian Revolution*, London: G. Allen & Unwin.

Resis, A. (1970), 'Das Kapital Comes to Russia', *Slavic Review*, 29 (2): 219–37.

Rokitianskii, I. A. and R. Miuller (1996), *Krasnyi dissident: Akademik Riazanov – opponent Lenina, zhertva Stalina: biograficheskii ocherk, dokumenty*, Moscow: Akademiia.

Rozhkov, N. A. (1923), 'K metodologii istorii revoliutsionnogo dvizheniia', *Krasnaia letopis'*, 7.

Rudiak, B. M. (1979), *Russkie knigi v bibliotekakh K. Marksa i F. Engel'sa*, Moscow: Izdatel'stvo politicheskoi literatury.

Ruge, A. (1840), 'Friedrich von Florencourt und die Kategorien der politischen Praxis', *Hallische Jahrbücher für Wissenschaft und Kunst*, 282: 2249–54.

Russkie sovremenniki o K. Markse i F. Engel'se (1969), Moscow: Politizdat.

Ryazanov, D. (1924), 'Mezhdunarodnoe Tovarishchestvo Rabochikh: I. Vozniknovenie Pervogo Internatsionala', *Arkhiv K. Marksa i F. Engel'sa*, 1: 105–88.

Serge, V. (1963), *Memoirs of a Revolutionary, 1901–1941*, Oxford: Oxford University Press.

Sieber, N. I. (2011), 'Marx's Economic Theory', in P. Zarembka and R. Desai (eds), *Revitalizing Marxist Theory for Today's Capitalism*: 155–90, Bingley: Emerald.

Skrebitskii, A. I. (1862), *Krest'ianskoe delo v tsarstvovanii imperatora Aleksandra II: Materialy dlia istorii osvobozhdeniia krest'ian*, Volume 1, Bonn na Reine: Pechatano v tip. F. Kriugera.

Skvortsov-Stepanov, I. I. (1930), *Izbrannye proizvedeniia*, Leningrad: Gos. izd-vo.

Stalin, J. V. (1937), *K izucheniiu istorii: Sbornik*, Moscow: Partizdat.

Stalin, J. V. (1949), *Works: Volume 12*, Moscow: Ogiz.

Stalin, J. V. (1953), *Works: Volume 6*, Moscow: Foreign Languages Publishing House.

Struve, P. B. (1893), 'Zur Beurtheilung der kapitalistischen Entwicklung Russlands', *Sozialpolitisches Centralblatt*, 2 (1): 1–3.

Struve, P. B. (1894), *Kriticheskie zametki ob ekonomicheskom razvitii Rossii*, Vypusk I., St Petersburg: I. N. Skorokhodov.

Takhtarev, K. M. (1902), *Ocherk Peterburgskogo rabochego dvizheniia 90-kh godov: Po lichnym vospominaniiam*, London: Tip. "Zhizni".

Tengoborski, L. (1855), *Commentaries on the Productive Forces of Russia*, London: Longman.

Thatcher, I. D. (1991), 'Uneven and Combined Development', *Revolutionary Russia*, 4 (2): 235–58.

Tikhomirov, L. A. (1885), *Chego nam zhdat' ot revoliutsii!*, St Petersburg: Izdanie gruppy tipografshchikov Narodnoi Voli.

Tikhomirov, L. A. (1886), 'Review of Plekhanov's *Our Differences*', *Vestnik Narodnoi Voli*, 5.

Tikhomirov, L. A. (1997), *Kritika demokratii: Stat'i iz zhurnala 'Russkoe obozrenie' 1892–1897 gg*, Moscow: Redaktsiia zhurnala 'Moskva'.

Tkachev, P. N. (2010), *Izbrannoe*, Moscow: ROSSPEN.

Trotsky, L. (1905), *Do deviatogo ianvaria*, Geneva: Tip. Partii.

Trotsky, L. (1909), *Russland in der Revolution*, Dresden: Druck und Verlag von Kaden & Comp.

Trotsky, L. (1915), 'Nash politicheskii lozung', *Nashe slovo*, 24 February.

Trotsky, L. (1917), *Chto zhe dal'she: (Itogi i perspektivy)*, Moscow: Priboi.

Trotsky, L. (1919), *From October to Brest Litovsk*, New York: The Socialist Publication Society.Trotsky, L. (1924–25), *Sochineniia: Volume 3. Part 1*, Moscow: Gosizdat.

Trotsky, L. (1925), *Sochineniia: Volume 2. Part 1*, Moscow: Gosizdat.

Trotsky, L. (1934), *The History of the Russian Revolution*, Translated from the Russian by Max Eastman, London: Gollancz.

Trotsky, L. (1962), *The Stalin School of Falsification*, 2nd edn, New York: Pioneer Publishers.

Trotsky, L. (1970), *The Revolution Betrayed: What is the Soviet Union and Where is it Going?*, New York: Pathfinder Press.

Trotsky, L. (1971a), *1905*, Translated by Anya Bostock, New York: Random House.

Trotsky, L. (1971b), *The Permanent Revolution. Results and Prospects*, Translated by John G. Wright and Brian Pearce, London: New Park Publications.

Trotsky, L. (1974), *La guerre et la révolution: Le naufrage de la IIe Internationale, les débuts de la IIIe Internationale*, Volume 1, Paris: Éditions Tête de feuilles.

Trotsky, L. (1979), *Our Political Tasks*, London: New Park Publications.

Trotsky, L. (1980), *Report of the Siberian Delegation (1903)*, London: New Park Publications.

Tsagolov, N. A. (1956), *Ocherki russkoi ekonomicheskoi mysli perioda padeniia krepostnogo prava*, Moscow: Gospolitizdat.

Valentinov, N. V. (1968), *Encounters with Lenin*, London: Oxford University Press.

Vasetskii, N. (1992), *Trotskii: Opyt politicheskoi biografii*, Moscow: Izd-vo 'Respublika'.

Volk, S. S. (1966), *Narodnaia volia 1879–1882*, Moscow: Nauka.

Volodin, A. I. and B. S. Itenberg (1983), 'Karl Marks i Nikolai Daniel'son', *Voprosy istorii*, 11: 83–95.

Vorovskii, V. V. (1919), *K istorii marksizma v Rossii*, Moscow: Gosizdat.

Waldenberg, M. (1972), *Wzlot i upadek Karola Kautsky'ego: Studium z historii myśli społecznej i politycznej*, Volume 1, Krakow: Wydawnictwo Literackie.

Wetter, G. A. (1964), *Dialectical Materialism: A Hisorical and Systematic Survey of Philosophy in the Soviet Union*, London: Routledge & Kegan Paul.

White, J. D. (1979), 'The Sormovo-Nikolaev Zemlyachestvo in the February Revolution', *Soviet Studies*, 31 (4): 475–504.

White, J. D. (1985), 'Early Soviet Historical Interpretations of the Russian Revolution 1918–24', *Soviet Studies*, 37 (3): 330–52.

White, J. D. (1996), *Karl Marx and the Intellectual Origins of Dialectical Materialism*, Basingstoke: MacMillan.

White, J. D. (1998), ' "No, We Won't Go That Way; That Is Not the Way to Take": The Place of Aleksandr Ul'ianov in the Development of Social-Democracy in Russia', *Revolutionary Russia*, 11 (2): 82–110.

White, J. D. (2005), 'M.N. Pokrovskii's Interpretation of Russian History', in I. D. Thatcher (ed.), *Late Imperial Russia: Problems and Prospects. Essays in Honour of R. B. McKean*: 168–88, Manchester and New York: Manchester University Press.

White, J. D. (2016), 'Rosa Luxemburg and Maxim Kovalevsky', in F. O. Wolf and J. Dellheim (eds), *Rosa Luxemburg: A Permanent Challenge for Political Economy: The History and the Present of Luxemburg's 'Accumulation of Capital'*: 93–121, New York, Secaucus: Palgrave Macmillan; Springer.

Zhukovskii, Iu. G. (1877), 'Karl Marks i ego kniga o kapitale', *Vestnik Evropy*, 5: 64–105.

Ziber, N. I. (1871), *Teoriia tsennosti i kapitala D. Rikardo v sviazi s pozdneishimi dopo;neniiami i raz"iasneniiami: Opyt kritiko-ekonomicheskogo isledovaniia*, Kiev.

Ziber, N. I. (1900a), *Sobranie sochinenii: Volume 1*, St Petersburg: Izdatel'.

Ziber, N. I. (1900b), *Sobranie sochinenii: Volume 2*, St Petersburg: Izdatel'.

Ziber, N. I. (1959a), *Izbrannye ekonomicheskie proizvedeniia: Volume 1*, Moscow: Izdatel'stvo sotsial'no-ekonomicheskoi literatury.

Ziber, N. I. (1959b), *Izbrannye ekonomicheskie proizvedeniia: Volume 2*, Moscow: Izdatel'stvo sotsial'no-ekonomicheskoi literatury.

INDEX